REPORTERS

To Khaul Ismail —
A young poet
from an old one,
who thrives upon learning
every day of his life.

Will Fowler
1993

REPORTERS

Memoirs of a Young Newspaperman

By Line: Will Fowler

ROUNDTABLE
—— Publishing, Inc. ——

Library of Congress Cataloging-in-Publication Data

Fowler, Will, 1922 -
   Reporters: memoirs of a young newspaperman / by Will Fowler.
      p. cm.
   Includes bibliographical references and index.
   ISBN 0-915677-61-X: $21.95
   1. Fowler, Will, 1922-   2. Journalists—United States-
-Biography.   3. Reporters and reporting—United States. I. Title.
PN4874.F587A3 1991
070' .92—dc20   91-17235
[B]   CIP

10 9 8 7 6 5 4 3 2 1

Photographs are from the private collection of the author.

*To the many newspaper reporters
who were always going to write a book,
but never got around to it.*

By Will Fowler

Reporters

The Second Handshake

The Young Man From Denver

Pico Street

The Fosterling

Julius Castro
(Off Broadway play)

Just completed:
Good Thinking

Bud and Louise

CONTENTS

Preface

No other profession, even that of soldiering, produces as fine a version of the selfless hero as journalism does. Unlike the profession of soldiering, journalism does not coerce and discipline its own into selflessness. The journalist's dedication to his craft is based on his own nature, the one he brings to it as a duck brings its webbed feet to the pond.

What I write is no blanket description of newspapermen. It includes only the kind I once knew and admired because I was somewhat like them. They were young, whatever their age. Their profession allowed them to remain exactly what they were — either stupid, elegant, profane, aesthetic, crooked, idealistic. And the newspapermen were accordingly as full of fierce gratitude toward their profession as toward perfect and indulgent parents.

A good newspaperman, of my day, was to be known by the fact that he was ashamed of being anything else. He scorned offers of double wages in other fields. He sneered at all the honors life held other than the one to which he aspired, which was a simple one. He dreamed of dying in harness, a casual figure full of anonymous power; and free. For the newspaperman, the most harried of employees, more bedeviled by duties than a country doctor, more blindly subservient to his editor than a Marine private to his drill sergeant, considered himself, somewhat loonily, to have no boss, to be without superiors and a creature always on his own. As the great newspaperman Duffy said: "Socially, a journalist fits in somewhere between a whore and a bartender but spiritually, he stands beside Galileo. He knows the world is round."

—Ben Hecht

Foreword

Will Fowler and I worked together as reporters on the old *Herald-Express*, before its ignominious merger with the morning *Examiner*. It was a Hearst paper, and generally demeaned by its competitors as a scandal sheet. It was a good newspaper; it had dash, guts and vitality. For getting on the street with the story it was hard to beat. We were all very loyal to our city editor, Agness Underwood, who had been a tough reporter herself.

Those days (the late 1940s and early 1950s) were the last gasp of "Front Page" journalism. The *Herald* city room was noisy; there was always a sense of urgency; we worked fast and we worked hard.

Will was almost the prototype. He was type casting. His energy was amazing. Among his several improbable talents was prodigious physical strength. His arms were like legs. He once dropped into a cop hangout in the San Fernando Valley and defeated eight cops in Indian wrestling, creating a legend that is remembered today.

Whenever any of us entered a bar in a bad neighborhood with Will, we felt safe. Will would protect us. He was probably one of the best of the great barroom fighters.

He was also gentle and compassionate. He could cover any kind of story, but sometimes, faced with tragedy, especially the death of a child, he suffered great emotional punishment. He was once assigned to cover a story about a mother and four or five small children who died of asphyxiation in the family station wagon. Will wrote the story with great emotional force, but with restraint; but he was an emotional wreck after that for a week.

Will loved fun. Occasionally tour groups would stream solemnly through the city room, getting a glimpse of the real thing. Will kept a pint of whiskey in his desk drawer for these visits. When the tour group was passing by, he would open the drawer with a clatter, shout "Boy!" to get everyone's attention, then tip the bottle up and take a big slug, wiping his mouth on his sleeve. The crowd was always impressed.

We were all comrades in those days. After work, if there was ever any after work, we assembled in the nearest bar to talk over the day's laughs and triumphs. We were not very good husbands. But we loved our work, we loved each other, and we loved our wives.

—Jack Smith
Los Angeles Times
Times Syndicate

I

Evolution In Overdrive

When radio news broadcasting was beginning to take shape in the early 1920s, one had the impression that we were a more literate society than we are today. Urbanly-speaking, this might be true.

At the start, radio programs in progress were never interrupted to flash fast-breaking stories. The station would wait for a break before cryptically offering the story on the air. And then it wouldn't be until the evening news segment when listeners would be filled in on the details.

But there was something missing for inquisitive listeners living in cities still obsessed with newspapers. The radio was unable to show pictures of the news disaster, victory or oddity. The newspaper *could*. And in regular or extra editions, it usually hit the streets before the scheduled evening broadcast went over the airwaves.

If anything, radio news gave newspapers a great boost in street sales and circulation. Papers filled the need for the person who wanted to *see* the gory details or vicariously gaze into a hero's smiling eyes.

And as a follow-up in order to closer study the already aging news event on the scene, one had to wait a few days until the weekly newsreel footage was disseminated, then projected on the screen at the local movie house. Although late, the novelty now was that one could watch news story subjects actually moving.

Years passed and the three mediums peacefully co-existed. There was no feeling of competition between them because none was singly capable of fulfilling the reader-listener-viewer's complete desires for news being served up in one package.

In the 1930s, radio began to display a stronger threat with its own "news magazines" such as *The March of Time*. And Walter Winchell's dynamic style of machine gun delivery was an event missed by few. But these were still once-a-week shows, and newspapers continued to thrive as the king of the hill. The real competition came from within the opposition papers, and it was *fierce* as their metropolitan sheet continued to publish several editions daily.

World War II was an historical calamity shaped for international news coverage. The voice of Edward R. Murrow, broadcasting with the sounds of great explosions in the background while London was being bombed by the German *Luftwaffe*, gave the listener as much drama as he could handle.

Then, on January 22, 1947, the blurred black-and-white image of a man magically flashed over Southern California airwaves, and the image spoke: "This is KTLA, formerly W6XYZ television, broadcasting on Channel Five. Good evening, everyone ..." It was an almost informal announcement of the nation's first commercial television station emanating from Hollywood, across the street from the Paramount motion picture studios.

News-wise, because there were only 300 receiving sets in the stretch of its communication, the medium's introduction was treated by the press more-or-less as a novelty. It might also have been dealt with in this manner because farsighted publishers could have been disturbed with the thought of the shape of things to come.

In 1948, there was an all-out sales campaign to offer television receivers to a nation that counted only 17,000 sets in all.

Public reaction was immediate and hundreds of thousands found themselves cashing in war savings bonds in order to be first in the neighborhood to own one of these wonderful mechanical contraptions with a small tube reflecting pictures and the sound of Hopalong Cassidy movies beamed directly into their homes. And it was all for free.

In regard to television news coverage, it was brief, time-restricted and in some ways, archaic. When there was a fire to report, a still photo of the scene was beamed out, and to offer a live effect, an offstage director would blow cigarette smoke across the camera's focus.

But it was only a matter of time until a big story would break and a shrewd TV station owner or manager would be ready to cover it with a newly devised mobile camera unit having the ability to transmit the on-the-scene event back to its mother station which, in turn, would feed it out into all the living rooms in its scope.

That day came on Friday, April 16, 1949, when a little girl named Kathy Fiscus fell into a dry well in South Pasadena, California, and KTLA's Klaus Landsberg sent his brand new mobile crew out into the field to cover the evolving story on the spot.

And cover it Landsberg did. For 50 straight commercial-free hours, the entire nation sat poised the whole weekend, glued to their or their neighbors' TV sets, foregoing sleep to be in on the latest bulletin about this little girl fighting for her life, a child they had never known before she had fallen into that well.

At the end of it all, these hundreds of thousands of now exhausted viewers throughout the country finally learned that Kathy Fiscus had died during the time feverish rescue workers attempted to reach her. It was as though the child's life had been sacrificed in order to alert the world that perhaps the second greatest *transition* in the past 2000 years was taking place.

This correlation to the Coming of Christ might be construed as vulgar and blasphemous to many, but the two events were amazingly alike in nature. When Christ first came, there was no fanfare and most were slow to accept him. But when he proclaimed he was the son of God, it so shocked the small world in which he lived that he was crucified.

The major difference between these happenings was that centuries passed before Christianity was accepted throughout the world. The Coming of Television took less than two years, and it was eagerly accepted.

This new medium, however, also spelled the death of the news-reel and temporarily put the motion picture industry on the skids. Television forever minimized radio's power down to mainly becoming a listening pastime for commuters.

The advent of television news coverage also condemned the lives of three-quarters of the world's newspapers.

There was something else radically happening at this time which would never have been so exhilarating if it hadn't been for the advent of World War II. It was doubtlessly the initial, yet inadvertent, time when women were literally thrust into respon-sible professional positions heretofore held only by men who had either gone off to fight or taken essential jobs with the War Department. These were the infant days which would eventually be referred to as Women's Liberation.

When women filled in some of these executive positions, many industries were surprised to discover that females were not only adequate, but—in some cases—even functioned better than the men they had replaced.

This was highly profiled when it came to newspapers always in need of good young minds to work in its editorial departments. And with the exception of the very few who arrived earlier—such as Polly Pry, Dorothy Parker and Agness Underwood (the first female city editor on a metropolitan newspaper in the world)—it payed off as women went to work as newspaper reporters.

When it was unpopular to do so in these early days, I was the newspaperwoman's champion, and often backed up my senti-ments by getting into fist-fights defending women's right to func-tion as full-fledged reporters.

All my friends in this profession witnessed these times when television news unlocked the front door of privacy and ultimately became the undisputed leader of the news media. We were also participants during the transition.

This is the story about what newspaper reporters used to be like, how we were effected, and what we evolved into, now that the cathode ray tube has become the ultimate monolith of modern communication.

II

Breaking the Cherry

By the time William Randolph Hearst had opened his fourth newspaper for publication, his corporate fortune was second only to Henry Ford's; he was building the most expensive private residence in history, and he had become the most controversial man in the country, if not the world.

These papers, in chronological order of publication were the *San Francisco Examiner*, the *New York American*, the *Chicago American* and the *Los Angeles Examiner*.

Of Hearst's initial six publications, my father and I had worked in the editorial department of four of them.

Between 1918 and 1928, Gene Fowler had become the foremost talented and colorful reporter ever to walk down New York's Park Row. He also flourished in The Big Apple as the youngest managing editor (at age 33) ever on a metropolitan newspaper. This was the *New York American*, and, finally—with the Chief's favorite editor, Walter Howey—created the *New York Mirror* in competition with the *Daily News*.

Between 1944-52, I also burned a two-wicked candle functioning as a hard-working, hard-drinking Hearst merry marauder on the flamboyant Los Angeles morning *Examiner* and afternoon *Herald & Express*. And I enjoyed a cornucopia of excitement that no ten men I know would ever have collectively experienced. It also had to be foreordained when I was born in 1922 that I would be named William Randolph Fowler.

My namesake began publishing the *San Francisco Examiner* in 1895. He gave the upper and middle classes what they were most interested in reading: scandal, sex and crime. The remainder of the newspaper's news was devoted to crusades "in the interest of the masses." Following the paper's stunning success, Hearst invaded Joseph Pulitzer's publishing world with his *New York American*. Then, like Sherman marching to the sea, Hearst took on Chicago. This was a tougher situation, and in getting his *Chicago American* going, there were those who accused him of fomenting that city's habitual gang warfare.

The formula for success on the West Coast was far easier. The remarkably prosperous San Francisco paper led the way for Los Angeles union activists to invite Hearst to start a newspaper in their city. It was planned as competition to Gen. Harrison Gray Otis's conservative *Los Angeles Times*. This, so that L.A. would have a paper representing the working man's interests ... so they said. Celebrating the *Examiner's* opening in 1914, union members paraded down Broadway and handed Hearst an initial subscription list of 50,000 names.

Success followed success and the flamboyant Hearst established the *Herald & Express* as the city's afternoon newspaper standardbearer.

The iron-willed publisher expected his five sons to quit college to become high-salaried publishers themselves in his newspaper empire. In an attempt to lock in his sons, his last will and testament stated that if any of them pursued other vocations, they would be reduced to receiving a $30,000-a-year income—tantamount to poverty considering their lifestyles.

Only two of the five, however, demonstrated a talent for the business: the eldest, William Randolph, Jr. and twin to David, Randolph A. Hearst, who my father claimed was the best editor of them all. David did become a publisher (the *Los Angeles Herald & Express*), but was not successful. George Hearst, Sr., survived well on the reported $30,000 yearly stipend by continuing to write large checks when there was no balance to cover them. When I met George at Charley Foy's Supper Club in 1950, this tall jocular gentleman who had the appearance of a freshly-shaved Santa Claus theorized: "Now, who would ever refuse a Hearst check, anyway?"

Unfortunately, the renowned publisher gave little or no corporate power to these sons, bestowing this on nonfamily executives. And, unfortunately, the nonfamily executives had financially and ruthlessly bled the newspapers, transferring their profits to continue investing in its magazine holdings, which—coincidentally—were thriving.

I tossed all night. My thoughts were unsettled about what my debut in the world of journalism was going to be like now that I'd committed myself to a job on Hearst's *Examiner* editorial staff.

I was 21 years old. My spelling wasn't too reliable, my typing went a blazing 45-words-a-minute, and my alliance with murderers, con men, skid-row bums, prostitutes and senators was less than limited. The only thing I had going was my enthusiasm and a bent for being inquisitive. I also possessed a strong stomach and leaned a bit toward being wild. Also, what other paper could I work for with a moniker like mine?

I drove slowly along Olympic Boulevard, not anxious to show up at all. Downtown, I crossed the trolley tracks and pulled up in a lot across the street from the *Examiner*. I was due in the city room at 7:45 A.M., but arrived a half-hour early.

The brooding five-story cream-colored stucco building displayed four blue and yellow tiled domes at each end, and at the center and overall, was a huge waving American flag. The structure occupied a half-block.

I crossed Broadway where a queue of people waited for the next streetcar to carry them uptown to local government offices.

Half of the *Examiner* building's street level floor displayed giant black presses through large plate windows.[1] The presses hummed loud and were awe-inspiring. More so were the stories in newsprint that came roaring out of the presses like sixty. At that time, the *Examiner's* circulation topped that of all other newspapers in the west.

---

[1] Today, those windows have been painted over since 1967, at the beginning of an extended union strike.

Inside, two long, dark mahogany-topped counters lined either side of the impressive lobby. There were column shafts of brown marble with architrave and cornice. And up toward the vaulted ceiling were heroic hand-painted and gilded figures "of the best Spanish sixteenth century period," as Mr. Hearst had put it. High and in the center there was (and still is) a large monogram carved into white marble reading "L A E" (for *Los Angeles Examiner*). I thought my voice would echo if I hollered.

A small wrought iron-decorated elevator was out of service at this time of the morning. It only tightly accommodated four people which made it necessary for large groups to hike up 38 marble stair risers to the city room on the third floor. It was a taxing and humbling experience, and perhaps was designed to be so.

I passed through a low wood-carved swinging gate to the reception area and looked through the open door that had the authoritative words, CITY ROOM, printed in black block letters on its opaque glass window.

The room was huge, with about 30 plastered-over steel bearing beams which allowed it to be open and accessible. The paper's several editorial departments were hived into autonomous sections of activity.

I waited until 7:45, then entered like an anchor was dragging from my rear end. I asked a guy looking through pages of copy where I could find the city desk. He jerked his thumb like a hitchhiker in the direction of two desks facing one another in front of a large window. There sat assignment editor Bill Gammon and general assignment reporter Sid Hughes.

I announced I was there for my first day's work. Hughes briefly looked up from whatever he was reading and Gammon said, "Oh, yeah ... Fowler?"

I nodded.

"Take a seat anywhere," said Gammon. "Over there." He pointed toward the bull pen, a double line of 12 desks. Attached, they were six-facing-six beat up pieces of furniture hidden beneath a pile of spiked foolscap and mangled editions of the previous day's newspaper. The ancient coffee-grinding typewriters were Royals and Remingtons. It looked to me like a titanic version of W.C. Field's desk in his 1940 movie, *The Bank Dick*.

Then I noticed something that looked like a human being wearing a trench coat and hat. It was spread facedown over two adjoining desks next to the society department. I was disoriented with the experience of being in an alien atmosphere and didn't want to appear like a rube so I wasn't about to ask what or who this thing might be.

More than an hour—that seemed like an entire morning in time—passed. A few reporters filtered in. The action gradually began to pick up. And nobody, absolutely nobody had even nodded in my direction.

By ten o'clock, City Editor James H. Richardson made his entrance, striding past the bull pen toward his window desk. Ceremoniously, he removed his coat and necktie and rolled up his white shirt sleeves. There was a quiet pause, and then he growled as though he was playing to me. Like an alternate opening to Ben Hecht and Charlie MacArthur's play, *The Front Page*, he roared, "Well, what the hell's going on that we can put in the paper?"

My instinct was to be as inconspicuous as possible.

The morning wore on, and coming on to noon, Associated Press and Hearst's International News Service printers were spewing out copy a mile-a-minute. Various editors had arrived and ten, maybe 20 typewriters were clacking and one rewrite man shouted, "Copy! Copyboy!"

During this acceleration of activity, a three-foot wire waste basket caught fire and burst into flames. A casually tossed match was suspect. I watched a bunch of milling people seemingly not knowing what to do ... except head copyboy Chuck Wells who aimed his handy fire extinguisher at the blaze. Everyone went back to what they were doing, which indicated that this was a chronic occurrence.

Right at 12 o'clock a young rewrite man was the first to address me directly. "How about some lunch?" he asked. "Name's Murray. Jim Murray."

"Sounds great," I said. "Name's Fowler ... Will."

"I know," said Murray.

I met another rewrite man, Gus Newman, and we walked north a block to Betty's Broadway Circle located on a pie-shaped slice of cement sidewalk where Broadway and Spring streets intersect. The place was big and open, and bright for a place where spirits were served. "How about a drink?" Murray asked. Even though it was early, I thought this was a great idea, and after a couple of bourbons, we ordered the lunch special: a ham on rye with two bottles of ale, all for sixty-five cents. This was the beginning of my uncalculated destruction of a perfectly healthy liver.

I had many questions I wanted to ask about the *Examiner*, but Gus and Jim were more interested in learning why the hell I wanted to become a reporter. I said my father had been one, and when I was a promising actor, he said he preferred I pursue "a more meaningful profession."

Murray and Newman already knew much about my father, a man who had lived in three enchanted eras: The tail end of the old west in Denver, the entire Roaring Twenties period as a reporter, and into the brief Hollywood Golden Age of the 1930s as a screen writer and script doctor, ending up (as reported by the IRS) as being the tenth highest salaried person in the U.S. during the pit of the Great Depression year of 1934.

Dave Brown, a reporter on the swing shift, joined us. He was young, rough-skinned and appeared hunkered from some random dissipation of the night before. Dave was on the way to work and stopped by for a shot of whiskey backed up with a beer.

When we headed back to the paper, I didn't feel half bad with the ale sloshing in my belly.

I filled in my new friends with a bit of information about myself. I said I'd been the third of three children and was the first born in a hospital.

"Following a 1931 trip to the Coast when Pop started writing movie scripts," I said, "we came to stay in 1935. But we returned to Fire Island for ten weeks each summer until we got

into the war. That's when Pop used to write his early books."
I added that in those days, Fire Island had no automobiles, tele-
phones or electricity, but we had indoor plumbing. "We even
had a lamp-lighter named Mr. Claus. And the boys who carry
their books in a funny manner hadn't yet invaded the sand bar."

I told them that I was only a high school graduate, and that
neither of my parents took much interest in guiding me or giving
me proper supervision regarding my education. "That sort of
disappointed me," I said, "but having been the third child and
nearly six years younger than my brother, I phased into becoming a loner at a young age."

As we climbed the 38 marble stairs to the third floor, I added
that I had enlisted in the Coast Guard on the Fourth of July, 1942,
when I was 19, and that our ship had pulled out to sea on convoy duty the following day. "We sank one Japanese submarine
each of my two convoys. On the way home from the South Pacific
and two days out of home port, I came down with a high fever.
When we moored, an ambulance delivered me to the newly com-
missioned Long Beach Naval Hospital. There, x-rays showed
my throwing up blood was caused by a hole in my right lung."
I was medically discharged and married in 1943, and now had
a son one year old.

On the third floor, rangy Alex Cuscaden, a man who had
whipped Tom Horn in Cheyenne,[2] lumbered across the city room
toward the office of managing editor R.T. Van Ettish. Richardson, picture editor Don Goodenow and others I didn't know yet,
followed. Behind the wainscoted, glassed-in partition, they conferred in the fish bowl office to decide what story would be featured in the headline. They would also choose where to place
subordinate stories and other apologues in order of importance.
A headline would be composed and the picture for the first edition
would be given its column size and space placement.

---

[2]After Cuscaden discovered he'd punched hell out of Tom Horn—one of the west's
last killers—in a barroom brawl, the kid hopped a freight and never looked back
until he arrived in Los Angeles.

As the 3:15 deadline neared and activity hit its peak, the atmosphere of urgency spread. Cowboys had geared up from lope to gallop. They quickly responded to cries from rewrite men ripping out copy and refeeding their typewriters with new sheets of paper. In complete command, city editor Richardson functioned like he was playing an instrument.

Sid Hughes was stuck with a sour story and was busy hyping the skid-row dead-body report to rewrite man Wayne Sutton. No money had been found hidden in the dead transient's shoes and there were no felony records matching his fingerprints. He hadn't been a man of notoriety like a few before him who had dropped out from society to disappear. And he hadn't left any notes to tell who he was. The deputy coroner who picked him up, a guy with a lot of experience in these things, said it was a bad liver that did him in. Sutton got all this information from police reporter Bill Zelinsky before Hughes returned with pictures of the dead body.

Catching Sutton scratching his head while trying to dream up a lead that could justify a three paragraph story, Richardson said, "Kill it, Sutton. If it's giving you that much trouble, the story's deader than the man."

All this time, two talented telephone operators deftly handled a glut of incoming and outgoing calls from their open cage. With old-fashioned earphones clamped over their heads, they spoke into gooseneck horns strapped to their chests. Their hands were as agile as a fencing master's as they worked with snakelike wire cords, replying to flashing red lights on their boards.

The gals, Jo Wise and May Northern, knew all the reporters' secrets. They protected them from unwanted outside calls. And when newsmen got in tight circumstances with the desk, Jo and May would give them an advance capsule fill-in of what they thought Richardson's barometric temper readings were.

Without a signal of any kind, activity quickly wound down, like a motorboat cutting its throttle and coasting in on its own wake. The first deadline had passed. Chuck Wells and company automatically returned to such menial duties as cleaning paste pots, sandwiching and stacking carbon paper books, sharpening pencils, changing typewriter ribbons and running down to Gallagher's hash factory for a ham and egg sandwich and coffee when a rewrite man was unable to leave his desk while working on a story.

During the deadline respite, reporters and the rest tilted back in their chairs, and waited for copies of the first edition to roll off the presses—like fresh loaves of bread from the oven—which would be circulated about the city room. This edition would eventually represent an historical chronicle of their day's literary output.

When the paper was distributed, the nearsighted Murray shoved his glasses up on his forehead and buried his nose a few inches from the print to check a story he had written. Then he looked up and asked me, "How are things?"

I mouthed, "What the hell am I supposed to do?"

"The desk won't forget you're here," I heard him say.

Richardson lit up a cigarette (spelled "cigaret" in the Hearst Style Manual) from the embers of his last one. He swiveled around to study a long sheet of foolscap pasted on the wall behind him. It contained a collection of expressions he had blue-penciled as being "untruths;" things like: "fires of unknown origin" or "hails of bullets." Also, on the list, he underlined that only royalty or whores were referred to as "ladies."

When I glanced across the city room in the direction of Lynn Spencer and his polished spittoon,[3] I noticed the thing in the trench coat that looked like a dead body had vanished. It probably was the remnants of a forgotten joke from the night before.

Afternoon editor Harry Morgan, a wiry and well-liked man in his fifties, took over the desk. He meticulously lined six cigarettes along the edge of his desk. This ceremony irked the chain-smoking Richardson as he watched Morgan set up his coffin-nail quota for the day.

---

[3]Spencer, a former police reporter, was a unique editor who used to chew tobacco while making up the society pages.

Originally from Kansas, Morgan worked for an El Paso paper in 1920 when Mexico's fat and oft-married revolutionary General Pancho Villa was leading his last revolt. Hero to the peons, Villa was shooting up the border town of Jaurez in the name of his *Presidente* Venustiano Carranza's crumbling government. This was the only story of national importance at the time, so quite a few big name U.S. journalists were covering Villa's raids.

Among the honorable newsmen working with Morgan were five who eventually migrated to Los Angeles after Villa had agreed to retire from the military and settle on a large Durango rancho which had been awarded him by the new government, provided the tarnished warrior would not bother them any longer.

The five with Morgan were Hy Schneider (a personal friend of Villa), Tim Turner, Jack Stevens, Bud Rowe and Cappy Marek. All but Marek joined the *Examiner*. Cappy went on to become L.A.'s *Her-Ex* city editor.

During the Juarez shoot 'em up, Morgan and four of the above-mentioned had been cut off from diplomatic immunity after illegally sneaking across the border. Villa had dispatched one of his subalterns to lead them to a haven which both warring factions wished to keep in reverential tact. It was Juarez's prime brothel-saloon which boasted "the longest bar in North America." The place was also stocked with spirits and female flesh. The only appropriate thing Jack Stevens could think to say when he saw all this was: "How lucky can you get?"

Around six o'clock, my stomach started growling. I was still sitting in the bull pen and yearned to join Newman, Murray and the others as they left for The Back Room bar, another *Examiner* hangout. But I didn't even have a clue if I would be going to dinner.

As I pondered this, Harry Morgan called up Dave Brown. He handed him a slip of paper with an address. "It's a shooting. Check it out," said Morgan. Then, "You might take Fowler along."

I followed Brown to the photo room. George O'Day, an ex-professional boxer with a large front gold tooth, grabbed his four-by-five Speed Graphic camera and a bag of negative plates and flash bulbs. We two-stepped it down a couple of flights of cast-iron stairways at the rear of the building and out to O'Day's car in the parking lot.

When we got to the scene, a police car and ambulance had already double-parked in front of a rundown apartment house. Red lights were blinking, but there was no urgency that I could see. A cop was writing in his notebook and an ambulance slowly unfolded a stretcher. My instinct told me whatever happened, it was all over.

At first the cops wouldn't let me pass. Then Brown explained I had just come on the paper and didn't have my credentials yet.

In the bedroom, there was a boy about 13 years old, his body thrown back over an unmade bed. Blood and gristle were splattered on the wall behind him. The boy's face was pasty and he had a hole in his belly as big as a grapefruit. His mother was sitting in a corner sobbing while his little sister stared at the floor as though she was being punished.

A police detective told Brown the boy had been playing with his father's shotgun. This was my first story and I was deeply moved. O'Day shot a picture he knew wouldn't get in the paper and Brown phoned the desk.

Morgan said that some dame had cut up a bartender's face in the classy Town Hall Zebra Room; the police had her in custody and they were on their way to Lincoln Heights Jail with her.

O'Day rammed his car across town and after we entered the jail, the first thing I noticed was the strong odor of Lysol. The composition floors were wet and a hushed trustee leaned on his mop waiting for whatever was going to happen. O'Day set his camera focus for an eight-foot grab shot inside the back entrance and waited.

I was wide-eyed, taking in everything. I had never been inside a jail before, not even as a visitor. Every insignificant thing impressed me. Never before had I seen people in such a raw state. Some were in deep mental pain and others didn't seem to give a damn being caught up in the snail-paced process of the law. I thought all these separate little stories really had an urgency to them, even though some of the players were unaware I was taking it all in for the first time. So they went about giving out their familiar lines to the jailers.

The gum-chewing prostitutes being booked were a flashy, exuberant lot. They seemed like a group of children enjoying themselves in spite of their adversity. They laughed and joked while standing in line to be fingerprinted. Their loud-colored, skin-tight outfits vulgarly brightened the dreary, over-packed booking room that stank of rancid sweat, cheap cigar smoke and a double dose of disinfectant.

The whores' faces I recall vividly. Their black eye makeup and exaggerated thick red lipstick reminded me of the hieroglyphics of women in colored relief on the walls of the tombs I had seen when I visited Egypt as a kid with my family.

Not that it was any improvement for the prostitutes, but they constantly stared into hand mirrors and commented to themselves while they added several more layers of this-and-that to their faces.

As a disheveled drunk was trying to locate the end of his bent cigarette with a burned-out match, one whore with a prize fighter's face hiked up her skirt, licked her thumb and straightened the seam of her one good stocking. Another tosspot listed as though on the bridge of a phantom ship and a rather handsome young, full-breasted girl grinned at me. She cupped her pantied crotch and said: "How'd you like to bury your nose in *this*, junior?" Then she laughed as a policewoman grabbed her arm and rolled her fingers one-by-one on a cold marble plate of wet ink.

Attempting to create a private corner for two, a bail bondsman who had offices across the street from the jail worked a toothpick around his mouth and conferred with his prisoner client who hadn't yet been deloused. He was coming off a drunk and the bondsman's garlic breath was making him sick, which added more to the pain of his broken nose and split lip. But, all-in-all, the shattered prisoner didn't look much worse than the bondsman trying to put together a deal. Added to his bad breath, the bondsman had a three-day-old beard and growled. He kept blowing his nose with an handkerchief that had been laundered so many times it refused to turn any lighter than the color of his worn gray overcoat.

Then something out of sight switched my attention. It was a howl and it kept growing louder. Shrieks, growls, grumblings. And when the shrill became audible, I figured I'd never heard an avalanche of polluted language come from a woman's mouth before.

As they turned the corner, I saw two hefty policemen trying to contain a bloodied female. Her silk dress was ripped down the front. She was jackknifing; kicking wildly like a Radio City Rockette out of control. Like the curious driver who slows down to see an accident, all those in the booking room riveted their attention on the raving woman who had suddenly taken center stage.

"You God-damned sons-of-bitches ... You fat-assed pricks ... You shit-faces," she yelled.

One of the whores in a relatively quiet voice cried back: "That's it, honey. Give it to 'em."

A nervous laughter of approval followed.

The two cops trying to control her just hung onto the wild woman.

O'Day was trying to get in rhythm with the woman's kicking. Then it happened—something I'd never seen before. O'Day's flash bulb popped just as the woman's legs flayed upward. But a split second before it went off, *I saw it as plain as day*! There it was: General Grant with his teeth out! ... The mad dog's tonsils! ... Her legs had flown apart to display what only gynecologists, obstetricians and trusted husbands have ever gotten a close look at.

I could hear O'Day say, "Oh, shit," realizing he was stuck again with a picture that wouldn't make the paper.

The bulb flash had now driven the wild woman, who had slashed a bartender's face with a broken glass, further into her madness. She knew her privates had been photographed. The eruption of searing words spewed out in swift batches of three-to-six at a time.

"... big-shouldered, short-cocked, hamburger-heads!" she roared, snapping the words off as though with her teeth, and waiting for them to scorch the walls before throwing out another salvo. "... couldn't satisfy me with your pencil-pricks ... a drought-going-on-inside your clap-ridden skills!" It was as though some other force had taken over her mind. "... fucking left-handed jabber shits ... explore all the cavities in my body!"

Most stood silently, unaware their mouths were hanging open.

"... your frappeed thigh-bolts all dried up now ... give me the half-nelson, you warn-out hog-heads!"

The filth of it had disappeared and the words began to sound like I was listening to John Barrymore in his finest theatrical tantrum.

The restraining cops' faces had turned sweaty with strain and red with anger. They had had enough. One slammed her down in a hard chair, grabbed a fistful of bloodied hair and yanked her head back. After getting what was the equivalent of whiplash, the slasher of the Zebra Room stopped thrashing and took in a long, quivering breath. Realizing she had been beaten, she slowly hissed with a carnal leer as O'Day finally got his picture, "... you couldn't make the pellet-transfer if your lives depended on it, you stone-scrotums."

At this, one of the cops knocked her senseless and all reacted with a communal, "Oh!"

O'Day took another shot of the face with her nose now pointed in another direction like a broken ship's rudder. A sergeant, the highest ranking there, snagged O'Day's last negative plate.

I looked at Brown and said, "Why the hell did you let him take the plate?" as a nurse led the broken woman away.

"This isn't going to be the last story I'll be covering up here," said Brown. "If I leave with incriminating evidence like that, something bad will happen to me one dark night when I'm all alone."

Brown made another call to the desk. Morgan told him we could break for a late dinner. In the excitement, I'd forgotten about my growling stomach. Jesus, I'd never been in such an exhilarated state before.

We dropped in at the Pantry,[4] a 24-hour eatery which opened in 1924. It was one block west of Figueroa on Ninth Street. Celebrating my first day as a reporter, Brown treated me to a ninety-five cent T-bone steak and potatoes and everything that went with it.

Driving home, I was bursting to tell anyone I could collar about the most exciting day of my life. But everyone was sleeping. There was no commercial television yet to keep them awake. That was still four years in the future.

The following day I read Gus Newman's embellished rewrite of Dave Brown's story about the Zebra Room bloody do. It was great reading, very fascinating, and I wondered if it was the same story Brown and I had covered the night before.

I began to search the paper for the story about the boy's tragic shotgun death. It wasn't on the front page as I expected it to be. It was buried back on page 16, next to a furniture ad. It had been reduced to one paragraph.

It hit me that I had a lot to learn about the value of stories.

---

[4]As it was yesterday, The Pantry accommodates 84 at a time, handles 3000 customers a day. Their statistics raise eyebrows. According to an anniversary brochure, they annually process 21,000 pounds of coffee, 90 tons of bread (461 loaves a day) and 7,200 head of cattle are needed to annually supply them with steaks. In addition, 2400 eggs are cracked daily, and each year, customers consume more than 6000 sides of bacon and a herd of 220 cows supply them with dairy products. Each year, 1 million jackets, aprons and towels are processed through their own laundry.

AUTHOR FOWLER—Ten minutes after enlisting in World War II, and two years before becoming *Examiner* cub reporter.

Photo by Frank Powolney

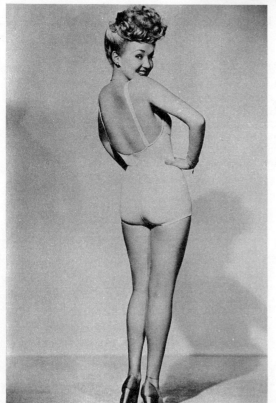

WORLD'S PREMIERE PINUP—In 20th Century-Fox photo department before heading for the *Examiner*, Fowler asked Betty Grable to strike a *derriere* pose (against rules of Hays Office censors). "You mean, like *this*?" Photographer Frank Powolney snapped his camera lens, and with a 1943 Stamp of Approval, the picture became the #1 pinup of all time during World War II.

III

The Rite of Passage

Testing the mettle of a cub reporter could be compared to one of yesterday's tough college fraternity hazings, but only in a vague way. The rite of passage for a newspaper tyro in the '40s was more intense, more brutal.

This was the "Jerkoff Era" in a reporter's life, the years when he was most impressionable and his ensuing miserable life was ordered and frozen in concrete.

When I was six, my big brother used to tell me I was an orphan, that the iceman was really father, and Mother was taking care of me for him. I thoroughly believed this and thought it was a great secret I didn't have to share with anyone else.

I began to notice that some of my features were like the iceman. I tried to get near to him; ask his advice about my small boy problems. I even made him peanut butter sandwiches, which he liked. But when I asked him if he knew he was my real father, the iceman never seemed to have time for me after that.

Every boy who wants to make something substantially good of his life should have a big brother with plans of sibling monopoly.

I became a grocery clerk during my adolescent Fire Island summers. I didn't socialize with the other rich kids lounging on the beach. They seemed too boring even though I still retained a Victorian fright to ask one of the girls what all the . . . you know what . . . was all about. The closest I got to seeing some sprouting female pubic hair was when I caught my sister in the shower. And that surely didn't interest me.

As a substitute for the cold shower, I took to rowing up the
Great South Bay, delivering boatloads of produce and canned
goods to Ocean Bay Park for Bohack's customers three miles
away. This unincorporated town had a U.S. Coast Guard station
during rum-running prohibition days. There were no sidewalks
and I made my deliveries pulling a wagon over loose, dry sand.
By the time I was 15, I'd grown so strong that there were times
when I thought my grandmother didn't know if I should be allowed in the house to sleep or be chained to a pole in the backyard. The girls at that time became interested in smiling at me
because they wanted to touch my arm muscles. And following
an insignificant incident, waist-deep with my big brother on a calm
ocean day, I didn't have to run for his glasses of water anymore.

My father had little time for me except when I was available
to drive him to his friends' homes when he was drinking and
had the urge to visit. I didn't want to voice it, but this situation
seemed great to me; I began reaching out for the friendship of
older, intelligent men. I began spending much time with my father
and he was introducing me to fascinating, erudite men I would
never forget: men like John Barrymore, W.C. Fields, artist John
Decker and the rest. By far, they were many years my senior,
but our mutual friendships grew and as a result, I nearly discon-
nected myself from those of my age.

I heard James H. Richardson was the best city editor ever to
operate on the west coast. He had been a badger covering fast-
breaking crime stories as a reporter. But as an editor, Richardson enjoyed breaking cubs in—or down. He savored undressing
us in front of others. He made it a point to do so if we came
back from an assignment without all the information needed to
feed the rewrite man. He looked down on the half-informed as
being idiots. And when a cub did return with the holes filled—or
even with a minor scoop--Richardson's handing out of compli-
ments came as hard as it was for someone to defecate mollusks.

Arriving in Los Angeles from Canada in 1914, Richardson got
his newspaper training on the old *Evening Herald* under the whip
of city editors J.B.T. Campbell and Wesley M. Barr. Fighting

for its existence, the *Herald* was barely meeting its payroll from week-to-week. There was a constant turmoil of firings and fist-fights going on all the time in the city room. By the early 1920s, Richardson became a star reporter. But the high-living pace was fast during these bathtub gin days, and in 1928, it got out of hand for him. He was eventually fired for boozing. Unable to get a reporting job in town, he left the newspaper business to take up a publicity post with a movie studio until he could get a handle on the sauce. He name was eventually mentioned as a possibility for city editor on the *Examiner*. At the time he'd been off the flit for more than a year and someone took a chance. He was hired and became a superior city editor and, also, a dedicated reformed drunk.

Like the twelve tasks of Hercules, there were four challenges Richardson put to all *Examiner* cubs. These consisted of going on a bogus meat-packing story at a slaughter house so the beginners would be exposed to a lot of blood and spilled organs; reporting a gory traffic accident; witnessing an autopsy; and— to humble even the stoutest of the lot—to take dictation from the famous syndicated Hearst movie columnist, Louella O. Parsons while she was in her cups.

First we were sent to the local abattoir to watch some big bastard cave in a steer's head with a sledge hammer. Then we followed an assembly line from where the carcass was strung up by its hind legs and split open with its guts spilling out, all steaming on a slippery floor. The ones who lasted through this first assignment would go on to the next story: accompanying a seasoned reporter who would write it. This was a suicide.

My first was that of a middle-aged husband who had been cuck-olded. By the evidence we found, he had been neat. Systematically the man whose wife had taken on a lover at a Woodland Hills school where she taught swimming, had rented a room in a swanky midtown hotel. His luggage consisted of a suitcase which contained shaving and tooth brushes, a necktie, clean shirt, a change of underwear, a bottle of good scotch, and a shotgun.

When the maid discovered his body the next morning, it was propped up like a gargoyle in the bathroom tub with the back of the head blown off. She noticed his neatly-folded glasses on top of a note that read: "I hope this hasn't caused you any inconvenience."[5]

The war was winding down and still hard-to-get rentals—with one exception—were handled by sharp real estate brokers. Their finder's fees by far exceeded the normal commission.

The "one exception" transaction took place before a suicide's body was removed by the coroner's office. Even before the investigating detective checked in with headquarters, he made a phone call to a listed prospective renter and made a lease deal on the spot.

Covering another messy suicide, I heard a homicide detective order the building's owner to "get this place cleaned up. I got someone moving in this afternoon." He had the upper hand, especially if the owner had a couple of good-paying *filles de joie* in residence.

My first accident story was thrown at me when I heard screams coming up to the *Examiner* city room and Richardson's eyes settled on me. He said, "Fowler, go see what the hell that's all about."

I ran down to the Eleventh Street side entrance. There I found a woman's body lying across the trolley tracks, a lot of blood and a few females sobbing and yelping. A man held his hand over his companion's eyes as I walked up to the body. As a courteous gesture, I lowered the skirt covering her head. But when I pulled it down, I found she had been decapitated by the express streetcar's wheels. Her head wasn't there and at the time, no one seemed able to find it.

When I reported this to Richardson, he thought I was joking.

The follow up to the story came the next day. A woman who sounded like she was so drunk she couldn't see through a ladder, phoned the desk and said she had read about the accident

---

[5]In my experience, when men committed suicide, they always removed their glasses first. When women did themselves in, they usually removed all their clothing, and *never* seemed to shoot themselves.

in the paper. Literally putting two-and-two together, she was presently keeping the missing head in her refrigerator.

Her call was turned over to me and I asked the lady how she came to have such a unique acquisition. "That God-damned 12-year-old stepson of mine brought it home yesterday," she slurred, "an' he lifted the God-damned thing up in the air an' said, 'Look, Ma!' " I heard ice tinkling, then told her she should phone the coroner's office, and I'd be glad to give her the number. "They'll take it off your hands," I said, "or from your refrigerator, that is."

"Not havin' a God-damned head without no body puts a lady in jeopardy, don't it?" she asked.

"I don't know," I said, passing up a comment on the malapropism. "Just call the coroner's office." I gave her the number.

"That God-damned stepson of mine sure don't have no respect," she said. "He's always playin' tricks on me like this." Knowing she would eventually get around to phoning the coroner's office, I hung up.

An accident of greater consequence came when a police siren drowned out a warning honk, causing two buses to collide. Injuries were slight with only three passengers being carted off the Georgia Street Receiving Hospital, where I'd been dispatched. The "consequence" part of covering a municipal bus accident came after ambulance-chasing shysters advised their newly-found clients to hobble over to Georgia Street and scream bloody murder about whiplashes and sore everything. "Borrow crutches. Steal them," cried the lawyers. "The buses are city-owned and *beaucoup* insured." Within an hour, the emergency hospital would look like the annex to Lourdes. In this set of circumstances, I had to take down names, ages, addresses, professions and phantom injury complaints suffered by the litigious-hungry ... And this, from every single one of them.

Accustomed to these sieges of disaster fiction, doctors worked hard to *administer*—instead of relieve—pain. They'd pinch and probe the fakers. They'd crack joints and twist toes and inoculate them with dull needles, informing some that immediate surgery was indicated. If a charlatan was Catholic, it would be suggested that a priest be summoned.

This atmosphere suggested it would be safer on the streets, and a majority of get-rich-quickers—including some who had jumped on the bus after the accident—would begin drifting toward the exits.

Georgia Street Receiving Hospital's facade was the same as the majority of city edifices built on a tight budget during the Great Depression: Red cinder brick with grouted cement joints. If you lined structures of this kind in a row and tried to locate a particular one on a dark night, it would be impossible.

Today, the Georgia Street building lies in slumber, no longer in use. Its carapace still bleaches in the sun but its sinew has long ago abdicated. I wonder how God's life-actuary tables read for this sanctuary of memories before it will be invaded by bulldozers to make way for some modern characterless structure.

But while the hospital building still stands dormant, before the rigor mortis of its destiny-to-be-forgotten sets in, it is worth eulogizing the doctors and nurses, ambulance drivers, telephone operators and Dr. Waldo Sebastian before they completely disappear from memory. It was Dr. Sebastian who ran the place and wielded a swift and accurate scalpel. But, especially, the building itself should be dwelled upon, this place of urgent healing that was once open all day and night to attend and ease confused pain.

The now aged building still stands a half-block south of Pico Street and three blocks west of Figueroa, the latter being the taw line where downtown Los Angeles officially begins.

The dormant structure sets back several feet from the street where three-or-four ambulances used to poise in their starting blocks. Dust now gathers at a downstairs entrance where Juvenile Hall used to be.

Then there's the entrance where two large elevators used to hum up to the spacious hospital lobby on the third floor. Again, painted with that city gall bladder green, the lobby had direct access to four treatment rooms. Next to the open entrance of each there was a desk, a sort of lectern where reporters—after becoming familiar faces—were allowed to study a patient's chart.

To the south side there was the telephone operator board and a room where the personnel had their coffee. It was also a sanctuary where they could lie down for catnaps. This was where the ambulance drivers hung out, waiting for calls.

To the north were cordoned sections. One was a patient's ward with six beds, used for city personnel undergoing emergency treatment, or other non-hostiles in hospital transit.

The second area was narrow and had three barred cells lined along one wall. This was where I used to grab needed sleep while working two back-to-back eight-hour shifts, or just plain staying up for several nights when pursuing a story that hadn't cooled off yet. I had slept on the same bed where a distraught boy had lain after shooting himself because he didn't know how to cope with his drunken parents who shouted at and hit one another. He had fired a shot into his head during a busy night at Georgia Street. Weirdly, his heart had stopped, but his brain kept his lungs functioning.

The third section, rather small for its function, was the emergency surgery. It still hangs a swinging screen door at its entrance and the door still has holes in it as it did nearly a half-century ago when Dr. Waldo Sebastian was performing his surgical miracles.

Sebastian was of medium height. The skin on his unusually handsome face was tight and I could swear it shined. His hair was pepper-and-salt gray, his moustache was waxed and its hairs were trained to come to a point, which gave him the look of a German field marshal. His eyes twinkled when he was enlightening reporters with his surgical procedures. They were gray, but not cold like those of an old western gunslinger. He was worshipped by his nurses. One, whom I only knew as "Molly," had followed Sebastian from the World War I battlefields of France to Los Angeles, just to serve with him.

Dr. Sebastian also found time to consult with ailing members of a newspaperman's family and treat them for free.

We used to marvel at this man who would dramatically appear from surgery in the middle of operating on the subject of one of our stories. He was aware what deadlines were and would update a patient's prognosis for a new lead. We enjoyed his ego which was not overbearing.

One time while removing L.A. Mayor Fletcher Bowron's gall bladder, Dr. Sebastian burst from surgery with wet blood on his smock to give an update. And, by God! he was holding a scalpel in his gloved hand. He was what could be described today as a fascinating son-of-a-bitch. Before reentering surgery where the Mayor awaited with open belly, Dr. Sebastian paused to pull down his face mask, and with twinkling eyes, said: "You know, boys, I perfected this procedure I am now employing by repeating it over-and-over again on dead bodies in the front lines."

There was only a single way we reporters could irritate the usually unflappable Sebastian. That was when we interrupted his sleep to settle a bet. It was always the same bet, and it started one day after a group of reporters were sitting on a death watch in the Lutheran Hospital in downtown Los Angeles. Specifically, we were waiting for a patient in critical condition—just molded into a body cast—to take a turn for the better or croak.

While biding time with us, Dr. Sebastian mentioned something he thought would interest us. "Do you know how we used to clean body casts back during the Great War?"

"What do you mean, clean body casts?" I asked. "You mean while the casts were *on* the patients?"

"Precisely," said the doctor.

"Impossible," said another reporter.

"Not at all," said Sebastian. "It was discovered by a fluke." Then, entering his clinical manner, he said: "Some soldier had died after rigor mortis had set in, and when the body cast was cut away in order that he could be fitted into a coffin, a French surgeon noted the area where the wound had been weeping was as clean as a hound's tooth." Sebastian gloriously smiled. "The maggots had eaten away the proud flesh and the dead man's wound was sterile clean."

"Maggots?" I said, screwing up my face.

"Maggots," said the good doctor.

From then on, when reporters happened to be partying, one in the group invariably brought up the subject with candor. "I'll bet you don't know how they used to clean body casts in World War I."

"No, I don't know how they used to clean body casts in World War I," some gullible guy would say. "How did they do it?"

"Maggots," the reporters would reply.

"Maggots? ... Maggots? ... You're full of shit."

"No shit, maggots."

"Prove it."

"How much?"

"Five bucks says you're full of shit."

"You can't afford five bucks. Show it to me."

"How can you prove it?" a collusive confederate would ask.

"One phone call," the perpetrator would say along with: "When I win this bet, I intend to collect and then we'll become enemies."

"Here ... Here's the five ... Now prove it."

"One phone call," the perpetrator would say.

"How the hell can you prove something like this at one o'clock in the morning?"

"One phone call to ... Would you take the word of Waldo Sebastian, M.D., head surgeon for the City of Los Angeles?"

"... City of Los Angeles ... I'd believe," the weaving guy about to be bilked would say.

Now, Dr. Sebastian never received phone calls late at night. These were relegated to one of his assistants. However —just in case—the conscientious physician felt it his duty to be available if some municipal emergency arose, or if the Mayor had a relapse.

The good doctor frowned upon these invasions as being dis-
respectful. In any event he would handle these thoughtless calls
in this manner:

"Hello. Dr. Sebastian?" an over-relaxed voice would inquire.

"This is he."

"Dr. Sebastian," the cotton voice would continue: "I have
a question about body casts ..."

Realizing what the sleep interruption was all about, Dr.
Sebastian would merely mention a single word, "Maggots," then
hang up and try to get back to sleep.

Georgia Street Receiving Hospital was a parking lot for tragedy.
There were so many episodes in life I used to witness being
played out on the third floor of this theater of pain.

There was the time when Detective Lieutenant Harry Freemont was questioning a captured criminal lying on a treatment
table in Room Number Two. The felon, who had been shot in
the shoulder while attempting to escape, had just killed Harry's
partner with a gun.

I knew Harry's temper. He was quietly interrogating the
prisoner. His quiet was a sign of danger to me. He said: "You're
not hurt bad. Sit up and talk to me." He had a trace of a smile.
I recalled this tall, wiry, rough cop when he got mad. Once he'd
nearly beaten a prisoner to death in a 77th Street substation and
I'm certain he'd killed a lot of criminals in back alleys.

Now, Freemont shoved the hospital prisoner off the treatment
table and growled, "Get the hell out of here, you son-of-a-bitch."
He shoved as other plainclothesmen backed away toward the wall.

It was a Mexican Standoff. The man was still handcuffed and
knew he was about to run for what was left of his life.

Harry was a marksman and there was nothing stopping him
from playing out his retribution for his partner's death.

I didn't go to the floor like other bystanders caught in a place
they hadn't planned to be. I just stood very still and quiet as
the cop killer ran past me. Somehow, I was fascinated by his

glazed eyes staring at the opened elevator door as the first of Harry's six shots ripped into his body.

Then there was the 12-year-old boy. It was the Fourth of July. I was working overtime. Georgia Street was the obvious place to be when fireworks casualties started coming in. And this was the human interest story the paper ended up using as an example of how people should be cautious when playing with firecrackers.

The youngster had been experimenting with homemade bombs. His injured right hand looked like a baseball catcher's mitt when he was brought in. He was French and was visiting his grandparents. He couldn't understand English, but the nurse who had followed Sebastian from the front lines was there. In translation, Molly was the only link between this child who was in shock and an alien world. As doctors arrested the bleeding and prepared to surgically amputate the hand, Molly tunnelled these pathetic words as he stroked his forehead: *"Je t'aime mon petit. Le bon Dieu avec vous."*[6] When she said this, the child reflected hope in his eyes.

"He says he can't find his guardians . . . and they will be cross with him." Then, "He says he is here to study with the great piano teacher, Roger Obert. He is a prodigy." Then, "He says if we let him go home, he will promise not to play with fireworks again."

There were also occasions when a smile could curl when something of less urgency occurred. There was the time when a bald-headed black man casually entered the third floor. He had a switch-blade wedged into the top of his skull like a watermelon plugger.

Most courteous, he articulately explained he had been "in an altercation with another gentleman . . . and you now view the remnant of our argument."

I tried like hell to remove it, but it was impossible to draw the knife from the man's head. It seems that human skulls, like greedy wives, have a penchant to clutch.

---

[6]"I love you, little one. The good Lord is with you."

There was no emergency, so the gentleman rested with his problem and waited. Legs crossed, he perused the morning newspaper as passers-by oogled and came up with several interesting comments when out of earshot.

A resident surgeon signed in for his watch, attempted to pull out the switch-blade, said, "I'll be damned," then called for a gurney. The human dart board was wheeled through the swinging screen door and into surgery where a small pie-shaped hunk of his skull (along with the switch-blade) was excised.

There were prospective patients in pain who would come crying to Georgia Street with several fascinating symptoms possessing hideous, yet humorous symptoms . . . such as the fellow with confusion written on his face and an incandescent light bulb (75 watts) stuck up his ass. Suction had refused to relinquish it and there was only one way to ameliorate his immediate succor: Shatter the glass orb, prescribe milk-of-magnesia and warn the stricken fellow not to have anal sex for at least six weeks.

Then there was a man who came into the hospital with a billiard ball he couldn't dislodge from his mouth. There was the hooker with syphilis so bad, she had a residual problem with her hip flying out of joint while humping. She was a revolving door patient and thus considered herself in the seniority category and used to castigate resident physicians. "You get this damned thing fixed right this time," she'd say. "It's cuttin' into my income. An' I'm too proud to go on the county dole."

There were the usual problems of poor souls getting their everreadies suctioned into the neck of a milk bottle, and the number of visiting servicemen requesting a shot of penicillin following a drunken blackout they couldn't completely recall. However, there was an interesting case regarding man's most treasured appendage which demands mentioning more thoroughly.

Awakened from my sleep in a jail cell next to that of an epileptic who had had a seizure and was embarrassed to go home, my favorite night shift nurse shook me awake and offered me a cup of coffee. Barbara wanted me to see what she referred to as a "big piece of salami." I followed her into Treatment Room

Three where a very confused man was in distress. His clothing was being cut away.

When the snipping got down to his midriff, it was evident that the man, indeed, had an enormous sexual organ. But there was a flaw; it had been cut halfway through.

"Oh, God," the stricken man cried when he viewed his injury. "It's my *thing*!"

Pretending not to notice the injury, his physician asked: "Where do you hurt?" Examining other parts of his body, he said: "Is it your arm? You seem to have a few cuts there."

"No, it ain't my arm," the patient cried. "You know damned well it ain't my arm . . . It's my *thing*!"

"What thing?" the doctor asked.

"What the hell thing do you think?"

"What thing?"

"My cock, you mother," he cried.

"Ah, yes," said the doctor. "Your penis . . . Well, now. We can fix that up for you . . . a few stitches about the circumference."

It seemed that the humiliated man had been caught by his wife while he was on the rise, making love to another woman. After his mate thrashed the other woman, she proceeded to get hubby very drunk. And after he had passed out, she took a razor and cut his penis halfway through. In the process, the invaded urethra had been severed and was in need of re-connection.

Taking the pain with Spartan courage, the man asked after the minor surgery: "Will I be able to use it again? . . . You know what I mean . . . Will I be able to . . . *use* . . . it again?"

Sorrowfully, the physician binding his precious wound assumed the attitude of a priest, and with compassion, he said: "Only for pissing."

My first autopsy took place in the County Morgue located uptown in the Hall of Justice basement. Even a long time ago the coroner's office was already considered too small for this growing city However, the population had not yet begun to explode, and crime was not so rapacious as in today's doped-up society.

There were only two embalming tables and four body refrigerators. Here autopsy surgeons used to stick their large knives in a thick, round piece of balsa wood. And when the American Legion or other national organizations came to town, about 50 extra gurneys were rented to accommodate the overflow of conventioneers' bodies, those of older men with heart problems and too out of shape to rump-thrash all night.

Later when I worked the Saturday sheriff's beat with a tall and good-looking reporter, Kendis Rochlen from the *Mirror*, we'd check our rounds, then I'd grab a nap on the flea-infested press room couch. Across the hall in the coroner's office, Kendis would prepare breakfast and we'd eat it on an unoccupied embalming table.

The autopsy performed this day was on a 30-year-old prostitute who had been beaten to death by her pimp for holding out money on him. It was suspected she died as the result of a fractured skull.

There she lay, defenseless. Only a small cloth, like a *petit doily*, covering her pubis. There was a tattoo across her stomach. Following an arched line were the words: *Many a bloody battle has been fought here*. A half-dozen blue arrows pointed toward her vagina.

Present were a few other new cubs. One, from the *Daily News*, was a gal. And it surprised me that when the autopsy surgeon made his initial incision that she didn't leave us.

After the surgeon incised the sides and rear of the woman's scalp in order to get to the skull, he peeled it forward and over her face, allowing a tuft of brown hair to jut out from her jaw. It looked to me like a Mormon bishop's beard.

I began to laugh. Not from anything humorous in my interpretation. Not because of the tattoo. But it was because I had never seen a human body (as battered as was hers) so ungraciously violated. I stared at the splayed-open monstrosity that once had been a little girl, probably once kissed by a loving mother and hugged by a devoted father. And, now, here she was, the remnant of a worn-out whore already forgotten by her pimp who had disappeared into the night.

The surgeon's saw took a second run around the skull before he could remove the top to examine the brain. The odor from the brain told us she'd been drinking gin prior to her death. It was finally decided she'd died from internal injuries of the peritoneum and not from a cerebral hemorrhage. Her skull was too thick for that.

The final—and not so amusing—Richardson trial by fire assignment for his cubs was that of taking dictation from syndicated columnist Louella O. Parsons phoning in an exclusive while in her cups.

I'd been working hard on my typing speed (which had climbed to 60-words-a-minute) when the desk called for me to take Louella's dictation. At first I thought I had a bad connection. I held my hand over the phone to tell the desk I didn't know what the hell she was talking about. Richardson said, "I don't care if it sounds like Choctaw, take it down." I did, and it still made no sense, but we'd gone on record as taking it down by putting it on the log in case Louella might have remembered phoning it in and called us on it.

When the work day wound down, Richardson seemed in an unusually genial mood to the old-timers. His euphoric state came as a result of hiring a new man out of Kansas, just on the strength of a story he'd written and sent over the INS wire. His name was Ted Thackery and the story that moved him to the west coast went this way:

(INS) May 22—Udall, Kansas:

> This little prairie town died in its sleep last night. A tornado wooshed through it like a biblical sword of wrath, and in less than 60 seconds, 60 years of growing was cut to sod.
>
> Tom Mathers, the town barber, was asleep in the back of his shop when the twister struck.
>
> He can't be found.
>
> Neither can his shop.

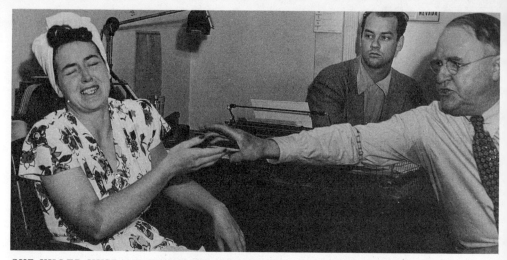

SHE KILLED HUSBAND WHILE HOLDING BABY IN HIS ARMS—Irish war bride Bridget Waters cries out in anguish at her 1946 Las Vegas coroner's hearing for shooting errant husband holding their year-old son in his arms. Reporter Fowler, exhausted from entertaining Chief of Police all night, sits at center as attorney L.O. Hawkins tries to quiet the 26-year-old nurse.

ARMED AND DANGEROUS—While on roadblock watch for a dangerous prison escapee, a bicycling itinerant fruit-picker is shaken down by variously armed *Examiner* newsmen (l to r) Phil Glickman, Fowler and Ben White. Back in 1946, Los Angeles reporters were licensed to carry concealed weapons, and oftentimes hurt themselves while trying to use them.

IV

Reporters: A Menagerie of Miscellany

"**N**ever have a hangover on your own time," was the most penetrating professional advice anyone had given me to date. This epigram emanated from Richard Vincent O'Connor who was a rewrite man on the *Los Angeles Herald & Express*.

O'Connor was reticent about his age, but was probably propelled into this world about the time the Poles led the last cavalry charge of history in The Great War, or when American women were allowed to begin voting.

In 20 years as a newspaperman, O'Connor had graced the city rooms of that many papers and was fired only twice. He never owned a car and probably never learned to drive one. I used to pick up the six-foot-four-inch redheaded Irishman each working morning, and if he was with hangover, Dick would curse the size of my small MG sports car as he twisted into its bucket seat.

O'Connor wrote the earliest of his more than 50 published books, squeezing in paragraph by paragraph between deadlines on the *Her-Ex*, where he functioned as a rewrite man. Three of his biographies were of generals Hood, Thomas and Sheridan. And he probably knew more about the War Between the States than any living man except Bruce Catton and Fletcher Pratt. When he died (too soon) at the age of 59, O'Connor was writing an encyclopedia on law.

Of him, columnist Jack Smith once said: "Our O'Connor sometimes gave the impression of living in an unreal world of his own construction, but nobody was more deeply rooted in the facts

. . . He loved dogs, women, drink, chewing tobacco and smoking cigars, sleep, food and humor. He was as fierce as a puppy with a belly full of warm milk, and he had more facets than a bowl of ice cubes.''

O'Connor had more theories on drinking than a Johns Hopkins psychologist. He had a fathomless respect and predilection for all forms of spirits, but when I met him, he had an almost excessive devotion to tequila. He drank it solemnly and maintained his own private bottles in a number of convenient watering places. When he had had too much cactus juice, Dick had a tendency to be hostile, but he struck out only toward the dead.

No one I knew could set at a bottle of tequila with such unbroken patience as O'Connor, which got me thinking upon his unequaled aphorism regarding the hangover: *Have I been leaning too heavily in my narrative about reporters in respect to their drinking escapade and habits?*

I think not.

I believe reporters' excessive toping image followed by the display of the racking hangover was overly misjudged by persons who took too little time to consider what made us the way we were. Most likely the ungentlest judgments came from those alien to our volatile way of life. Those people only read about what was going on in the world rather than living it—mortals who predictably played bridge on Tuesdays, had sex on Fridays, and didn't really know how to do either very well. They were incapable of calculating the thrill a superior reporter used to experience while living on the edge to pursue his scoop.

To ease off the afterglow, the newsman would visit the only club he could afford, his corner bar. Here, he celebrated his surviving on a ridiculously low salary paid in tariff to be allowed to gaze firsthand through a dark window where the spectacle of life was observed. These capon critics had never—nor would ever—be thrown into as many bizarre situations during their entire earthly term as we did in a week's time.

In the beginning, Murray, Newman and I worked weekends and this Monday, Gus had asked Santa Anita horse race caller

Joe Hernandez to fill in as a fourth. Gus was good at fading his shots around oil well derricks planted in the middle of the Inglewood Golf Club fairways. Jim was just learning the game, and I liked to see how far I could hit a drive, no matter where it went. Hernandez was erratic, too. And when his drive sliced across the street and onto cemetery property, it was necessary that he reappropriate his hard-to-come-by wartime re-covered *Wilson* ball.

As it worked out, Hernandez's ball settled three feet inside a chain-link fence where a Catholic burial was taking place. Joe tried not to be intrusive, but he was. There came some throat-clearings and the priest—obviously not a golf enthusiast—leered at Joe poking his two-iron through the fence, probing for his golf ball. As the priest blessed the remains, a compassionate mourner adroitly flicked the ball within Joe's reach while genuflecting. Nodding a "thank you" to the gentleman, Hernandez said to him: "If it wasn't for the war, I wouldn't have had to bother you."

Refreshed by two days off, I reported in on Wednesday. Night editor Jack Lait, Jr. (son of noted Hearst reporter Jack Lait, Esq., who had covered the Lindbergh kidnapping and trial), was heavy-lidded, exhausted and suffered stomach cramps. His usual night of sucking on a pint of sloe gin didn't help alleviate the pain instigated by too much spicy Mexican food. I couldn't help but notice that Jack was attached at the ankle to a length of clothesline. I asked him what he was trying to prove. "If you're trying to hang yourself, you're going about it at the wrong end," I said.

"Spent the whole god-damned night on the can," said Lait while untying himself. "Really had a bad dose of diarrhea."

"What's that got to do with a hunk of rope around your ankle?" I asked.

Lait explained that it was impossible for him to leave the toilet for more than a few minutes at a time, so he had a copyboy rustle up the clothesline which he had stretched from the men's room, all the way down the hallway to the city room. "Whenever there was a call I couldn't get out of answering," he said, "someone would yank the clothesline and I'd run to the phone with my pants at half-mast."

Such an emergency came that night. It was a three-alarm jerk
that had Lait hobbling into the city room with his sloe gin in one
hand and a fistful of toilet paper in the other. He answered the
phone with a disturbed, "Well, what is it?"

"This is Mr. Hearst," came a high-pitched answer.

"And I'm the Queen of Sheba," said Lait.

"Who *is* this?" Hearst was known for his alto voice.

"The Prince of Wales," Jack mocked in falsetto. "Who's
this?"

"This *is* Mr. Hearst," came the answer, "and I want ... "

When a copyboy insisted it really was the Chief, Lait said his
colon jerked in preparation for another rectal rebellion.

Jack expected the worst after making his way back to the can
where the remainder of his watch was spent contemplating
immediate dismissal, which never came.

By this time I had three weeks experience on the street on
my own and I was beginning to feel more confidence with myself.
I'd begun to learn the patterns of certain stories that also contained human interest sidebars—a separate, lesser story, but
still associated with the main one.

One of the most disappointing times to a reporter was when
a sidebar was passed over for various reasons. This was such
a story.

I was covering a San Pedro fire where arson was suspected.
A heavy advertising mercantile company's warehouse had been
torched. All was not lost because the establishment would be
able to write off its warehouse's losses with the IRS, making
up for the previous year's deficit. At full value, it could rid itself
of the merchandise it was unable to move.

During the blaze, I became interested in the plight of an old
couple sobbing into one another's arms. Hot cinders from the
warehouse had ignited and burned their little home to the ground.
They were not insured. My photographer, Al Brett, took a shot
of the couple who couldn't hold back tears. They had lost the
only house they had ever owned.

I sounded like a passionate pulp writer when I unloaded the sidebar to my rewrite man only to see it tossed into Richardson's basket. Marjorie Driscoll, the best rewrite woman west of the Rockies, had written a compassionate story about the old couple who had lost their home, but the reason Richardson had to pass on it was because the mercantile company was a prominent advertiser and the publisher didn't want anything to distract from the company's loss.

There were many graces and ingrained customs which even a roughshod reporter used to conform to nearly 50 years ago which have all but been forgotten in today's society. We always wore coats and neckties to work or when attending social functions. We stood up when a lady entered the room and we opened car doors for them. And when in their company while walking, we always assumed the protective side nearest the street. We never shook their hands unless a hand was first offered. We asked permission to smoke and never offered a cigarette unless asked for one. Oh, yes, and we never used blue language in their presence, unless we were drinking.

I've noticed that when customs change, this is done in order for things to be made easier for people. The main exception is that today, we've been weaned from being referred to as "man" and "woman." In substitute, "person" is the demanded word to be used, sexlessly referring to both male and female. All must be accepted as a single entity. This was a blow to me in the beginning of the age of the person. My parents and their ancestors all came from the Midwest where ladies were not only defended and looked up to, but even duels were fought for their affections. Therefore, I was brought up to be a gentleman, and I'm damned if I'm going to die a *person.*

Because of society's strict Victorian moral facade in those days, newspapers never printed suggestive phrases or words like the forbidden ones commonly read in today's periodicals. Even the four-letter word "rape" was taboo. We wrote around it and the code word for "raped" was "attacked." So when some unfortunate lady was raped, we would be compelled to write the lead something like this:

As she was walking through a dark alley, Miss Vel-
veeta Devlan, 19, of 16157 Morrison Street, was
struck a stunning blow on the head with a blunt instrument. Then, as she lay helpless on the pavement, she
was kicked and stomped upon and hit with rocks. When
she tried to struggle to her feet, her assailant knocked
out six of her teeth, tore her clothes from her body,
and began to pound her in the stomach with his fists
until she fell once again. Just as she was lapsing into
unconsciousness, the assailant proceeded to attack her.

Then there were the tragic stories that wars bring about—
especially those which have to do with infidelity. A soldier went
overseas, and after a long absence, often began wondering if
his wife was still being faithful while he was at the front.

Throughout World War II, many callous wives sent "Dear
John" letters to their overseas mates in uniform after running
into a handy civilian she found fun playing with in the bedroom.

One particular story I covered involved a young lady who had
been little more than a bride when her husband was called up
and shipped out to serve as an infantryman in the European
Theatre of Operations. The two were deeply religious and
believed that God would safely deliver him back home. She was
no "Dear John" letter writer, but two years after the bridegroom
had taken the mandatory ocean voyage for Uncle Sam, she came
down with pregnant.

This was not an uncommon wartime affliction. Some wives
often covered their fooling around by backdating a child's birth
certificate. And in one reported case, an overseas soldier had
been convinced his wife's child had been a divine presentment.

While interviewing this girl, I wanted to be convinced that
something was not exactly right. Had it not been for her deep
spiritual quality, she said that the thought of suicide had entered
her mind. She hadn't yet written to her husband about her quan-
dary, and was now considering an abortion.

Then I came up with a lead that literally had teeth in it. Three
months earlier, a local dentist had removed an infected back molar
for her. He had used gas as an anesthetic. She supplied me with

his address and I checked police records to see if the dentist might have a felony record. He didn't, but there was a notation that he had been taken to civil court on charge of rape but the charge had been dropped. Police reporter Bill Zelinsky ran it down and said the dentist's attorney had won the jury over in proving the plaintiff was a loose woman and had repeatedly been unfaithful to her husband before he went overseas.

Not true in the instance of my lady. The *Examiner* followed it up and the district attorney issued a warrant for the dentist's arrest. The oral surgeon broke down under intensive questioning—which was more intensive in those days—and confessed to "attacking" his anesthetized patient.

Supreme court Justice Charles E. Fricke became famous to the general public long before when he sentenced an elderly man to 35 years in prison for murdering his wife. "But I'm an old man, your honor," the old felon pleaded, bending over with rheumatism. "I can't serve all that time," to which Judge Fricke uttered the classic line, "Well, you just do the best you can."

In the case of the bloomer-japing dentist, Judge Fricke was unflagging. He sentenced the D.D.S. to 25 years, which were served as San Quentin's resident tooth-extractor. Ergo: Dentist Fills Wrong Cavity.

One day Ted Thackery was laboring to come up with a lead matching in quality of the story he'd written about the Udall tornado. Richardson was hard on Ted's hide and the former Kansan was on the fourth rewrite, but determined to satisfy his city editor.

"Do you still have the carbon of your first try?" Gus Newman asked.

Thackery pulled carbons from his spike. "Here" he said.

"Just turn the first story back in," Newman advised.

Richardson studied the first take, then grinned: "Now, *that's* more like it."

Another rewrite man, Walter Brooks, had one of his stories rejected so often that he finally thumbtacked his copy to

Richardson's desk. The copy was rigged with a rubber band, and when Richardson picked up the story, the elastic band snapped Brooks' copy back to him.

In one way or another, all of us reporters were labeled as being characters. Most often we were looked upon by outsiders as a sort of *menagerie of miscellany*.

We once had a copy reader who could blow smoke from his eye, and the aforementioned jealous man in the art department who took his wife's wooden leg to work with him. Then there was Tom Towers. Tom was a stringer out of Palm Springs before becoming a staff regular. He was what we used to refer to as a "spiffy dresser." Once, covering a fashion show, Towers won the prize as Best Dressed Reporter. The following year, Tom missed out on the award because he was wearing the same suit and necktie.

Regarding Towers and neckties, I'd like to focus on a prank I played on Tom. It was on Christmas Eve day, a time when many lonely folks grew melancholy and did themselves in.

This December 24th found photographer Al Brett and myself riding in the back of the coroner's newest Black Mariah. We were trolling for stories with life's sadder aspects during the abundant Yuletide time of celebration.

The Mariah answered a call and we headed out for Pomona to pick up an exercise jockey's body. He'd hanged himself from a shower curtain-rail above his bathtub ... with a necktie. We found his body wedged facedown between the toilet and tub. When the deputy coroner collected him, I asked if I could have the necktie. He gave me a nasty sneer, then handed me the tie.

That afternoon I had the colorful tie cleaned and pressed at a Chinese laundry and an acquaintance at Saks Fifth Avenue boxed it for me. Then, after I was sure Al Brett had circulated the photo of the jockey's body and the necktie throughout the city room, I ceremoniously presented my gift to Towers during the peak of our staff Christmas party.

"Golly," said Towers, "I didn't get anything for you."

"Open it," I urged. He did, and I said, "Put it on."

He did, and when the revelers discovered the necktie had belonged to the dead jockey, men broke into uncontrolled laughter, and a couple of women experienced the vapors.

We also had a member of the menagerie at the Christmas party who was a resident horse bettor. If he couldn't be found in the bull pen, Frank Finch would be in a cubicle occupied by telegraphers. This dying breed used to receive the earliest Wall Street reports and horse race tote board returns via the sparking dit-dit-dah-dit Morse code.

Finch was in his late fifties and spoke painfully in low tones. He was as close to Damon Runyon's *Sorrowful Jones* horse tout character as anyone could be. One late afternoon when the city room was quiet, I watched Frank shuffle by. He had had a bad day of small time betting. In utter dejection he looked at me and said: "If I only had two dollars, I'd be exactly destitute."

We also had our house bookmaker named Lou "Cockey Lou" Gregorius, who divided his action between the *Examiner* and the *Her-Ex*. Cockey Lou walked as if he was keeping one step ahead of the bunco squad. His black-dyed hair was plastered down and he looked faintly like Rudolph Valentino. Cockey Lou used to hang around the sports department where the Associated Press printer tapped out the latest results from Santa Anita. Working out of the sports department, Sammy Schnitzer was getting *quid pro quo* under the table from Lou for the privilege of ingress. But when we reporters tried to get to the printer, Schnitzer would have us tossed out. Management eventually had a low wooden railing installed to keep us out. The day it was completed, we reporters took turns throwing Schnitzer back into the corral until the front office put a stop to it.

One of our more dignified parlay bettors was named Walter Naughton. Walter came from a line of newspaper reporters and editors of note and had the portly appearance and carriage of humorist Irvin S. Cobb. Years earlier Naughton had given up on whiskey because it began to make him sick. And now, suspecting he might have developed some residual *mal* from youthful enthusiastic imbibing, Walter's doctor suggested that a urine test was in order to check if he might have an excess of sugar coursing through his vascular system.

Unable to properly match a pronoun with a noun in his copy, or keep his syntax in order that day, Naughton gave up waiting for the test results and phoned his physician. "Well, Doc," said the sweaty Naughton, "did you find any sugar in my urine?"

"What time are you off?" The practitioner asked.

"Five o'clock," said Walter. "Why?"

"Well, when you're off," said the doctor, "come on down to the office and we'll have a taffy-pull."

Jim Richardson did have a leer that scared most reporters, and he took advantage of every physical aspect he had to get this across during his intermittent outbursts on the desk. What made his leer so eerie for the new men was that he had "wall eyes." His left eye had a weak muscle, and when he flashed the right one in the direction of a staffer, it took the left eye about a half-second to catch up and swim into position. "It was like a riveted boxer watchin' a hay-maker comin' at him," said a circulation department man. "He knew it was comin', but he couldn't do nothin' about dodgin' it."

Although Richardson never managed to intimidate me, another reporter who seemed to have been, Robert Epstein, developed a routine when turning in a piece of copy to Jim. He said: "Each visit to the desk required a serious look, a steady eye, a ready voice and a quick escape."

V

One Woman, Two Murders, Three Suicides

On April 11, 1947, Jackie Robinson broke the color barrier in professional baseball when owner Branch Rickey signed the athlete as a member of the Brooklyn Dodgers team. That was a time I would never forget because it was the very day I witnessed the execution of Louise Peete in San Quentin's gas chamber for committing murder after being paroled from a life sentence for killing yet another person.

During the years I put into this favorite apostrophe of my profession life—1944-52—the maximum sentence in the State of California for committing first degree murder was 17 years.

Louise Peete had already spent the equivalent of a full life term plus one year for the 1920 murder of 49-year-old millionaire mining engineer Jacob Charles Denton. The trial made national headlines for a month.

Denton's second wife, Dolly, had died shortly after he had completed building her a three-story mansion next door to another millionaire, Marco Hellman, in the blue stocking Wilshire district. Denton eventually advertised the house for rent. Louise Peete leased it.

At midnight on June 1, 1920, Hellman's maid heard a shot. Denton disappeared. A daughter, Frances (by Denton's first marriage), resided in Phoenix, Arizona. She became suspicious when her father failed to visit during a regular period. She hired a private detective to find him.

Searching his home, Los Angeles police found Denton's body in a musty niche in the cellar. He was identified through a rusty belt buckle which was initialed "JDC." His large diamond ring and Hamilton railroad watch were missing.

Denton had been shot through the back of his neck. The bullet penetrated his brain. Police deduced that his body had been tied up, then rolled down the basement stairs to where it had been sealed in a vault made from an old wine cabinet.

For two months, Louise had slept in the mansion, directly above Denton's "crypt." Then, when things began to get hot, she traveled to Denver. However, following an indictment, Mrs. Peete was persuaded that it would be better to bolster her claim of innocence to return to Los Angeles on her own.

She was tried, and during the trial, began to profusely quote the Bible. "I am being crucified upon a cross. But I can say as did Christ, 'Father, forgive them, for they know not what they do.' "

Louise was convicted by Superior Judge Frank R. Willis of first degree murder "for profit."

Two weeks before Christmas in 1944, Richardson decided I was ready to cover my first story of consequence. He called me to his desk and handed me a slip of paper with the address, 714 Hampden Drive, Pacific Palisades, scrawled on it. He didn't tell me what the story was, and I wasn't about to ask. He had recently looked at a piece I had turned in, one of the hundreds he would throw in the waste basket throughout the four years I would work under him. He had remarked, "You sure as hell can't write like your father."

"Neither can you, you damned fool," I answered. I knew a personality conflict was in the offing.

It was nearly an hour's drive west from the paper, a few miles from the ocean. When my photographer George O'Day asked, "What the hell are we covering . . . a cotillion?"

"I don't know," I said. "You know Richardson. He hands you an address and expects you to go blind into it."

When we arrived in this middle-class neighborhood, I saw a police car and a coroner's mariah parked in front of the address Richardson had given me. We weren't covering a cotillion.

A uniformed cop told me it was the home of a Mrs. Margaret Logan, and that a body had just been exhumed from a shallow grave in the backyard. Neighborhood dogs had been digging to get at something there.

Detectives had just wrapped the preliminary investigation and told the deputy coroner he could remove the body. It was that of a woman and it had been sprinkled with lime so it would quickly decompose. After O'Day got his pictures, I phoned in.

Later in the day, the body was identified to be that of the house owner, Mrs. Logan. She had been a real estate broker and was the benefactress of Louise Peete, who had been paroled to her. Taken into custody, Mrs. Peete claimed that Mrs. Logan had been done in by her husband, Albert Logan, who had recently died in the Patton State Hospital for the Insane two weeks before his wife's body was discovered.

Due process of law was swifter then before superior courts eventually became over-courteous to the criminal. The District Attorney handed down an indictment for first degree murder and Louise was brought to trial in short order.

Covering criminal proceedings became a passion with me. It seemed the bloodiest of bloodless sport ... to watch a deputy district attorney battle a vociferous and caustic defense attorney ... with neither speaking directly to the other. How beautifully they could throw invectives at one another in the third person.

In a way, I felt like a jury of one; for I was not allowed to offer my opinions to anyone with the exception of my rewrite man.

The State had charged that Mrs. Peete had shot the 60-year-old Mrs. Logan *in the back of the neck*, fractured her skull twice with a pistol butt (which had been identified as the murder weapon), then buried Mrs. Logan in the shallow backyard grave.

This is when Louise interjected that Albert Logan had done it, "and I buried the body, because I was afraid." Afraid, obviously, because she had already served time for the previous murder of millionaire Denton.

I was intrigued by the facets of this woman's character which were revealed during the course of the trial and by what I had observed of her, although she didn't testify. All this, along with her past erratic record, led me to believe that she had to be insane. I figured the State had put her in the wrong facility to start with. She should have been spending her time in the nut house all along.

By trial's end, it was obvious to the jury that this Bible-quoting woman had been the direct cause of five deaths which prosecuting Deputy District Attorney John Barnes brought out. She had murdered two persons to enrich herself through subsequent forgery and masquerade, and all three of her husbands had committed suicide.

Louise's first husband, R. Henry Bosley, a Waco, Texas, hotel manager, killed himself after being cleared in a $20,000 gem theft of which Mrs. Peete, then Mrs. Bosley, was suspected. This was in April, 1906, shortly after the San Francisco earthquake.

Her second husband, Peete, had been a wealthy automobile dealer. He committed suicide in Tucson, Arizona, on August 25, 1924, a year after he had divorced Louise and won custody of their five-year-old daughter, Betty. He had lost his health and his fortune.

When circumstances of the death of her third husband, Lee Borden Judson, were read into the trial records, I found myself drifting with the sound of his middle name, Borden. I was trying to recall the four line limerick. It was about grim New England many years earlier and another sensational murder mystery from whence came the provoking rhyme which I finally pieced together:

> *Lizzie Borden took an axe*
> *And gave her mother forty whacks.*
> *When she saw what she had done,*
> *She gave her father forty-one.*

In this case, Judson was a gentle man, and an innocent victim who had married Louise on May 2, 1944. He had known her by the alias of Jo Ann Lee, a widow. Judson was a susceptible

67-year-old bank messenger. He had been arrested with Louise in the Logan murder investigation. He was cleared and freed during the preliminary hearing which was held on January 10, 1945.

Shamed and humiliated, two days later, he took a crowded elevator to the top floor of a downtown Los Angeles office building and leaped to his death.

The State proved to the jury's satisfaction that Mrs. Peete had killed her benefactress in an effort to obtain property worth a few thousand dollars, and $2,500 in life insurance.

On June 1 of that year, and coincidentally on the 25th anniversary of the Denton murder, Superior Judge Harold Landreth sentenced her to die.

Convicting Mrs. Peete, the State pointed out 37 parallels between the murders of Denton and Mrs. Logan, notably: She shot each victim on the premises. She had also forged their names to checks and deeds to their property.

Between the time Louise Peete was sentenced, then executed on April 11, 1947, only 22 months had elapsed. Had this trial taken place today, appeals could have dragged the case out long enough for this insane woman to have died in prison of old age.

Two days prior to her execution by cyanide gas at San Quentin, Agness Underwood interviewed Louise. The two women had become friends during these extended months. Aggie wrote that Louise had dyed her hair brown, and had kept her figure trim. "For her age, she was an attractive woman. Her complexion was clear. Her gray-green eyes sparkled. She was calm, and her sense of humor was incredible."

Just before Louise was to be transferred from the State Institution for Women to San Quentin Prison, she had refused to be interviewed by reporters. "I don't want to see any of them. I won't, either, not at this end or the other," she shouted. "They don't care if I lose. They're just like everyone else. They want me to lose. Some of them are responsible for that dirty razor blade story." (A razor blade had been found in Louise's cell just before she was to be moved, and a rumor had it that she had tried to take her life).

Then a letter arrived from her attorney telling her to cooperate with the press. She recanted and shortly thereafter, entered a large room at the institution, enigmatically smiling and carrying an imitation gold-plated box filled with chocolate candy. Now, she was enjoying holding court. She called most of the reporters by their first names as she circled the room and shook hands. "Now, are there any I don't know?" Louise asked as she sat down and opened the conference with a, "Well?"

She apologized for having reprimanded a particular reporter about the razor story, then chuckled that she had "got to thinking, why should I be like the mother who spanked all ten of her children to make sure she had the right one?"

After Mrs. Peete said she was sleeping and eating well, she went into the usual question and answer section of the interview where she repeated that she was innocent of either of the murders.

Then, ending the session, she rose from her chair, opened the candy box and passed it around, smiling broadly. "I don't care if it makes me fat," she said.

Making her way toward the door, Louise said: "Why is there so much fuss about me right now? Don't people realize that there is one person dying every three minutes in this world from cancer alone?"

Then, in parting, she said, "Don't forget: my chin's up. I feel better than I look. I've made my peace with God and the world."

It was unusual for Aggie Underwood not to have delved into Louise's past. This was her specialty: acquiring a woman's confidence then extracting good exclusive stories from her.

During the investigation, few papers went into Louise's past. Her age was a mystery to the press at the time. She was passing for 59, but actually was 64. She had run away from home at an early age—as the saying goes—to make her living as a prostitute. She eventually phased into hard crime by blackmailing her clients in several states. The reason she killed Denton never came out in the trial, but she had done in her newly widowed millionaire because he had refused to marry her.

It was before the State Institution for Women was constructed in Tehachapi when Louise was sentenced to life. Therefore, she was delivered to her quarters in a new cell block outside the walls of the San Quentin California State Prison. The building, which is now the prison hospital, was referred to as the Bayview Apartments. It had a panoramic view of the San Francisco Bay.

Because of the close proximity of the sexes, there was continuous unrest on both sides of the wall. It was worse in Bayview where there were fewer inmates who had too much idle time. Lesbianism was rampant and divided factions waged war to establish social leadership there. And since California had not yet executed a woman, there were more dangerous convicted killers in Bayview than in the men's compound.

Two of the women competing for this leadership were plump: the intelligent 38-year-old Louise Peete and a beautiful lifer who had hammered her unfaithful lover to death. Her name was Clara Phillips. Clara had been rescued from her cell earlier by a gallant admirer, then was recaptured and returned to prison. And when the 25-year-old winsome looker arrived the second time, the brainy Louise had become the undisputed leader of Bayview society during Clara's absence.

Unintimidated by the comely young woman, Louise snubbed her and—with her followers—indulged in whispering campaigns so vicious that Clara once attempted suicide. However, the feud smoldered until 1933 when the girls were transferred to the new Tehachapi women's prison.

In his book, *88 Men and 2 Women*, San Quentin Warden Clinton T. Duffy mentioned that he had accompanied Louise to Tehachapi and when they arrived, she tearfully held out her hand and thanked him for his hospitality. "You have no idea how much I will miss my little gray home in the west," she told him.

Duffy thought he'd never see Louise again, but she showed up 14 years later. "She had returned to her little gray home in the west," said Duffy, "to die in the gas chamber."

Thirty-six hours before the scheduled execution, Sid Hughs and I boarded *The Lark* at Los Angeles' Union Station and the train started winding up toward San Francisco. The reason Richardson secured a second pass to what was expected to be a limited group witnessing the execution was economic, just as was the mode in which we traveled. My father had a friend, Baron Long, who owned the Los Angeles Biltmore. Long had a reciprocal agreement with the San Francisco St. Francis owner, therefore, I was offered free lodging along with what went with it.

The Lark was a slow commuter that paused at every milk stop. Hughes and I were handcuffed to hard-time felons. By accompanying a prisoner to San Quentin, the *Examiner* wouldn't have to pay for our travel expenses. In addition, Sid and I were each paid $3 for our custodial services.

Into the early leg, I began thinking the engineer had a heavy personal problem and taking it out on the whole train. Each time *The Lark* made one of its frequent stops, passengers the length of the train were given a good jolt. I began to call *The Lark*: "The Lurch."

During the second hour of the trip, Hughes got into enough trouble with the conductor to have us thrown off the train. He had packed his baggy pants with several two-ounce bottles of bourbon and was sharing his whiskey with his charge, a three-time loser.

After we had eaten some cold chicken and apple pie from a box lunch, I got acquainted with the prisoner I was nursemaiding. He was a second degree murderer. He hadn't killed a paramour in a jealous rage. He hadn't gone berserk and slain a friend in an unfriendly card game. He hadn't even killed a pedestrian while driving drunk. He was a 58-year-old barber named Bert who had been married for 35 years. Bert had no prior criminal record until he woke up one night, still drunk from some celebration. He said: "I'd listened to my wife farting in bed for the last 20 years ... Jesus, how she farted, and I was always a light sleeper ... Well," he went on, "I got so damned tired listening to her breaking wind, I vaguely remember going to the bathroom, getting my straight razor and slitting her throat."

Bert told me he had had his murder-one sentence reduced because a jury had been convinced that he had been intoxicated and had blacked out.

Bert's final words before he settled down to sleep were: "Only thing she ever did well was fart and play bridge."

Now I pulled an envelope full of newspaper clippings I'd gotten from the *Examiner*'s morgue. They all had to do with the San Quentin gas chamber. I got as comfortable as possible, with my left wrist cuffed to the wife killer, and started reading:

> *Loti Louise Preslar Bosley Peete Judson* was to be the second woman executed in California's history. The first was Evelita Juanita "Dutchess" Spinelli, a 52-year-old robber and murderess. In the mid-1930s, the diminutive Dutchess had organized a gang in the San Francisco area. She was myopic, had incredible strength, could wrestle a tough henchman to the ground, and throw a knife with unbelievable accuracy.
>
> The gang included her husband, Mike Simeone, Gordon Hawkins, Albert Ives and Robert Sherrand. Their specialties were auto theft, burglary and robbery. In 1940, after killing a man during a robbery, the gang split up. And because Sherrand showed signs he might squeal in trade for a lighter sentence, they killed him. Then Ives was arrested for some petty crime, broke down, and told detectives of the gang's activities.
>
> Dutchess Spinelli and her mob were apprehended, tried and sentenced to die in the California gas chamber for the two murders.
>
> Ives was judged insane and was committed to the Mendocino State Hospital where he died in 1951.
>
> Though her execution was delayed by appeals for nearly two years, The Dutchess entered the gas chamber on November 12, 1941, with a photo of her children and grandchildren pinned over her heart and next to the stethoscope diaphragm that would record her death.

During a long night on the train, the deputy sheriff in charge of our grim caravan purchased (for next to nothing) clothing and valuable personal articles from our ten prisoners. "The cash'll come in handy for spendin' money at the joint," he said. (Not true. All monies brought by prisoners to San Quentin were confiscated).

I remained awake most of the night as *The Lurch* bounced us northward to a rendezvous I would have with a woman I had interviewed only twice. This time we wouldn't have contact at all as the state fulfilled its public obligation. I started looking through my reference material again.

The very first execution in the California gas chamber happened to be a pig.

The gas chamber came into San Quentin under duress from then Warden Court Smith, a man with large reputation and size (Court was six-feet-six and weighed 250 pounds). He was against substituting the gas chamber for the gallows. He predecessor, Warden Holohan, had returned to his seat in the State Senate, wrote the gas chamber bill which had eventually become law.

Once the bill was passed, a professional bug exterminator who had built the Nevada gas chamber—a Captain D.B. Castle from Denver—was contracted to construct the same for San Quentin prison for the price of $5,000.

The gas chamber arrived at Quentin in March of 1938, and after its installation, two pigs were purchased with money from the prison's slush fund. The first was scheduled for execution in order that officials might study the chamber's effectiveness.

Newspapers had a field day with columnists referring to the condemned pig as "smoked ham."

I was bone tired by the time we detrained and were bussed to San Quentin. Three times I'd nearly fallen to sleep on the train, but the killer I was handcuffed to either had bad kidneys or a swollen prostate. He had me up three times. Handcuffed, I followed him to the men's can where I stood outside an ajar door while he relieved himself.

We were met at the prison entrance by a guard I had heard much about . . . and also found it difficult to believe what one of his duties was. He didn't have a front name. He was a fighter pug called *Canvas Back Kelly*. He was tall, about 20 pounds over-weight and was awkward in his carriage. He fancied himself as the public relations liaison between the prison and the visiting press.

Kelly showed us around the execution area which was actually outside the prison walls and in a corner near the guards' mess hall. Behind the gas chamber, there was the lethal machinery room where the guard assigned as executioner prepared the sulfuric acid solution. From this hidden partition, he would pull the bright red lever which would drop cyanide pills into the acid, activating the catalyst that would form the gas to kill Louise Peete.

He said Louise had just arrived from Tehachapi and was in one of the two death-watch holding cells. These were small cubicles furnished with only a toilet and mattress. Here she would spend her last night under surveillance of two female guards. Her last dinner would be cooked to order in the guard's kitchen and after the meal—if she chose—she would be visited by a chaplain and the warden. From then on, no one from the outside would be allowed to speak with Louise.

Executions were always scheduled at 10 A.M. but a last minute stay coming from the governor's direct line telephone on the wall next to the execution room often moved it up into the afternoon.

Fifteen minutes before the hour of execution, the chief medical officer would tape the stethoscope diaphragm to Louise's chest and examine her to be certain that she knew what was happening.

At the initial signal from Warden Duffy, the very short death march would begin at the holding cell. Supported by guards, if necessary, Louise would walk barefooted over a narrow carpet leading directly into the gas chamber. If everything went on schedule, it would take less than three minutes to secure her to her chair with six buckled straps (two about the upper arms, two around the forearms and two securing her legs).

Now, what made Canvas Back Kelly unique was . . . well, this is how it came about:

The first time when Cannon and Kessell were gassed in 1938, the blowers were turned on following the execution in order to evacuate the deadly cyanide fumes before a guard could enter and remove the bodies. And as accustomed in most capital punishment cases, a physician would immediately perform a postmortem. The doctor who did the first autopsy on a gas chamber victim was overcome when he incised a lung. The residual cyanide trapped in the deceased's lung had escaped and nearly killed the physician.

From then on, in order to keep the autopsy surgeon from possible death, Canvas Back Kelly—who had never had a knockout to his credit—would enter the death chamber wearing a gas mask. And after the venetian blinds were drawn, Kelly would punch the corpse hard in the belly several times until he figured all the gas had been forced from the decedent's lungs.

After the death house tour, I was anxious to get to bed early. The worse day was still ahead.

Hughes and I got into the bus along with several other out-of-town reporters. I asked a few from a small town paper to visit us for a drink. And when I saw we had a two bedroom suite, I invited them to stay the night; save per diem money for themselves. This put Sid's nose out of joint and he was filled with objections. His attitude was trying, mainly because he had already ordered four bottles of whiskey and some sandwiches from room service (on the cuff) and was acting as though the suite was exclusively his. He got me in a corner and whispered like a spy passing on secret information to the enemy. "Jesus Christ, Fowler, you can't invite these guys here for the night. After all, they're the competition."

"Jesus Christ yourself, Hughes," I said, "how the hell is the competition going to scoop anyone on a fucking *execution*?"

We both were up tight and I was relieved after Hughes passed out from pouting and pouring. Then the rest of us settled down and had as pleasant an evening considering the circumstances before turning in.

Hughes was quiet the next morning as we ate breakfast in the room.

The bus picked us up in the ever-present San Francisco fog and we headed toward San Quentin for our last appointment with Louise Peete.

I was surprised at the number of witnesses waiting to be ushered into the death chamber. "My God, are *all* these men[7] here to witness the execution?" The official total ended up being 80, the largest group ever to witness an execution by gas in the State of California.

At 9:50, just before we were to enter the death chamber, Deputy Warden Clinton T. Duffy joined us to make a short statement. He said that none of us would be searched, but reminded us that at the 1928 electrocution of murderers Ruth Snyder and Judd Gray[8] at Sing Sing, a New York *Daily News* photographer had strapped a camera to his knee and shot a picture of Snyder

---

[7]Women were not allowed to witness executions at that time.

[8]It was an atrocious crime with mundane principals. Ruth Snyder was a bored housewife living with a hard-working middle-aged husband. Judd Gray was a corset salesman who met Ruth in a speakeasy. He had a wife, a child and a house in East Orange, N.J. First there were the luncheons, then the dates and eventual mutual seductions. Over a period of two years, Ruth encouraged Albert Snyder to increase his life insurance policy while she plotted his murder with her paramour. On the night of the murder, Gray came from hiding and bungled pounding Albert in the head with a window sashweight as he cried out: "Mommie! Mommie! for God's sake, help me!" Ruth snatched the lead bar from Gray and finished the job. The alibis were weak and the lovers were condemned to death in the electric chair.

My father's harrowing account of powerful guards thrusting Ruth—whose body once throbbed with the joy of her sordid bacchanals—was to be recipient of the Pulitzer Prize for Journalism for his story that year. Instead, however, members of the Decency League revoked that direction, stating that Fowler's narrative in itself was "unwholesome and offensive."

In vehement objection, author and newspaper editor Ward Greene wrote: "You may find Gene Fowler's story florid, and you may find it more shocking than the picture of Ruth in the chair. If it makes you a little sick, why, that should be good for you. It takes a Fowler sometimes, to show us Death as it is."

The story lives on today as a powerful force against capital punishment.

dying. "Warden Lewis E. Laws had taken the word of newsmen that they were not carrying hidden cameras," said Duffy. "I hope there won't be such a recurrence here today."

Duffy told us to remain silent while inside the death chamber. Then, single file, we entered the green witness partition.

In those days, witnesses did not sit. Rather, we stood on one of three tiers of planks facing the lethal fish bowl which had six hermetically-sealed windows, each about two-and-a-half feet square. And at its center, there were the two metal-meshed chairs, each with its designation in block-letters: "A" and "B."

At 9:55, three guards led Louise from her steel cage. In the quiet I heard one man gather in his breath.

Louise had already been attached to the stethoscope diaphragm. A section of tubing hung out of her simple blue-and-white flowered cotton housecoat. Her hair was neatly arranged in small tight curls. Although she was carefully made up, the makeup couldn't hide her pallid complexion. However, she was remarkably calm and seemed eager to get on with it as she sat down to be strapped in.

Within 30 seconds of their entering, the guards had departed the round chamber that looked rather like a sea divingbell. Then the door was sealed shut.

Brief as was the time for the State to slay Louise, it seems in retrospect to have been a long, haunting blur.

No tasteless predilection should be employed on lady murderers we are told, but somehow I did not think of what this woman had done, but of what was being done *to* her.

The first cyanide pellet was dropped at 10:01. The second, 30 seconds later.

As the vapor started curling up toward Louise's face, we lost one witness through fainting.

Faithfully following instructions given her by Warden Duffy, Louise breathed in deeply. Then her head violently jerked backward and her eyes rolled up into her head.

The initial contortions exaggerated her pasty appearance. Then, a peaceful expression quickly replaced the wan look.

As her hands strained against the arm straps and her mouth fell open, we lost another witness. Louise's woeful wreck began to pass from life.

Five minutes after she had been led into the gas chamber, Louise's hand pitched forward on her breast. Then she twitched and began to cough.

At 10:13, Warden Duffy pronounced her dead after two physicians nodded to him. What a sorry gift the State had made to Eternity.

The venetian blinds were shut and Duffy turned to the crowd to say: "That's all, gentlemen. It's all over." But it wasn't really over. Canvas Back Kelly had yet to punch Louise in the belly.

As an example of the number of unregistered who got in to witness the execution, Warden Duffy said there were several friends of the doomed woman who had been present.

Louise's body was taken to an undisclosed private cemetery for burial. Its location was kept confidential.

Up to the last, Louise, almost coyly at times, declined to discuss her age.

The prison supplied the press with phones in order to file our stories. In this case, it was Sid Hughes giving notes to a rewrite man.

Whatever we talked about as we were bussed to the train station to catch *The Lurch*, the conversation was nondescript and we never mentioned Louise Peete's name.

Then it came to mind that I had forgotten to ask Duffy about a legendary death row story. San Quentin has a tall chimney that releases the lethal cyanide fumes following each execution. It is said at this time that a sea gull soaring above the chimney falls to earth, as though in token of the executed's soul making its passage into another world.

Of late, television station KCET is attempting to have an actual capital execution aired to the general public from nearby San

Francisco's San Quentin Prison. Its reason being under the guise
that television is being denied its rights under the First
Amendment.

I am against this sensational *Barnum & Bailey* "service" being
rendered to a thrill-seeking public.

Being on the scene to watch and feel and smell what's going
on as your heart pounds when a witness faints is a difficult for-
bearance. But sitting in a sybaritic's living room and watching
the obsequies with an electronic mechanism separating the viewer
from the real thing is a prophylactic experience which would—
but for its novelty—carry no more impact on the emotions than
a gory made-for-TV movie.

The second execution I covered was that of a 27-year-old black
murderer Robert O. Pierce as he paid his debt to society.

Pierce managed to smuggle a piece of broken mirror into his
holding cell and as he knelt to receive the chaplain's benediction, Pierce reached out and cut a deep gash in his own throat.

Kicking and clawing, I watched four guards muscle Pierce into
the gas chamber as he screamed: "I'm innocent, God! You know
I'm innocent! Please, Lord, I am!"

Then as guards began strapping him in while he was virtually
bleeding to death, Pierce momentarily phased into quiet suppli-
cation to utter, "All right, God. If you want to let me go, I won't
curse you."

Then as the chamber door was about to close, his violence
returned and he shouted: *"God, you son-of-a-bitch! Don't let me
go like this!"*

I wonder how KCET would have justified this being sent out
on the airwaves for young and old to see.

VI

The Enemy
at Close Range

Like my father, I never carried a watch with me in my youth, but when referring to the time, I was always able to come within three minutes of hitting it on the head. To this day, I don't use an alarm clock to awaken me at a certain time. I just register this in my mind and always wake up right on schedule. But when something of sudden shock, impact or import struck, I always referred to the clock on the city room wall or asked someone near me what time it was.

On the morning of Thursday, February 20, 1947, there was a great explosion that rocked the *Examiner* building so violently that all of us along the bull pen stopped typing and talking and exchanged eye contact with one another. Then we looked up at the clock on the wall. It was 9:45, exactly.

Richardson was away from the desk and Leonard Riblett glanced over at Gus Newman and said: "That's your assignment for the day."

Then Riblett called out: "Fowler, Massard." Nothing more to say. Jack Massard and I ran for the photo room and pulled out two photogs.

I got in Bob Hecht's wagon and we headed east, directed by a tower of smoke rising into the sky so dense it clouded the sun.

The center of the blast that had rocked the city was in a manufacturing district only a quarter-of-a-mile away from the newspaper offices. The first few blocks were easy, but all at once, it was like a bunch of billiard balls heading for the same corner pocket. Vehicles jammed together as police and the first Georgia

Street Receiving Hospital ambulances began arriving. The sound of sirens so close up was nearly deafening.

Then I saw a row of four motorcycle officers wheeling tightly together. Coming up alongside us, they drove our wagon right up on the sidewalk. They were playing interference for Mayor Bowron's black limousine. I told Hecht to pull back onto the street and tailgate Bowron right in.

We managed this without stopping because no barriers had been put up yet to keep unqualified people from slipping through. As a result, we were the first reporting team on the spot while everything was happening and changing by the second.

The trouble with covering a story this big was that the on-the-spot team was completely in the dark as to what was going on elsewhere in association with the emergency. All we could do was document what we were in the middle of, hoping we wouldn't miss anything even though we didn't know what it was all about. The advantage Hecht and I had going for us right now was that we had beaten the other papers in. We would be able to shoot pictures of the first emergency rescues.

With a quick sweep of the eye, I saw I was standing in the epicenter of whatever the hell had happened. The tremendous blast had flattened everything in a one-block area and blew a ten-foot hole in the ground. What used to be the O'Connor Electro-Plating building at 922 East Pico Boulevard wasn't there anymore.

The heat, steam and confusion was intense.

Then I became aware of people screaming as stretchers were being carried in. Two of the rescue workers ripped away a large sheet of corrugated iron to expose three bodies that were puffed up like out of shape balloons. They were boiled and their clothes had been blown from their bodies. One of them was in several places, and I turned to Hecht and yelled over the din:

"For Christ sake, get that! I'll keep feeding you plates! Shoot everything that moves!"

Then I saw that Hecht didn't have his camera with him. "What the living hell are you doing?" I screamed, as another stretcher passed by carrying an oriental woman with one arm missing and the other dangling from the side. Her eyes caught mine, and we both knew she'd soon be dead.

"I'm looking things over," said Hecht.

I knocked him down and ran to the wagon for his camera and plate holders. I started shooting pictures myself until Hecht got up. Then I shoved the Graphic in his hands and said: "You shoot every fucking thing as fast as you can, or I'll kill you!"

Hecht used up the remainder of his negatives as the other papers began making it in. Helen Brush of the *Daily News* was mad because the police who had, by now, started to set up barricades, had given her a hard time.

I shoved Hecht in the wagon and drove back to the newsroom myself. His left cheek was beginning to swell and I left it up to him to explain.

Without parking the wagon, I went to the photo room, dumped the plates and ran into the city room to report to Richardson. Massard hadn't made it back yet. Jim told me to unload what I had to Gus Newman before I went back where bodies and the living were still being exhumed from the rubble.

When a rewrite man covered a disaster of this dimension, he was given total consideration in the city room. Any conversation always had to do with the story at hand because it was easy to derail his concentration. He was treated more-or-less like an opera diva about to make her grand entrance. It was still ahead of him to weave together the many facets in this complex story. The *who, what, when* and *where* lead paragraphs in those times didn't read like those of today that start out more like an installment from a brooding Charles Dickens novel. Now when a paper's first edition is published, it is taken for granted the public is aware of what the story is about, so the printed intent is to offer an in-depth version. In the winter of 1947, it was a competitive race to be first on the street in the form of an *extra*, and the more it was in *fortissimo*, the better.

With a run-of-the-mill piece in the 1940s, a reporter was trained that his wasn't the only story of the day, no matter how much in love he was with it. So, it was routine that he give his rewrite man a quick rundown about what he was going to write. Being concise was of the essence. For instance, I once gave Newman an introduction like this:

"This is the story of a two-year-old who wanted to play in the water. Locked in the house while her mother was shopping, the little girl got her foot stuck in the toilet bowl. The fire department was called and was unable to free her foot. To do this, they had to remove the toilet and crack it open." Then, "We have a great picture of a fireman holding the pot up high looking like he wanted to be holding his nose while crossing the yard. You can't believe the look on his face, and the child in bright curlers is screaming like hell and covered all over with shit."

"I always enjoy taking stories from you," said Newman.

This day there was only one story: The deadly explosion disaster. Everything else, including new clues on the latest murder were subordinate and buried in the back part of the paper while makeup men were clearing more space for the picture editor to fill page three with photos.

As I waited my turn with Newman, he was simultaneously taking notes from police beatman Bill Zelinsky and being handed hot copy off the wires that kept him updated with stories emanating from nearby the explosion. His only relief would come from other rewrite men doing the side bar pieces and the casualty list.

Gus had his first four paragraphs typed on a book by the time he got to me. With this commotion, I thought I'd never seen a rewrite man with such imperturbable poise under fire.

"What've you got?" he asked me.

Joshing, like I was giving him a run-of-the-mill, I opened with: "This is the story about an explosion."

"Oh, really?" he laughed, temporarily breaking the pressure.

I gave him my word picture account of being first on the scene. Then: "I didn't have time to talk with any of the victims yet. I was busy kicking Hecht's ass around; getting pictures."

"I've got that stuff coming in," said Gus. "You going back?"

"Not with Hecht," I said.

Then Gus filled me in with what else was going on. He said the first estimates of the dead ran around 30, with about 300 injured. Deputy Police Chief Reed said he thought the death toll would reach 75 ... Battalion Fire Chief Tynan said the whole area went up in smoke like the newsreel pictures he had seen of the atomic bomb blast.

An early report stated that the Army was working on some secret chemical compound in the area that caused the horrendous explosion. Gus also said more than 200 of the injured were being treated at Georgia Street and the overflow was being taken by taxi and private cars to Good Samaritan and other hospital facilities. "It's a hell-of-a big one," he said.

I started back with George O'Day at 10:45, just after 300 more policemen were called up to augment a force of the 250 already there. The first reports of looting began coming in.

O'Day made his shots as I went into the field to talk with individuals about their personal experiences when the explosion happened. About 300 homes had been leveled, along with apartment houses, small hotels and office buildings. Many of the structures left standing were being condemned.

Now, only a few hours after the conflagration, this disaster was being compared by Mayor Bowron to the 1933 Long Beach earthquake that took 107 lives and injured more than 4,000.

While the first morgue was being set up at the California Hearse Service on Washington Boulevard, Georgia Street surgeons said of the 43 remaining patients, 25 weren't expected to live.

As I was interviewing a woman who said she had literally been blown off her toilet seat, I noticed a wagon parking alongside a partially destroyed building. On both sides and the rear double doors were printed in white bold letters: "W6XYZ." I knew these were amateur radio ham call letters, but couldn't figure out what that big ventilated metal umbrella was doing on the truck's roof. It appeared to be tilted sightly upward as if it was pointing to the north.

I couldn't see what was inside the truck which had its rear doors open. Next to it and connected to a tripod was a very large box, again with the W6XYZ call letters stencilled on its side.

Next to this thing which I figured was a different kind of news-reel coverage setup, I saw a ruddy-faced man of medium stature dressed in a gray suit and necktie. He was talking into a hand-held microphone. At once, I recognized him as being motion picture character actor Dick Lane. I walked closer to get a better look.

When I went past the truck, I peered inside where a man was cramped sideways on a bench. He wore earphones and concentrated while adjusting several knobs on a collection of electronic equipment. There were wires everywhere. And as he leaned forward, I saw an illuminated tube about one-foot-square. The darkness inside enhanced the bright sharpness of the picture it was transmitting. I realized that—for the first time—I was looking at a television set. It was reproducing what was going on directly outside.

I walked closer to Dick Lane who was broadcasting a steady description of the scene. He fascinated me with his monologue informing whoever might be on the other end of the camera what had happened here. He went on non-stop, briefly checking notes in his free hand as this clumsy camera on its tripod slowly panned across the scene.

When Lane took a break, I introduced myself. An outgoing fellow, it took little encouragement for him to go into his message about extolling the new medium.

"Ah, television," he said, as though describing his loved one. "It's the news of the future . . . You see it while it's happening . . . It's gonna change the world . . . My boy, it'll make the newspaper obsolete . . . I got into it while it's young . . . Not much money, but lots of room . . . Everything's looking up . . . A peon today and an executive tomorrow!" God, that man sounded like a gifted drummer.

Lane filled me in on how the unit functioned. He said the metal parasol on the truck's roof was an antenna pointed to the nearest high point where its beam was sent on to W6XYZ in Hollywood. This transmission came from atop a bulldozed ridge dividing the city from the San Fernando Valley. The high point was called Mt. Lee.

I told Lane if television wanted to be competitive with newspapers, it would have to figure a way to get its remote outfit set up quicker.

Lane was convinced this could eventually be worked out. "What the hell," he said, "it's only been about 30 years since the photographic process was introduced to the newspapers. And where the hell are all those quick-sketch artists today?"

"How many private receiving sets are you getting to right now?" I asked him.

"A couple hundred, I guess," he answered. "When this thing gets into high hear, there'll be millions."

"Millions of homemade television sets?" I said. "Come on."

Most reporters who had covered the explosion were still on the job at various locations. Either at hospital emergency stations, getting first-hand stories from survivors, or trying to run down the answer to the explosion from the fire departments fire prevention officials. The rest of us were taking a lunch, waiting for the *extra* to be sent up to the city room. We wanted to see what our baby looked like.

It arrived at 12:30, just short of three hours since our building had been rocked. The story took up the entire front page. The headline read:

DOWNTOWN BLAST
KILLS 30, INJURES 300

Below the headline and masthead was a six-column, eight-inch picture of the overall scene with rescue teams at work in the vicinity of the *O'Connor Electro-Plating Corp.*'s building, which was thought to be from where the blast emanated. Newman's roundup story ran across two columns in bold face. The two-column lead went:

> In an explosion that rocked downtown Los Angeles and was heard for miles, the one-story brick building of the O'Connor Electro-Plating Corp. at 922 East Pico Boulevard was blown up at 9:45 a.m., killing at least 30 persons and injuring more than 300.

Private residences were blown completely from the
face of the earth in the mysterious blast that devastated
an area of one-mile square.

Also on the front page was a second disaster photo along with
the first of three side bar stories and the early Dead and Injured list.

After questioning surviving O'Connor plant employees the following day, the fire department's arson squad came up with the
answer to the disaster. It was laid to exploding *perchloric acid*
concentrate used in a new process developed by Dr. Robert
McGee, chemist and metallurgist at the demolished plant. The
concentrate, which fire officials said was "nearly as deadly as
nitroglycerin" was used in plating aluminum chairs and daven-
ports for use in government service hospitals.

It was imperative that the acid be kept under constant refrigeration. But one hour before the blast, the factory's refrigeration
unit had broken down. And warmed to room temperature, anything organic coming in contact with it would cause it to explode.

Later that day some of us were winding down at The Back
Room. I told Newman of my meeting with Dick Lane. "Have
you ever seen television?" I asked.

"Not yet," said Gus.

"I can only say it's spooky," I said. "You look at it and there
it is, right now."

"But what if you're not looking at a television set when it all goes
on?" Gus asked. "You miss the whole thing, unless you happen to be with one of those few who owns one of those things."

"I guess so," I said.

"It's gone forever," said Gus. "So what do you do? You read
it in the papers."

"Maybe you're right," I said. "But what if they find a way
to show it later? Christ they'd beat our asses as far as the news
time factor goes."

"Well," said Gus, "that's a long way off."

"It all sound like Buck Rogers, doesn't it?" I laughed.

VII

The Black Dahlia

It was 1947 and only five months and one week before commercial television would be introduced in Southern California and along with live entertainment and movies, there would be segments of news reports which would begin a slow climb to become the prime source of instant communication throughout the world.

Jan. 15, 9:05 A.M.

The morning started out like a day stolen from the pocket of a classic Indian Summer. It had rained three weeks earlier, and the fields and vacant lots displayed a crew-cut length of fresh grass. The air was snappy cool, but would soon heat up and become muggy.

My photographer partner for the day was Felix Paegel. He was thin and intense and proud of his professional talents.

We were returning from our first assignment. It had to do with one of the Barbee mirror twin brothers. The two were sole franchisers of Southern California's *Coca Cola* outlet. This short fellow was well into his fifties and had just announced his engagement to a sexy, svelte dark-haired French girl in her early twenties.

"Love at first sight," Barbee told me, the only reporter to show up to cover the story in a Beverly Hills Hotel bungalow.

Our freeway system was still on the drawing boards, and Paegel leisurely drove east on Venice Boulevard on the way back to the paper.

"Why the hell didn't Barbee give us both a bottle instead of us having to split one?" he griped over the car's police radio calls.

"That's why he's rich," I said.

Also monitoring radio reports were two uniformed policemen we would meet later. They were patrolling the nearby Leimert Park section.

Some miles father west, homicide detectives Harry Hansen and Finis Brown were checking out a dead body report. They were in the city's southwest area waiting for the deputy coroner to pick it up. They were away from their car radio at the time.

As Felix and I approached Crenshaw Boulevard, a voice cracked over the shortwave: "A 390 W, 415 down in an empty lot one block east of Crenshaw between 39th and Coliseum streets ... Please investigate ... Code Two ..." (Code Two meant to proceed in all haste without red light or siren. A 390 W meant "Drunk Woman," and a 415 designated "Indecent exposure.")

"I don't believe it," I said. "... a naked drunk dame passed out in a vacant lot. Right here in the neighborhood, too ... Let's see what it's all about."

Felix turned south on Crenshaw. "I still can't figure out why that rich son-of-a-bitch didn't give us each a bottle. How the hell are we gonna split it?"

"I tell you what," I said. "If she's dead, you take my picture with the body and I'll give you my half."

Within a very short time, we arrived in the area given over the radio. Paegel slowed and turned east onto 39th Street. I kept looking along the strip of vacant lots which were staked off every 30 feet for retail stores to be built facing Crenshaw.

Then an ivory-white thing caught my eye. "There she is," I said. "It's a body all right ..."

There's something about a dead body you couldn't mistake. I approached it like I half-expected it to jump up and run after me.

As I got closer, I called back to Paegel who was pulling his Speed Graphic from the car trunk: "Jesus, Felix, *this woman's cut in half!*"

The body lay only a few feet from the cement sidewalk on this stretch of back street. I took a few minutes to get used to the look of this gargoyle lying there like a discarded marionette, separated from itself by about one foot. There was no blood on the grass and her body was exceptionally clean. I figured it had been bisected and scrubbed somewhere else, then transported to this spot off the main drag during the dark hours.

Here were two hunks of flesh laid down like sides of beef; two pieces of perhaps what could have been a good looking young woman.

I had only a short time to examine the body closely before the police arrived.

It's difficult to describe two parts of a body as being one. However, both halves were facing upward. Her arms were extended above her head. Her translucent blue eyes were only half-opened so I closed her eyelids.

By this time, I had been a reporter for three years and had learned a lot about the human body from Ray Pinker, head of the Los Angeles Police Department's Crime Scientific Laboratory. Pinker taught me subtle things about body attitudes when found, leaving little signatures of disclosure to inform the keen eye the manner in which some poor bastard might have checked out.

The top of this young woman's right breast had been cutaneously excised along with its nipple. Her generously formed left breast had been horizontally incised (about 12 millimeters) to the left of and away from the nipple and exposed an outer sheet of muscle.

Viscerally, the transversal colon and liver between the point of the body's bisection were palpable and soft to the touch. Neither organ had been invaded by a scalpel.

The dark blood coloring and its coagulation on her forehead and slashed mouth told me in advance of Ray Pinker's arrival that these wounds had been inflicted while she was still alive; while her blood was still coursing her body.

She had purple bruises around her neck, arms and wrists, specifically denoting she had been tied fast before being tortured.

There was a vertical incision (about 13 millimeters) in imitation of a hysterectomy scar between her navel and "Mount of Venus" directly above the exit of her urinary duct. In that area, I noticed that many pubic hairs had been pulled out, leaving minute pimply eruptions.[9]

A section of her left leg had been cut deeply through the muscle sheaths between her hip and knee, and there was a small section of her femur bone exposed. An equilateral triangle (about 10 millimeters) marked where a large piece of muscle and skin was missing.[10]

Her fingernails had been poorly cared for. Also, her chestnut hair, as it appeared from the roots, had been dyed black. And while looking closely at her hair, it seemed to me that her ear lobe was missing. It's been so many years now, I can't recall which one it was.[11]

While I was kneeling next to the body, Paegel took a picture documenting that absolutely no one was in the immediate area. His two principal photos showed the body alone in the barren field, and the second of me stooping beside the body. Before it was published on the front page, it was necessary for an *Examiner* artist to air brush a large blanket covering all but the upper arms and lower legs. He also removed the deep slashes on either side of her face.

While I was noting that a lower thoracic vertebrae had been neatly severed (and not sawed, because I could see no evidence of bone granules), two uniformed policemen pulled up in their

---

[9]The post mortem disclosed the first of three pieces of hidden evidence held back from the press in order that homicide might use same with which to question prime suspects. There was a small ball of pubic hair found inside the vagina, whose entrance was found by the autopsy surgeon to be *infantile*.

[10]The second piece of undisclosed evidence: The missing section from the body's left leg was located in her rectum. And it had a *rose tattooed* on the skin.

[11]The missing ear lobe, along with the location of the ball of pubic hair and the piece of her leg, was of general knowledge in the *Examiner* city room, but it was agreed that the paper wouldn't publish this knowledge in order that homicide could use the secret information when questioning the validity of a prime suspect. After 43 years, this is the first time it has been published.

patrol car and came our way. One undid the safety strap of his revolver holster. "Take it easy, pal," I said.

Now he removed the gun from the holster.

"I'm a reporter on the *Examiner*," I said, reaching for my police identification.

The cop raised his revolver and eye-balled me.

"Jesus, man," I said, snapping my hands up over my head, "I really am a reporter . . . Fowler's the name . . . Fowler."

His partner reached inside my coat, then checked my I.D. He was satisfied and the other cop put his gun back into its holster.

As they started their investigation, I pointed toward Crenshaw. There was a pre-teenager straddling his bike a block away. "Why don't you question that kid over there? Maybe he knows something," I said. I was anxious to get to a phone.

They gave me permission to leave the scene and I ran for a public phone. I stuck a nickel in the slot and dialed the desk, and when he heard me say, "cut in half," Richardson told me to get the hell in with the negatives.

The city room was already buzzing about the story as Paegel disappeared into the photo lab to develop the negatives. When he emerged, he was carrying a large dripping wet 11x14 print of the body. Several people gathered around to get a first look.

"Take a good look," said Richardson. "This is what a lot of you will be working on today." Then he disappeared into Van Ettish's office. He was back in a few minutes to tell us we were going to put out an extra and beat the afternoon papers to the street. Then he told me to get back to the scene with Felix. Next, he turned to assignment editor Leonard Ribblit to call the afternoon watch in early.

What a difference it was when Paegel and I got back to Crenshaw. Now the place was crowded with uniformed policemen, newspaper photogs and their reporters. Agness Underwood from our afternoon paper squatted near the body. She looked up and

said: "How come you let the *Times* beat you here, Fowler?"
When our extra hit the street, Aggie would find out this was
my second trip back to the vacant lot.

Detectives Harry Hansen and his sidekick Finis Brown had
arrived. Hansen was checking notes with Ray Pinker when I met
them.

This was the first hour of Hansen's assignment. He would officially remain on the case after his retirement and until his death—a
period of more than 35 years.

Hansen was very tall, red-haired and balding. Of Danish
heritage, he had joined the LAPD in 1926 and worked his way
up to homicide within a few years. He was meticulous and his
quiet manner often wooed suspects into confessions.

Hansen told me the first phone call regarding the case had come
in from a woman walking her dog. "She hung up before we could
get her name," he said. He gave me the name of the boy with
the bicycle. It was Bobby Jones. Then, "The kid told me there
was someone here earlier with a camera."

"That was Paegel," I said, "but I'd appreciate it if you didn't
let this get around."

The coroner's Mariah arrived and eventually, a deputy asked
me to help him pick up the lower part of the body. I took hold
and cupped her heels in my hands and braced myself to lift. But
being only half-a-body, it seemed as light as a feather.

11:35 A.M.:

The rear basement entry to the Hall of Justice looked like a
wholesale grocery receiving dock. I met our Sheriff's beat
reporter Howard Hertel there while Paegel recorded the body
being unloaded and weighed on a black floor-level scale. "When
we were told the body had been cut in half," said Hertel, "the
coroner said the autopsy would be performed right after lunch."

Our extra run beat the afternoon papers to the street by two
hours. It ended up being the second largest run in the *Examiner's*
history, bettered only by the VJ Day extra in 1945.

4:35 P.M.:

The autopsy completed, fingerprints were inked and transferred to a card to be special delivery air mailed to the Federal Bureau of Investigation for identification.

With no pictures other than the body of the unidentified girl to publish, artist Howard Burke created a likeness of the dead girl's face from Paegel's photos. "It'll give the cops something to go on when they start hitting the night spots for someone to try to identify her," he said.

While Burke was working on his sketch, Captain Jack Donahoe—recently transferred from robbery to head the homicide department—returned Richardson's phone call. Jim told him Assistant Managing Editor Warden Woolard had an idea to get the fingerprints identified in a very short period of time if Donahoe could supply the *Examiner* with a copy.

Donahoe was transferred to Woolard and told him the prints were already on their way to the FBI. "Well, until we get an identification," said Woolard, "we'll all be stymied with the investigation."

Pointing out that winter storms were grounding planes in the east, Woolard said it could take as much as a week—perhaps more—to find out who this dead woman was. "We have this new *Soundphoto* machine," he said. "What about sending the prints over the *Soundphoto*? It's never been done before, but I don't see why it wouldn't work." Donahoe agreed it was worth a shot and sent over the prints.

When International News Photo wires opened at four o'clock the next morning, the fingerprints were the first item transmitted.

In Washington, waiting to take the prints off the machine was Ray Richards, former *Examiner* city editor and now head of the Hearst Newspaper's Washington Bureau.

Then the paper ran into a snag. FBI experts were unable to work with the transmitted prints. They were blurred and couldn't be properly read.

At our end, photographer Russ Lapp suggested reversing the lab process and use the prints as negatives. He did this, then blew the prints up in size with a minicam enlarger. The resulting

8x10 prints were large enough now to be readable on the other end. The *Examiner* leased a special circuit to Washington and the slow process of transmitting the prints began. This time it was a success. Within a matter of minutes, FBI experts identified the prints as being those of an *Elizabeth Short*, who had last lived in Santa Barbara, California.

This scoop put the *Examiner* so far ahead of its opposition, they were never able to catch up. Hours before other papers had a clue that the body had even been identified, our crews of reporters and photogs were digging into Elizabeth Short's life. The competition actually had to read our paper before they knew what step to take next in the investigation. Richardson's crews worked so effectively with the clues we were digging up on our own that we were able to start making deals with LAPD homicide. This made Donahoe fume, but he had to go along.

One reporter from our afternoon paper, the *Her-Ex*, came across a man in a Long Beach bar who had been acquainted with Elizabeth Short. It was this reporter, Beverly "Bevo" Means, who gave the murder its moniker. Phoning in from his favorite place away from home—a bar—Bevo said, "They used to call her *'The Black Dahlia'* down here because she had black hair and everything she wore was black."

Today, so many years later, the public doesn't have a clue as to who Elizabeth Short was. But mention the name, "The Black Dahlia," and right away a lot of people who weren't even born at the time of the murder usually say something like: "Oh, yeah. That was the gal in Los Angeles way back . . . the woman who was cut in half."

When the Santa Barbara Police Department desk sergeant handed me Elizabeth Short's file photo, I was struck by her eyes. They reflected a sort of inquisitive innocence. Her skin looked as though it had the quality of alabaster. Her dark, curly hair loosely draping this inculpable stare suggested she might have been a beautiful woman.

The paper learned from the Santa Barbara police that Elizabeth Short had also been sent back home to Medford, Massachusetts, in 1943—as a delinquent. Jim Richardson assigned rewrite man

Wayne Sutton to locate her mother, Mrs. Phoebe May Short, in Medford.

"And I get the privilege to break the news," said Sutton.

"Don't tell her right out," said Richardson. "First say Elizabeth won a beauty contest . . . in Santa Barbara . . . Get what we need in background . . . I'll give you the sign when to tell her her daughter's dead."

Massachusetts information gave Sutton Mrs. Short's home phone number and Jo Wise at the switchboard plugged the city editor in on Sutton's line before dialing the long distance number.

"Hello," said Sutton. "Mrs. Phoebe Short?" Then, "Ah . . . ah . . . Mrs. Short, this is Wayne Sutton on the *Los Angeles Examiner* . . . I called to tell you . . ." He stared over at Richardson and the city editor nodded for his rewrite man to get on with it.

"Ah . . . I just wanted to be the first to tell you that your daughter . . . Elizabeth . . . had won a beauty contest . . . in Santa Barbara," said Sutton. He reflected that Phoebe was delighted and began to extol Elizabeth's beauty and charm and that her daughter had won other beauty contests in Medford.

Sutton glared over at Richardson again, waiting for "the sign."

By this time, Jim was crouched forward in his chair. "Keep going," he mouthed to Sutton.

Sutton was finally drained of questions and eyed Richardson a third time.

Jim Richardson sat upright in his chair and said: "*Now.*"

Sutton cupped his hand over the mouthpiece and said: "You lousy son-of-a-bitch."

Then the rewrite man went on to give Mrs. Short the *real* news, which was followed by several long and short pauses.

Somehow, Mrs. Short remained on the line, mostly because she wanted to know exactly what had happened. Sutton enlisted her cooperation, promising to pay her fare if she would fly west. This way, the *Examiner* would be able to keep Mrs. Short away from the police long enough to explore any new leads she might have to offer.

Before he hung up, Mrs. Short located a letter Elizabeth had recently written to her. She supplied Sutton with her dead daughter's San Diego address.

This information made way for another scoop: The disclosure that Elizabeth had left San Diego with a man known only as "Red." Richardson wasn't about to pass this information on to Donahoe. Not before *Examiner* reporters had a good shot in locating this man only known as "Red."

Within minutes after Sutton hung up, we had two reporter-photog crews heading north and south along the Pacific Coast Highway, the single main route along the California coastline before the advent of freeways. Stopping at every motel along the way, we checked each registry book.

Up to this point, the Black Dahlia story had been pictorially weak. There were the usual pictures; the routine art department "X marks the spot" kind. The only *art* we had to go with were the Burke composite drawing and the head-and-shoulders shot of Elizabeth supplied us by the Santa Barbara police.

It was then that Richardson received a tip from an anonymous caller that the Dahlia had had several "memory books" filled with pictures of herself and friends. Moreover, Jim learned these books were in her trunk and that the trunk had been lost in shipment to Los Angeles when it was sent out from the east.

"Find the trunk," Richardson told two reporters.

We started checking railroads, freight depots, and every likely place where the trunk might be stored. It was reporter Baker Conrad who located the luggage at the Greyhound Express station in downtown Los Angeles. From then on, the Black Dahlia became the best illustrated crime story in newspaper history. And it all emanated from the *Examiner*.

The day our new information hit the street, Richardson called Donahoe and said, "You're welcome to the luggage, but I want it understood that story is ours, exclusively." What could Donahoe say? If he didn't agree, Richardson said he could damned well read about the cases's progress in the *Examiner*.

The luggage turned out to be a suitcase and some bags, not a trunk. One suitcase in particular contained dozens of Elizabeth

Short photographs in romantic settings with several of her admirers. Photo copies were hand delivered to our crews working the coast highway in hopes that a motel manager would be able to identify the Dahlia as being one of their recent overnight tenants.

Earlier, the desk was tipped that Elizabeth had lived in Hollywood at one time. We were supplied with names and addresses in that area, and several of us started working the bars at night. Locating and questioning roommates and men who had dated her supplied us with good human interest stories. (Years later, when I was with 20th Century-Fox, actor Paul Burke told me he'd known the Dahlia when he was a Hollywood bartender. He had corroborated the fact that lesbians had been interested in Elizabeth, but she hadn't responded to them.)

In the meantime, the crew of George O'Day and reporter Tom Devlin continued checking hotels and motels, looking for anything that would lead them to the identification of "Red." And coming up a winner, Devlin located a motel where a red-haired man had registered the previous December. Unbelievably, he hadn't signed in with the usual Mr. and Mrs. Smith. He had actually entered Elizabeth Short's real name at the motel a dozen miles north of San Diego. He also signed his name: Robert Manley from Huntington Park.

10:00 A.M., Jan. 18:

Baker Conrad recalled he had seen a telegram among Elizabeth's belongings. He went through her effects again and located it. The Huntington Park address in the wire was 8010 Mountain View Avenue. Jim Richardson sent me out there without a photographer.

A strikingly beautiful red-haired young woman answered the front door and I flashed my Los Angeles County Sheriff's badge without saying I was an officer of the law. She was nervous and was cooperative. She was Robert "Red" Manley's wife, Harriet. She told me her husband had telephoned her from San Francisco after seeing his name in the papers—in connection with the murder—and that he was presently being sought out. She said

Red told her he was still in the Bay City with business associate
J.W. Palmer representing a pipe and clamp company. He said
he would be returning to Palmer's Eagle Rock home the following evening to pick up his car.

While I was there, the phone rang. It was Red, and Harriet
put her hand over the mouthpiece and asked: "Do you want to
talk to him?"

"You'd better not tell him I've been here," I said.

Harriet remained calm, but seemed to want to warn him I was
there. And when she hung up, I asked her if she had any photos
of Robert. She pulled out several pictures "we just had taken
by a professional photographer." They were exquisite portraits
of Harriet, Robert and their year-old-son. She didn't seem to
object when I asked for them all, and instructed her—a bride
of only 15 months—not to talk to anyone, especially if newspaper
reporters started coming around the house.

10:00 P.M., Jan. 19:

Ferde Olmo and I sat in the back seat of a homicide stake out
car being used by sergeants J.W. Wass and Sam Flowers. We
were parked at the curb of Palmer's Eagle Rock house, waiting
for his car to drive up.

Eventually it arrived and when Manley stepped out, the
detectives with guns drawn, darted toward him. Manley raised
his arms and Olmo flashed pictures. Manley said, "I know why
you're here, but I didn't do it." Dressed in a heavy gray overcoat and broad-brimmed hat, he was frightened out of his wits.

As Olmo shot a picture of Manley being handcuffed by Sgt.
Flowers, Sgt. Wass followed Palmer into his house. I was surprised when Flowers allowed me to get away with shooting questions at Manley before he was interrogated downtown by
homicide. I didn't take out a pencil or pad. An experienced
reporter never does this under these circumstances because
suspects have a tendency not to talk when they see someone
making notes.

Manley told me he'd phoned his wife from San Francisco two
times after he'd read his name in the papers. "The first thing

she said to me—crying—was: 'Did you do it?' Manley said. "I told her, 'Of course not, honey. Whatever made you think I did?' I told her I loved her more than any man ever loved his wife."

Olmo drove back to the paper and I asked him not to talk to me while I made notes of all the quotes Manley had given me.

Wayne Sutton was napping in Ray Van Ettish's office when I returned to the paper. He was taking a breather while putting together a complicated roundup story about the case, so I let him sleep. There was time enough before the home edition deadline.

Half an hour later while night editor Pat Hogan and I were talking, Sutton came out of the managing editor's office and said: "Well, what've you got, Will? Let's wrap this thing up."

I gave Wayne what I had in pictures and story of Manley's capture. Then he began chronologically sewing together this complicated roundup piece.

The story was dated January 20 on the home edition. The front page carried a two-column, seven-inch picture of Sgt. Flowers handcuffing Manley. There were three sets of headlines:

'RED,' SLAIN GIRL'S FRIEND, HELD;
GIVEN LIE TEST; LUGGAGE FOUND

FORMER AIR FORCE MUSICIAN
TELLS OF TRIP FROM SAN DIEGO

Parted With Miss Short
at Hotel; Went North

In the story, Sutton wrote that Manley had voluntarily submitted to a lie detector test because he had been identified as the man seen with Miss Short fourteen hours before she was found slain.

The long piece also added that Manley had been discharged from the Army Air Force as "menatlly unfit for the service."[12]

---

[12]An Air Force psychiatrist's report stated that Manley possessed homicidal tendencies.

It was mentioned that Red's black 1940 Studebaker was being
checked for fingerprints and any possible blood stains ... that
Short's luggage was located "through the efforts of the
Examiner" ... that the luggage consisted of two suitcases and
a hat box found by "an *Examiner* reporter" ... that Manley
had let Elizabeth out at the Los Angeles Greyhound bus station
... that he had been an Air Force musician, and that his father,
William Manley and his wife, Harriet, 22, went to police headquarters to give him moral support.

Sutton wrote that Manley was quoted as having first met Miss
Short at a San Diego bus stop in December and "ran into her
again in January."

Manley said Elizabeth had an Italian boyfriend with black hair
"who was intensely jealous of her."

Red also said that he had driven Elizabeth to the Biltmore Hotel
in Los Angeles.

Other leads mentioned a Railway Express Agency clerk,
William E. Sullivan, who had identified Elizabeth from a picture
shown him by Baker Conrad. He said she was inquiring about
shipping her luggage to Ketchikan, Alaska, on the day before
her body was found. Sullivan also said he noticed a black-haired
man impatiently waiting for her, but couldn't identify him. (This
in itself is exactly one of those vital instances that could have
completely turned the case around: People with shaky or no identifications at all; those who couldn't correctly read or remember a licence plate at the very second a suspect's car speeded
off, or a detective failing to notice an essential piece of evidence!)

The story also carried the name of a Mrs. Elvera French who
had seen a "red-headed man drive away" from her Pacific Beach
home on January 8. Short had lived with Mrs. French the previous
month.

Wrapping the story, the last paragraph said Mrs. Phoebe May
Short was expected to arrive in Los Angeles from Berkeley,[13]
and that no date had been set for the coroner's inquest.

---

[13]The *Examiner* had already met Phoebe in Los Angeles earlier, before she flew
up to Berkeley to be with her sister, Mrs. Adrian West.

New exclusives were coming to the *Examiner* so fast, the paper began placing otherwise front page stories on page three.

In a single edition, we ran six exclusive Dahlia photos, including one of myself interviewing Phoebe who thanked the *Examiner* for speedy identification of her daughter when she arrived at the Los Angeles airport at Mines Field. There were also glamorous portraits of Elizabeth and pictures of her posing with friends at unidentified locations. The most interesting side bar that day had to do with several of the letters the paper had taken from one of her suitcases. The stack, tied together with red ribbons, was given to Marjorie Driscoll to assemble and fit into a sob story. The most tragic of these love letters were those from Elizabeth to a Lt. Joseph Gordon Fickling. They were signed and sealed, but never sent. They read:

> *Your devotion is my most precious possession ... how many lips have joined with yours since ours last met? Sometimes I go crazy when I think of such things.*

But in an unmailed letter dated December 13, after Fickling's passion had cooled, Elizabeth had written:

> *I do hope you find a nice young lady to kiss at midnight on New Year's Eve. It would have been wonderful if we belonged to each other now. I'll never regret coming West to see you. You didn't take me in your arms and keep me there. However, it was nice as long as it lasted.*

A week earlier, Fickling had written her:

> *Time and again, I've suggested that you forget me as I've believed it's the only thing for you to do to be happy.*

Elizabeth wrote, but once again, pride—or futility—kept her from posting the letter:

> *If everyone waited to have everything all smooth before they married, none of them ever would be together.*

On January 3, five days before Elizabeth left San Diego, she was brushed off in a letter written by a Lt. Stephen Wolak:

*When you mentioned marriage in your letter, Beth,
I get to wondering. Infatuation is sometimes mistaken
for true love. I know whereof I speak, because my ardent
loves soon cooled off.*

The tone of the letters she never mailed reflected that Elizabeth had been deeply hurt many times as she almost desperately looked for one man after the other, seeking someone who would love her. I believe all these rejections came after she had gone to bed with her lovers, and when they discovered they were unable to have sexual intercourse with her . . . because of the infantile entrance to her vagina.

Manley's alibi—being in San Francisco with Palmer at the time of the murder—checked out with police and he was released. But what had started out as his stiff resolution in a clandestine affair had put him in the middle of a notorious and heinous slaying. Not only had his face been displayed and his story published in newspapers throughout the country, but the wife he had betrayed eventually divorced him.

Not so long afterward, Robert Manley was remanded to an asylum for the insane, and shortly thereafter, committed suicide.

With the elimination of Manley from the case, the investigation bogged down. But this was after the *Examiner* had kept the unsolved murder on the front page for 32 consecutive days.

Scores of vagrants and psychotics continued showing up at various precincts to confess the murder. Throughout the years, there were more than 500 counterfeit confessors.

As Elizabeth's name faded from the front page, startling news came from a post office inspector. The Black Dahlia's killer had mailed the *Examiner*—not the police—an envelope containing a notebook and other items from the dead girl's purse. These items proved to be authentic, and they offered the stark reality that Elizabeth's killer was alive and still out there somewhere.

The evidence found in her bags at the downtown Greyhound bus depot contained more pitiful keepsakes and photos of unrequited loves. They seemed to back up the love letters; and that she was a lonely girl desperately searching for companionship. It also seemed that the killer of this once beautiful youth with her hidden sexual flaw had committed the perfect crime.

Through time, writers theorized as to who could have been her slayer. Much of the dreamed-up evidence has proved to be more sensational than authentic.

A reliable nonfiction author must always deal with facts, even though he has the privilege to dissect and conjecture them. The author must not ever be tempted to stray from the basics in a moment of weakness to dream up these pieces of sensational noninformation in order to entertain his readers.

As for myself, through serendipity, I happened to be the first person at the scene with Elizabeth Short's body. (Photos by my photographer bear this out). Next, I was fortunate enough to have been part of the finest crew of newspaper reporters and editors ever grouped to cover a murder case of this proportion. These are my credentials.

However, there still remains this insuperable rash of would-be writers who have defiled this code. In all cases, they lacked recognized literary track records simply because they also lacked talent.

These frauds believe their passport to immortality is to leave counterfeit prints of fame on the sands of time, hoping no one will notice they have been wearing someone else's shoes.

Unfortunately, I have given too freely of my time in order to help a score of seemingly honest and enthusiastic writers. But early on I discover they have insincere motives and lack a natural talent.

As an example of the types of pretenders who have approached me through the years in regard to the Black Dahlia, there was a mysterious-looking woman who treated our meeting at the Hollywood Drake Hotel as being clandestine. She slipped me a motion picture scenario written by an *Ibycus Crane*, hoping for me to help get it produced for her. Aptly titled, *The Black Dahlia*, it was a fictitious treatment of how Elizabeth Short's murderer had lured her to a San Juan Capistrano motel where he strangled her; drove the trunked body to a Los Angeles leather establishment, the *Clark Factory*, situated in the alley behind 1823 South Hope Street, where he cut the body in half with a "jackknife" leather-cutting knife, then washed it clean before depositing Elizabeth's two body parts on the vacant lot a block east of Crenshaw between 39th and Coliseum streets.

The Crane script even cameoed me in the early part of the picture, arriving as the first on the scene. But the entire scenario was too bloody and gory ever to be produced for the screen.

Crane, however, did follow the *Examiner* accounts closely, and he must also have had access to the homicide closed records, pointing to me, at least, that he must have been a member of the Los Angeles Police Department.

Then there was a 13-year-old boy named John Gilmore, the son of a Los Angeles policeman at the time of the Dahlia murder. The elder had little to do with the case then. But after many years of listening to his father recount the unsolved slaying over-and-over, young John finally published a Black Dahlia piece in what is know in the industry as a "junk magazine."

It is my impression that John finally succumbed to the fictional bizarre when he claimed to have met Elizabeth's killer, "Mr. Jones." And . . . heavens-to-Betsy . . . John's informant who led him to Mr. Jones was no other than the reliable source: nationally-respected "Mr. Smith!" Now, how about *them* apples, kid?

This was the only gauzed unsubstantiated offering upon which John based his short magazine piece . . . But there was more heavily laid-on falsehoods to come after John met up with my next and final example of how far these fraudulent identifications with the notorious can go.

It was during the late '80s when I was drafting this very book that I met Mary Humphrey. She fascinated more than fooled me.

"Bette Short . . . I call Elizabeth 'Bette' . . . Bette Short used to baby-sit for me when I was eight-years-old back in Medford,

Massachusetts, and I'd like to meet you and tell you about it,'' she said over the phone. She had a marked Boston accent.

I was under the impression Mary Humphrey had wished to pass this information on to me. But that wasn't how it turned out.

Mary told me she didn't drive a car, but asked if I might pick her up at a bus stop near my home in the San Fernando Valley.

She was waiting when I drove up to the newsstand at the corner of Ventura and Van Nuys boulevards.

Mary looked to be in her mid-fifties. She was a bit on the heavy side, and had a long straight nose. She wore long loose dark clothing, boots, a black scarf over her head and carried a bag larger than a purse. Beside her face, the only bits of her skin to be seen were from the wrists to her poorly polished fingernails. She looked either like a hippie or a gypsy. I never could quite make that differentiation.

Before we met, Mary told me on the telephone that she had a decent reputation as a master *erotic* printmaker and had had her work shown in several Northern California art galleries. She had promised to bring me some examples of her work, and, to be honest, this fascinated me far more than her having told me the Black Dahlia had been her baby-sitter.

It came as a surprise when Mary told me she had been researching Elizabeth Short's life for *ten years* and that she was planning to write a book on the subject. And having the life-long reputation of trusting people at their face value, I believed Mary when she told me she didn't expect to get around to the actual writing until she could document the killer. Instead of taking this as *caveat emptor*, I uncorked a bottle of Napoleon brandy and asked if I might take a look at what she had in the portfolio.

I handed her the rough draft of my Dahlia chapter to read while I perused her dazzling artwork.

It was obvious when she poured herself another brandy that Mary had been shocked with my description of Elizabeth's body, and the secrets Harry Hansen had shared all these years.

Now it was Mary's turn to fill me in on what she had known about Elizabeth. The Dahlia had attended Roberts' Junior High and Medford High schools. Mary said "Bette" had dropped out of Medford High at 16 when she was a sophomore. Eventually she went to Hollywood "to become a movie star" when Mary, herself, was only eleven, and too young to have become emotionally involved, considering she'd known Elizabeth hardly more than being her baby-sitter.

Mary and I talked long into the late evening and a characteristic began to surface. Over these long years she had interviewed almost everyone in Medford and its environs regarding Elizabeth. Because she had lived a quiet and sheltered life, Mary's little interviews allowed her to at least break into a more expanded world. At the same time, she realized she would be the center of focus as long as she could talk about Elizabeth Short, as though in deep confidence.

As a downpayment in order to more closely study this woman who desperately yearned for some kind of recognition, I offered to guide her along the difficult route of writing a first book. In good faith, I handed her my Dahlia chapter, the Crane scenario, some photo negatives and John Gilmore's erroneous magazine piece. This, with the proviso that the material would serve only as a guide, and that she would not publish or publicly refer to any of the same until after *Reporters* was published.

It was too late to send Mary off on a bus so I drove her to Pasadena where she was staying with a friend.

Among the several prints Mary gave me was her interpretation of Adam and Eve standing naked in front of *The* apple tree, ripe for picking. Overpowering the entire composition was Adam's enormous erection, ready for battle.

"My God," I said, "that's not an erection. It's a telegraph pole!" Then, "Can you imagine what he might have said while experiencing creation's first hardon? . . . (If it were me, I guess I'd have said, 'Stand back, Eve. I don't know *how* big this thing's going to get!')"

In the following weeks after she left for her home of Oakland, a plethora of long inquiring letters about Elizabeth followed. They often interfered with my work at hand, but I answered with the spirit of a teacher, encouraging her to start writing. But she simply didn't do this because she was unaware of how to attack the project.

It wasn't until 1990 when Mary sent me her final letter. She wrote that she and John Gilmore had met and the two were going to collaborate on her Dahlia book.

"My God," I thought, "now *two* confused Dahlia nonentities have coupled."

Some time later I happened to catch the two on a television talk show where they starred as the ultimate Black Dahlia authorities. They had unblushingly enlarged on their fancies. Now John claimed the murderer had confessed to him before death, and not to the police. And Mary had raised Elizabeth in her social station, having had her double-dating with Marilyn Monroe and appearing at fashionable Hollywood nightclubs with the likes of Franchot Tone, Richard Carlson and other motion picture luminaries. She even had Elizabeth acting in movies and on the radio.

Due to rankling, Humphrey and Gilmore have lately split. Mary recently contacted me and wrote that she'd retained a lawyer "to protect my rights after receiving a very intimidating letter from Gilmore's attorney with a threatening 'request' to sign a *Release and Acknowledgment*," which would prohibit her from using the expression "Black Dahlia." Since, Mary has begun writing her own book alone.

This is an unfortunate example of how protracted squabbling among pretenders overestimating the value of their literary eggs—which have long-ago become over-ripe—renders their information archaic.

Unless Elizabeth Short's murderer of 45 years ago miraculously emanates to confess the crime, this chapter closes the case for good and all.

In all, I considered I had learned more from Mary Humphrey than I did from the other lonely souls who continue their pitiful efforts to earn their fifteen minutes of fame.

Intense interest lingers regarding this murder mystery simply because it *remains* a mystery. And by this fascination, it has earned its niche in the annals of crime history as being the most notorious unsolved murder of the twentieth century.

Elizabeth Short's slaying might be solved in the distant future, but I sincerely hope not. It's like an unopened present. The present always remains a wondrous thing, as long as it remains unopened.

The Black Dahlia murder still remains "a riddle wrapped in a mystery inside an enigma."

"THE BLACK DAHLIA" SCENE - Los Angeles Examiner reporter Will Fowler kneels before bisected body of Elizabeth "The Black Dahlia" Short at scene of pre-eminent unsolved murder mystery of 20th century in Los Angeles. Fowler and Los Angeles Police Detective Sergeant Harry Hansen (with loud necktie) kept three secrets pertinent to the slaying until Hansen's death in the 1980s.

Photo by Felix Paegel

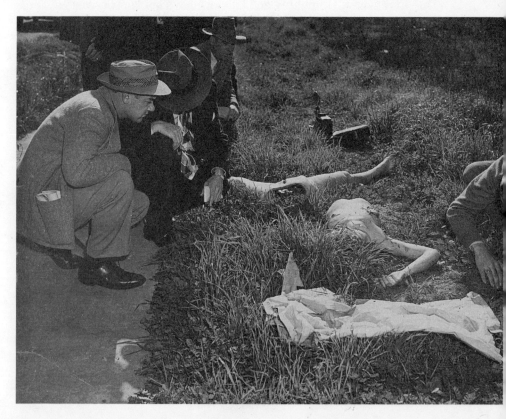

"THE BLACK DAHLIA" BODY—Once beautiful 22-year-old Elizabeth Short came to Hollywood seeking fame on the Silver Screen. Instead, the raven-haired girl's eventual celebrity would name her "The Black Dahlia" of the 20th century's most celebrated unsolved murder.

BEAUTIFUL VICTIM—Dressed in her usual black and with black-dyed hair, Elizabeth Short poses for nightclub photographer. When her murder received appellation "The Black Dahlia," it would become "a riddle wrapped in a mystery inside an enigma" for the rest of time.

ATTENDING TO PATRON—Artist John Decker and Paulette Goddard at famed Hollywood Mocambo nightclub in 1945.

DECKER-FLYNN OPENING—Artist John Decker and Errol Flynn opened a Hollywood art gallery just after World War II. It ended up more a gatheirng place for friendly wassailers. From left: Ward Bond, Decker, Phyllis Decker, Flynn, Mrs. Alan Mowbray, Harry Hays Morgan, Red Skelton, Georgia Skelton and Will Fowler, who rarely posed normally.

THE TIME W.C. FIELDS WENT ON THE WAGON—"It was the worst weekend of my life!"

VIII

Uncle Claude and the Mutinous Artist

Whenever palm trees come alight with multicolored globes, and Salvation Army Santa Clauses tinkle bells along the avenues, I tend to dwell on the memory of Uncle Claude, known to the world as W.C. Fields.

I had known the great comedian for ten years and as a boy, was his occasional caddy at the Westlake golf course in the San Fernando Valley. In his final years, he lived on DeMille Drive in Hollywood, the town which supported him, but which he scorned both philosophically and emotionally. "Hollywood," he once told me in his cracking voice, "is the gold cap on a tooth that should have been pulled years ago."

His aversion to holidays was equal to his dislike of the film capital. The one he detested most was Christmas. He once swore that anyone who observed this yule celebration would be stricken from his will. "Sleigh bells give me double nausea!" he exclaimed.

Why W.C. Fields always comes back to memory at this time is that he died on Christmas Day in 1946. And because of this sad event and a string of circumstances, I received my first by line.

But I didn't write the obituary. My father wrote it.

Newswise, Christmas Day was usually slow and reporters were most often sent home early to be with their families. But this time there was a breaking story about a missing Western Air Lines flight from Los Angeles which had been scheduled to land in San Diego the previous evening. Last radio contact was made from 50 miles east of San Diego over the Laguna Mountains. It was presumed that the DC 3 had crashed and the 12 aboard were probably dead.

I was grateful I didn't have to go mountain climbing with search parties. Maybe I could still get home in time to meet my father and go out to visit Uncle Claude at Las Encinas Sanitarium in Pasadena where he had been drying out for the last nine months. But there was a side bar to get at our end of the story.

Harry Morgan assigned Ferde Olmo and me to get some sort of picture story at the home of the missing flight's stewardess Glenda Wade.

It was Wednesday and Jim Richardson was enjoying the mid-week day off at home.

When a group of reporters turned up at the home, we were refused pictures of Glenda and were not allowed in the house for an interview. We left empty-handed, but with a little enter-prising scoop in mind, I told Ferde to drive around the corner and wait until the others had gone. Then we returned to the Wade residence where I talked our way into the house with the sug-gestion that there was still hope that the stewardess was alive, and that a story and picture would encourage more people to get into the urgent search for the missing plane.

There was a modest Christmas tree in the living room. It was on a coffee table and had unopened presents at its base. The family was waiting for Glenda to return home before opening them.

A master with the artistic photographic touch, Ferde took Glenda's portrait from the mantelpiece and placed it on the table beneath the tree.

There was little to say. We all seemed to feel that the worst had happened, but by not talking about it we thought it would disappear.

Back at the paper, I gave my notes to Gus Newman who wrote:

> Before a modest Christmas tree at 1720 North Whitley Avenue a mother placed one more decoration yesterday.
>
> It was a picture of her daughter, Glenda Wade, 25-year-old flight stewardess missing with 11 other

persons aboard a Western Air Lines plane in the mountains east of San Diego. "I won't give up hope," said Mrs. Jessie Wade. "I just won't, although something in my heart . . ."

The girl's brother, Jack, 24, gripped her hand.

"Don't, mother. Don't . . ."

The way things were going, all but one of the stories that would appear on the front page the next day would be coming from the wires. The local piece would be the holiday traffic roundup. Slippery streets from the rain and drunken drivers had already cost 24 lives in accidents over the Christmas holiday. It was the worst 24 hour record in Los Angeles County's history, according to Coroner Ben H. Brown.

All was quiet around 2 P.M. and Harry Morgan sent me home early. If Richardson had been on the desk, he would have had me running around town covering stories that wouldn't get further than overset type.

When I got home, my father was waiting for me to go out to Las Encinas and he said Fields' mistress, Carlotta Monti, had phoned to say that Uncle Claude had died just after noontime.

Pop also said he had phoned in Fields' obituary to Harry Morgan. He told Harry that I had written it but he would dictate it as a favor because "Will's out wassailing with his friends." He also suggested that if there was a by line, it would be nice if Harry gave me one.

"What the hell will I say when I go to work tomorrow if I do happen to get the by line?" I asked him.

"I have a feeling Harry won't expand on it," he said. "You've been watching Jim Richardson tossing your stories in the basket for three years now. Maybe getting a by line will rankle him a bit."

"A *bit*!" I howled. This evil theory leaped into my mind as being a good possibility. Wouldn't it be extraordinary if Richardson bought it that I'd actually written the obituary?

When I arrived at the paper the next day, I'd already seen
a copy of the *Examiner* home edition. It displayed a fine two-
column, five-inch portrait of Fields centered on the front page
and the straightaway, unflowery story was carried under my by
line in bold face type. The tail of the story bled over to page
three. And when Richardson made his morning entrance, it
wasn't dramatic as usual. He was very quiet and very pissed.
And for that day and the next, he never called on me to cover
a story. He wouldn't even let me take dictation. Obviously, Harry
Morgan, who had been aware about my frustration in getting
stories I'd written in the paper, hadn't raised an opinion about
the piece. The by line ramifications remained a secret that I would
keep until after I left the *Examiner* a year later.

On Sunday, December 29, Magda Michael, W.C. Fields' longtime secretary, phoned me. She said she had to file Uncle
Claude's Last Will and Testament at the Hall of Records in downtown L.A. the following morning. "I'm not sure where it is,"
she said. "Could you take me there and guide me through the
routine?"

I phoned Pat Hogan on the desk. I told him what Magda wanted
and Pat said: "Go ahead. I'll give you the assignment on my
watch. I'll leave a note for Richardson."

"I don't think he's going to like it," I said.

"Don't worry about it," said Hogan. "I've got my retirement
years in."

I got in and out of the Hall of Justice first thing on Monday.
We left as soon as she got her filing receipt and the story
remained exclusive. But after our peach edition hit the streets,
the competition, as a follow up, bore hot-and-heavy on the torrid
Paragraph Fourth, b, of the will which read:

> Upon the death of my said brother, Walter Duken-
> field and my said sister, Adel C. Smigh, and the said
> Carlotta Monti (Montego), I direct that my executors
> procure the organization of a membership or other
> approved corporation under the name of W.C. FIELDS
> COLLEGE for orphan white boys and girls, where no

religion of any sort is to be preached. Harmony is the
purpose of this thought. It is my desire the college will
be built in California in Los Angeles County.

This eyebrow-raising paragraph walloped the dead comedian
in two basic areas: racism and religion.

Editorialists in newspapers and on the radio throughout the
country struck out against Fields' character, and I advised Mickey
Mouse (Fields' nickname for Magda Michael) to take the receiver
off the hook for a few days.

At the same time, I phoned my father to be ready with an
answer to the press which might help enlighten inquiring
reporters and radio newsmen. Television news was operating
at the time, but the thousands of pounds of remote equipment
still restricted this medium to cover any story unless it was
on-going and the stations had time to set up.

With the exception of Magda Michael, my father had been the
only person to read Fields' will before the comedian's death.
Reviewing Paragraph Fourth, b, Pop said to Uncle Claude: "Such
a narrow gesture will make you misunderstood and much
disliked."

"I've always been misunderstood," said Fields. "Besides,
did you ever hear of a corpse complaining of unpopularity?"

When the press gathered to interview my father at his Brentwood home, he said: "If I were to apologize for W.C. Fields,
or for any other member of our group for that matter, or attempt
to justify his or their wayward actions, their shades would cry
out with indignation. False praise is the province of the epitaph-
maker and is best done with a chisel on a stone seldom visited."

When Magda Michael was discharged as executrix to the will
on April 20, 1954, it had been eight years, three months and
22 days in probate, the longest in entertainment world history.

Shortly before his death on Christmas Day in 1946, W.C.
Fields' divorced wife, Hattie, and their son, W. Claude Fields,
Jr., had taken up residence in Beverly Hills.

The sensationalism demonstrated during the probate hearing to determine heirship provided the newspapers with good hard copy and pictures. And the damned thing never really got going until sixteen months later in May of 1948.

Among the twenty-four people who had to be notified before the hearing could get under way included Mabel Clapsaddle (a bank teller whose name fascinated Fields, and to whom he left $2,000), and my father (to whom Uncle Claude designated a trunk filled with the comedian's original stage skits and other hand-written material).

After notice of filing was served the following press report appeared:

Widow Harriet sued for a half-million of the estate estimated at $771,428, which she claimed the comedian had given away. She named Mildred L. Blackburn, Fay Adler and Grace George (as his former lovers).

Fields' cremation was also ordered on November 19, 1949, but it would be two years more, over widow Hattie's Catholic objections, before this was carried out.

Also, a William Rexford Fields Morris filed a request claiming he was the illegitimate son of W.C.

When Superior Justice William R. McKay finally got the hearing under way, Hattie fought for her fifty percent share of the estate under California State community property law. She said she and Fields had been married in 1904 or 1905[14] and was aware that her husband was "romancing" a Broadway showgirl, Bessie Poole, who had given birth to young Morris in 1917.[15]

And when Carlotta Monti got to the stand, this dynamic Latin beauty said she had a "thing-or-two" she wished to be put in the record regarding W.C.'s widow and son. Displaying impressive dynamics, Carlotta—who made the best media copy of all—said:

---

[14]W.C. and Hattie wed in San Francisco, and the fire following the 1906 earthquake had destroyed their marriage records.

[15]When Morris showed up at Fields' Hollywood home in the early 1940s, the comedian's butler announced that Morris claimed to be his illegitimate son, and was waiting to meet Fields downstairs. Fields replied to his butler: "Give him an evasive answer: Tell him to go fuck himself."

"Mr. Fields had his own ideas about the funeral. He wanted his friends like Gene Fowler, Dave Chasen, Gregory LaCava and fellows he used to play golf with to be his pallbearers.

"Instead of that, they had some cadaverous looking characters carry his coffin!" She also added that under her supervision, Fields' estate had thrived and increased considerably in value. "And all I got from the will in return," she said, "was a $50 weekly income from trust."

(Word had it that Fields had had bank accounts throughout the world, but Magda Michael listed only twenty-three containing a total of $566,107, all in the United States. However, Fields had often joked: "I have $10,000 in the Bank of Berlin just in case that son-of-a-bitch Hitler wins!")

The court adjourned the first time with the following questions yet to be answered: When did Fields take up legal residence in California? And was William Morris really the comedian's illegitimate son and entitled to one-third of W.C.'s estate? While this conjecture was going on, *Examiner* street sales went up nearly ten percent.

Over the following years, there were reconvenings, adjournments and more reconvenings. During this time, Carlotta asked for partial distribution of the estate so she might begin receiving monthly payments. Harriet wanted an additional $100,000 she alleged was given to Carlotta by Fields. Greed was making this probate extremely messy.

Mickey Mouse, obviously not a money-grabber, requested $17,500 for "extraordinary fees" while functioning as executrix. And Judge McKay ordered that Hattie be paid half of Fields' earnings after he had become a California resident in 1927.[16] He also ruled that W.C.'s brother Walter would receive $75 a week for life; his sister, Adel, $60, and Carlotta $25.

McKay also threw out the will's plans for setting up the W.C. Fields College for white boys and girls, stating that "Mr. Fields

---

[16]Uncle Claude's taking out a membership in the Automobile Club established that his California residency had begun in 1927.

in his lifetime could have discriminated against other races, but he cannot in death.''

The scope of intricacies, deviousness, circuitous, delaying, tricks and dishonest ways by several of the attorneys representing their clients plagued Justice McKay who nearly suffered a nervous breakdown during the seemingly endless trial.

Hattie had entered litigation at age 66, and was 75 when it concluded. She won a total of $120,000, but had to pay William Morris $15,000 for not further contesting the will, plus attorneys fees of a reported $80,000 (conservative these days), exorbitant inheritance taxes levied by the State of California, not to mention her living expenses during the many years of litigation. The inconveniences and frustrations she suffered were certainly not worth going through this marathon. It cost her more than she received, by far.

Carlotta, who had remained inconspicuous and in the background during Uncle Claude's lifetime, had ended up the true star of the show with her outspoken attitude which was laced with a sailor's vocabulary. In the end, Carlotta, who has been my friend these many years, had her annuity reconverted into a lump sum and drove away in Fields' 16-cylinder Cadillac with its built-in bar in the back. A retired negative film cutter, Carlotta, as of this writing, lives in a comfortable West Hollywood apartment and spends her leisure time creating oil paintings.

In all, it was the press, and in the later years of the probate, television news who had enjoyed the legal proceedings most.

A few months following the will probate's final adjournment, Judge McKay ended his life by swallowing a bottleful of barbiturates because he feared he was going blind.

Fields always made good newspaper copy, but when he and a select few of the movie industry wanted to hide out, escape and talk and drink without being annoyed by the news media we used to gather at a small house Pop and I found for artist John Decker after he'd been thrown out of his Hollywood digs. It was a·small, rundown Tudor place north of Sunset Boulevard in Brentwood. It had a prolific avocado tree in the backyard, nurtured by a leaking cesspool. There he penned a sexual deviate duck which exclusively practiced *flagrante delicto* with chickens. The rent was only $35 a month.

Gathering at Decker's at 419 North Bundy Drive were Fields, John Barrymore, Thomas Mitchell, Errol Flynn, Burgess Meredith and Anthony Quinn. We were referred to as "the mad Bundy Drive Group." Quinn and I are its only survivors.

Here, Decker set up his easel before a modest paned bay window where a huge pine tree shaded the living room so thoroughly that it was necessary for the artist to paint by electric incandescent light. His judgment was: "What the hell. People look at my paintings that are electrically lighted. Why not paint under the same conditions?"

John was a man of medium height with strong features accented by a poorly set broken nose. He had a whisper of a moustache over which he applied brown crayon to make it subtly visible. He usually wore a leather-buttoned camel's hair sports coat which he failed to keep free from his tube paints.

Not having enough money at one time to impress a bank teller, Decker lacked a savings account. And the checks he wrote were returned for insufficient funds more often than they were successfully cashed by his landlord or the gas company. With such an imbalance in his credit, John kept his available currency hidden in a cigar box behind his bed. When in need of alcohol, he would descend to his hiding place (much like a squirrel in winter) and extract enough cash to purchase a bottle of booze. And when the eventual day arrived, John would disappear behind the bed to tap his stash only to re-emerge wearing a surprised and pathetic expression to say as though it couldn't possibly be true: "It's all gone ..."

This was when Decker would adorn himself with cleric temperament and abstemiously flagellate himself. During this time of self-inflicted sobriety, he would shut himself up, and like a man obsessed, attack every available canvas before unlocking the front door of the Tudor house, upon which he had painted his own coat of arms proclaiming he was a "Poor, insignificant poet."

John would then contact Francis Taylor, a Britisher and proprietor of an art gallery in the Beverly Hills Hotel. Taylor, the father of a captivating black-haired child named Elizabeth, would set a date for Decker's one-man show, have a brochure printed and mailed to collectors of the Hollywood ilk. During the show's first hour, diminutive dark-eyed Elizabeth Taylor—who would eventually emerge as one of the motion picture industry's most dynamic stars—would circulate among the adults, charming the men and causing the ladies envy with her beauty.

And when the always successful showing came to an end and actors, directors and producers had stripped the gallery's walls of his paintings, Decker would ceremoniously partake of his first glass of champagne. From then on, it would be smooth sailing until the artist once again ran out of currency stashed in the cigar box behind his bed.

It was here at Bundy Drive when Decker spent his happiest times. There were always interesting friends dropping in and John, a fine chef, would cook rare dishes for them.

One evening after dinner found Decker, Thomas Mitchell and the Johns Barrymore and Carradine simultaneously attempting to read *Hamlet* from opposing editions of *Shakespeare's Collected Works*, absolutely confused why one page number didn't coincide with that of an edition put out by another publisher.

There was a constant visitor to Decker's named Sadakichi Hartmann. He was half-German and half-Japanese. And during World War II, it was the great fear of the Bundy Drive Group that the United States Government would discover they had this man blooded by both the country's enemies sequestered on an American Indian reservation in Banning, California. This admixture seemed to spell out triple-jeopardy, not to mention that Hartmann was somewhat of an addict and was continually putting my father's physician, Dr. Sam Hirshfeld, into fits over writing prescriptions for Hartmann.

Taking on the emulation of either a praying mantis or a stalk of bamboo when he removed his heavy woolen gray coat, Sadakichi's thin, long face was as wrinkled as a prune. But in the early part of the century when he was an Apollo striding the streets in his black felt crush fedora and flowing red silk-lined Inverness cape, Hartmann was an art critic who proclaimed himself the King of Bohemia in New York's Greenwich Village. Author of several important books and portfolios on art, the "Gray Chrysanthemum" (so named by Barrymore) was the first to showcase such great photographic geniuses such as Steiglitz, William Crooke and Albert Edward Steiner in his published critiques.

But for some reason—perhaps because he demanded strict attention be paid him—Sadakichi was despised by W.C. Fields. So much so that when Uncle Claude appeared at Bundy Drive to find Hartmann there, the comedian would immediately depart. When he spoke once of Sadakichi, Fields said: "This Eurasian belongs in print only among the pages of Steckel or Krafft-Ebbing. He has been a Peeping Tom, a cap-and-bell interloper at all the art shrines." Fields so much eschewed Sadakichi that he never allowed himself to correctly pronounce his name, and it would euphonically emerge as "Itchy-Britches," "Hoochie-Koochie" or "Catch-a-Crotchie."

Shortly before Uncle Claude's death, Errol Flynn moved John and his delicately feature wife Phyllis to a studio of remarkable modern architecture at 1215 Alta Loma Road, situated on a steep street just south of the Sunset Strip in Hollywood. Set sideways to the street's entrance, the studio was in full view of the rear of Charlie Morrison's Mocambo nightclub and restaurant. There were strewn bottles, boxes and garbage haphazardly littering the landscape. When Decker viewed this panorama, he posthaste abandoned the moving-in functions, set up his easel, squeezed some paint tubes and furiously began work on a large canvas to paint his impression of the devastation cursing his vista. On completion, he had the oil delivered to Morrison at the Mocambo. Morrison immediately had his backyard put in order and made presentable. And in return for his unwitting transgression—and as a gesture of apology—Morrison picked up Decker's bar and restaurant tabs at the Mocambo for the remainder of the artist's life.

As I slowly drove past the Alta Loma studio several times in recent years, I found it to still be in tempo with today's modern architecture. The garage and store room were on the ground floor, and one flight up, there remains the huge studio with its residence to the rear. I had an urge to knock unannounced, introduce myself to the present occupants, and fill them in on the studio's history.

But by doing so, I would have had to surrender my well-cradled memories of more than 40 years ago. Everything would be new and alien at the same time, with absolutely nothing associated with the shade of a John Decker wandering about the studio's high-vaulted ceiling with natural light flowing in from the overhead and reflecting down onto large cloth brown walls with the paintings of modernists that had hung there; the likes of Gauguin, Braque, Modigliani, Dali, Picasso, Van Gogh, Chagall and Lautrec.

Uniquely in those post-war days, the spacious studio contained a tall steel stairway mounted on rubber wheels and placed before an upstairs landing where there was an office-bedroom. This contrivance could also be used as a movable staircase for artists painting heroic canvases.

The Alta Loma studio was an attempt by Flynn to begin trying to recoup monies he had been successfully throwing away. At the least, the Irish actor hoped for the place to generate enough of a cash flow to make house payments and pay the taxes. To do this, it would be necessary to have continuous showings exhibiting works other than those of Decker, and where profitable art sales could be transacted.

An uncomfortable occasion arose while Flynn and Decker were planning their gala studio opening. It came to light when the *Times* published a story about a Van Gogh painting purchased by 20th Century-Fox Studio executive William Goetz. An argument had brewed between the U.S. Customs Department and an authority on Flemish paintings who claimed the incoming work was a forgery.

The question had arisen when customs was attempting to put a reasonable value on the painting. The stickiest part of the situation was that the Van Gogh had been purchased by Goetz through a Dutch third party secretly representing John Decker and W.R. Valentiner, the latter being the Director of the Los Angeles Museum of Art.

Fortunately, Valentiner had previously placed his stamp of authenticity on the work of art. And because of Decker's foresight (or usual practice), he had had Valentiner pass the painting through customs for backup authentication by close friends in Amsterdam. And when customs was presented letters of reliability and previous international shipping receipts, William Goetz and U.S. Customs came to an amicable agreement. Customs disallowed—over great protest—the Flemish appraiser's cries of "fake," and the Van Gogh was placed at a value of $50,000.

Actually, I had sat by the hour in Decker's Bundy Drive studio watching this multi-talented master *create* this Van Gogh. In order to faithfully copy the brush strokes of this mad painter who had killed himself in Arles, Decker deliberately injured his painting hand, spraining it badly enough that it was painful for him to apply Van Gogh's technique. He said it was "agony when I worked on the canvas. I wanted to put myself in the mind of this crazy Dutchman who was nuts enough to cut off his ear for a whore."

After allowing the paint to dry sufficiently, and his hand to heal, Decker presented it to Valentiner who, knowingly, authenticated the oil as being an original Van Gogh (for a price). Today, the work is accepted as being as true Van Gogh and is valued at millions of dollars.

One objet d'art Flynn continually tried to part Decker from wasn't a painting, but a late 17th century Italian wishing chair. It had a rococo ladder back and the original needlepoint was blighted by a small cigarette burn. It came from when John Barrymore dropped a burning ash while steadying himself to take a drink.

Flynn placed great sentimental value on the rickety piece that Rudolph Valentino had given to The Great Profile because Jack was the only man the flamboyant Irishman ever looked up to.

Years after I'd inherited the museum piece, I continued the
chair on its Odyssey by giving it to Barrymore authority and art
critic of the *Ft. Lauderdale News*, Roger Hurlburt. Along with
it, I sent this note:

> Imperfection can often add historical signification to
> an otherwise archaic object. Look what Jack's hot ash
> did for this chair.

My first professional trial regarding my friendship with Decker
as opposed to my fidelity as a newspaper reporter came when
I had to decide how far I would allow myself to go while attending the Alta Loma studio's opening.

Present at the affair were my father and mother, Diana Barrymore (a great brawler), Jack LaRue, Alan Mowbray (a compul-
sive thief), Anthony Quinn, Ida Lupino, Thomas Mitchell, Paulette
Goddard and Burgess Meredith. My father departed early after
giving Mother his alternative suggestion: "Well, shall we go home
now, or should I get drunk?" Errol Flynn had left earlier with
a young female prospect.

The gala subsequently turned into a drunken bash. And when
uninvited actor Lawrence Tierney—who had recently starred in
a film portraying gangster John Dillinger—arrived, it turned into
a brawl.

After Tierney socked the feeble Jack LaRue and it was reported
to the police, I knew I'd have to alert the paper before it was
reported by a beatman. So I called the night city editor and let
the whole thing evolve by itself from there.

There were several versions of the set-to. The drinkers only
vaguely remembered bottles being thrown. And as Decker was
trying to protect his plaster of Paris nude model, Mona, LaRue
was delivered to the nearest emergency hospital to have a head
wound stitched.

Flynn, who happened to be an exceptionally good boxer, kept
a low profile in view of the bad press he had been receiving of late.

By September of 1946, Flynn had spent $76,000 renovating
and rigging his second sailing yacht, the *Zaca*, for a marine voyage

down the coast of Mexico with his father, Dr. Theodore Thomson-Flynn, a zoologist and dean of the School of Science at Queens College in Belfast, Ireland. Accompanying them was Professor Carl L. Hubbs of the Scripps Institute of Oceanography at La Jolla, California. He was a noted ichthyologist and hoped to discover new forms of marine life on the trip.

It was as simple as that at the beginning. But with Flynn, nothing, absolutely nothing, was ever pursued in a simple manner. The purpose of the voyage branched into several objectives:

Swiss composer Ted Stauffer came aboard with his camera, planning a *National Geographic* photo story. Archer Howard Hill and toxologist Jerry Courmoyay joined the crew. They were equipped to shoot a short subject movie of the trip featuring Hill's exceptional talents with the bow and arrow. They also brought along two actor friends to appear in their picture.

And with Decker—who had been filled me in with information the *Examiner* planned to use in feature stories—the crew swelled to seventeen.

Flynn had invited John so he could record the voyage with field sketches he would later paint for a one-man show at the Taylor Galleries.

"But the fly in the ointment," Decker reported to me, "was Flynn's 20-year-old bride, Nora Eddington . . . if she was a bride at all."

Not exactly a sailor himself, Decker complained at the outset:

"Just as soon as Nora got her sea legs, she took over command of the boat and started shoving everybody around . . . This was the first time she started playing the role of Mrs. Errol Flynn and it has gone to her head . . .

"It's too bad this little mosquito came between Errol and myself," said Decker. "Hers was a constant pin-pricking process calculated to wear me down." He said that when something went wrong, ". . . Nora had screamed it was my fault."

The serious fishing began at Socorro Island off the west coast of central Mexico. Among ichthyologist Hubbs' prizes was a hitherto unknown small specimen; a fish with fascinating camouflaged eyes at its tail, put there by evolution to confuse other predatory fishes.

To Decker's dismay, Dr. Hubbs had named the new fish after Nora. "That's going down in history!" John exclaimed later as I took notes over the phone. He then compared the youthful "matron" on the quarterdeck as Bounty's Captain Bligh . . . and himself as a beleaguered Fletcher Christian only hoping to mutiny at the first port the *Zaca* hit.

The discord came to a head in a Socorro lagoon where the yacht anchored. Seaman Wallace Beery (no relation to the late actor) dove into the water with a spring harpoon gun. And instead of spearing the shark he was aiming at, he impaled himself.

Dr. Thomson-Flynn and Prof. Hubbs operated to remove the harpoon from Beery's leg without the help of a general anesthetic. However, there seemed to lurk the danger of infection setting in. This was an opportunity for Decker to persuade Flynn—over Nora's protests—to head for Acapulco for competent medical aid. Now Nora accused Decker of caring nothing about the wounded Beery, but wanted to sail to Acapulco 1,000 miles away for a drink.

"So the bitch locked all my insulin in the refrigerator and hoped I would lapse into a diabetic coma," Decker reported over a poor phone connection after he landed. "When we moored, I broke the lock on the refrigerator, got my insulin and abandoned ship along with the wounded Beery and the two actors, who were also seeking a Pitcairn."

The ongoing story made great copy for the paper right up until the *Zaca* landed back in California.

This final escapade was more-or-less the beginning of the end of Decker's life. Too many of Flynn's parties had etched their toll on him. And after the yachting trip when the artist and Nora Eddington had become mortal enemies, Flynn threatened to evict John from Alta Loma and refused to allow him to have his Acapulco show in the studio. Therefore, John went to Francis Taylor who extended courtesies and financial aid.

The show, described in Taylor's lengthy title as being "Moods of tropical Mexico painted on a recent trip on Errol Flynn's yacht 'Zaca,' " was held on January 29, 1947. It was hyped by Arthur Millier of the *Times*, Kay English of the *Examiner* and Alma May Cook of the *Herald-Express* and was a usual Decker-Hollywood success.

Shortly before Flynn's death, he showed my father his *My Wicked, Wicked Ways* manuscript, in which the perfidious prank of "stealing Jack Barrymore's body" was fantasized. I had also read it, and when Flynn phoned Pop for his critique, my father asked why he'd written the odious squib. The actor (who had been heavily into drugs and alcohol at the time) said: "I just wrote it in for laughs because that's what I wish my friends would do for me directly after my final curtain."

John died five months later, plainly as the result of what happens to a diabetic who drinks alcohol. The process of dying, however, took long. And the physician attempting to halt the bleeding of varicose veins in the artist's stomach had gone into surgery way beyond his talents.

I served in my father's stead at Decker's funeral which was held in the Alta Loma studio. Pop had been recovering from a recent heart attack. Ben Hecht's posthumously published book, *Letters From Bohemia* (Doubleday: 1964), described at length the trouble I had arranging the funeral and getting it paid for.

The Decker-Flynn friendship had outdistanced itself so I had to go elsewhere to get the damned funeral financed. Only a few of us knew John was broke, and this was when I discovered the majority of actors who attended the parties had only showed up to drink Decker's whiskey. Now, they were turning their backs on me when I broached the subject of money. They would either say, "I'll get back to you," or never even had the courtesy to return my phone calls.

Phyllis told me John had decreed that his body be displayed among the easels. He wanted the deathbed picture of Barrymore propped upon the casket beside the dutch-door lid of the receptacle—the upper half of which was raised. He thought this would be better composition. This done, I watched Phyllis tenderly trace brown crayon over his slight moustache.

The boys at the funeral parlor wanted $4,000 for the obsequies, thinking that our John died as rich as he had lived. But John, of course, always spent everything he made faster than he could paint.

I descended upon the morticians with the wrath associated with the true journalist. I hammered the body-snatchers down from four grand to $500, then proceeded to raise this amount. Director Raoul Walsh was the most generous with his financial assistance.

But there were additional expenses; bills for example, totaling $2,500 from Cedars of Lebanon Hospital in Hollywood.

When Decker was taken ill, he was placed in a deluxe suite at the hospital, a circumstance that no one would have denied him, except that the charges were exorbitant for that time. He had three nurses around the clock whom he abused roundly. And there were frequent resignations on the part of the shocked nurses. Numerous suggestions to them by the dying man as to where they could place the bedpans and what they could do to themselves in general (and in particular) caused complaints such as to rouse the faculty to threats of expulsion.

The ceremonies at the studio included a phonograph recording of John's voice reciting the "No thank you" soliloquy from Rostand's *Cyrano de Bergerac*. There was a spray of red roses hanging on the Barrymore deathbed sketch and, so help me, God! at the very moment the minister said, "Let us pray," this spray of flowers came down with a plop upon the unopened half of the casket lid. If anyone could come back from what is known as the Great Beyond, Barrymore could do it. Perhaps this was some kind of benediction—or its antithesis.

They were going to display John's body in his famed red evening suit, a garment that always made him appear like a merry huntsman when rolling among the bars of our cafes, roaring imprecations. But it seemed that John, when making his dying plans, had asked to be buried in a darker suit, with his white muffler under his chin.

There were flowers, and about 100 pals were present—a few weeping at the loss of a really picturesque man. I listened to the minister from the kitchen with Decker's sister-in-law, Blanche, who cried as I held her in my arms. She sobbed: "He was such a great piece of ass."

The presence of newspaper photographers made it unnecessary to enlist aid to carry John's casket out the back and deposit it in the hearse. There were more than enough actors present and available.

Rather than follow the hearse to where Decker was to be cremated, I remained back at the studio to enjoy the quiet that had come at last. I relaxed for the first time in several days and had some drinks with Ida Lupino and her then husband, Louis Hayward, at Decker's little bar in the rear living room.

Now, I would have to hit the bricks to raise money to pay the considerable hospital bill of $2,500—which in present times would translate to about $50,000. I'd known Fanny Brice when I was a kid at Fire Island; knew she was of the old school and would at least return my call. She did better than that. She paid the entire hospital bill with the proviso that I would not make public this gesture.

Now I would have to lure some 30 of John's friends to give the hospital a pint each of blood in payment in kind for the 30 transfusions doled the artist. He had practically bankrupted the blood bank at Cedars of the rare type of blood he needed. Only Tony Quinn seemed to have had the kind that matched, and this generous fellow—who once before supplied a quart of his blood to John in an earlier illness—seemed to regard this whole matter with a look of haggard apprehension. The vast total of 30 pints staggered his imagination.

Quinn reported to me after witnessing John's cremation. He said he hadn't expected to see the body rise to a sitting position during the burning (a common manifestation due to contraction of the stomach muscles). "There must be a better way," said Quinn, still building himself back up after having surrendered a hefty draft of blood to the hospital. "Couldn't they have buried him under a tree or something? Maybe give the tree some sustenance?"

For some unexplained reason, John's ashes ended up on a shelf at a cemetery away from where he'd been cremated. This came to light when Phyllis received a bill from Westwood Memorial Park Cemetery[17] . . . for three months rental.

Checking this for Phyllis, I learned a friend I'd known since boyhood, Bob Yeager, had recently purchased the West Los Angeles cemetery and was merely "clearing the books."

After tracing the charge, Yeager sent Phyllis a successive statement marked "Paid in Full," and informed her that John's ashes had been scattered in the park's colorful rose garden. At the bottom of the statement, Yeager scribbled: "Anything for a friend."

It was ironic that Decker had been chronically in debt all his life . . . and now, also in death.

I was young then, compared to the men with whom I most associated. Therefore I felt I had lost more friends at an early age than others of my generation I knew. But I seemed to have possessed the persuasions and outlooks of these older friends and would not have had it any other way. Therefore, I was saddened greatly when they left me. Uncle Claude had to have included my sentiments when he said, "The ranks are thinning."

Jack Barrymore, with whom I had lived for many months, had died when I was 20. But I felt no finality to this. It was not until I was 25, when John Decker left the scene, that I began to feel that I was a survivor, alone without my toys.

---

[17]Through the years, Bob Yeager told me Westwood Memorial has turned into a West Los Angeles graveyard of the stars. In addition to Marilyn Monroe, Natalie Wood, Donna Reed, Christopher George and Darryl F. Zanuck and his wife, Virginia, are buried there. And Armand Hammer has had an impressive family mausoleum built there, across the street on Wilshire Boulevard where the billionaire spent close to $50 million on construction of a museum to house his private art collection. His body rests there today.

IX

Jim Murray:
Surrogate Brother

The finest raw newspaper writing talent I ever ran into upon arriving at the *Los Angeles Examiner* in April of 1944 was 24-year-old Jim Murray. This intense, slim Irishman with black wavy hair and explosive laughter was planted at the front of the city room bull pen. He was the youngest rewrite man the paper ever had. And he was better than the rest. At the outset, he was loaded with quick metaphor and turned phrases much after the style of Ring Lardner, and sometimes, Arthur "Bugs" Baer, which was good for a Hearst rewrite man in those days of dramatic, high-passioned reporting.

Jim graduated from Trinity College in 1943 and had already broken in as a campus correspondent for the *Hartford Times*. He worked as a reporter on the *New Haven Register* while living in his grandfather's house which was sporadically shared by his two sisters, divorced father, two cousins and "Uncle Ed who cheated at dice and was so bored with work that he couldn't even stand to watch people working."

Fanning on the police beat, Jim picked up a tip from Connecticut State Police head Leo Carroll. An heir to the wealthy Almandon family in Danielson had been shot by the husband of a lady this now dead young man had been sleeping with. There were only three or four murders a year in Connecticut and they were all kept as low-key as possible. Thus, the *Register* didn't want to disturb the peace and passed on the murder of this philandering fellow who had been in line to inherit a lot of money, a string of polo ponies and other things of precious significance.

Confused by this decision to bury such a good story, Jim handed
his tip over to AP's local chief Walt Cochrane. New York and
Washington went for it in a big way and when Murray moved
to Los Angeles, Cochrane sent a glowing letter of recommen-
dation to AP's west coast man, Hub Keavy.

"Hub couldn't hire me right then," said Murray, "so the only
sensible thing to do was to take a room out in Ocean Park by
the Pacific and fritter away whatever money I had left."

On his second visit, Keavy told Jim to see Bud Lewis of the
Times. Lewis said to return a week from Thursday, but this was
no solution. The displaced reporter from Connecticut had now
blown his last $106.

On his third contact, Keavy said, "I hate to do this kid, but
go down to see Jim Richardson on the *Examiner*."

Murray sat in a corner for a long time, wearing his big overcoat and reeking of the East. The man whom he later described
as "hardly beloved" and "a combination of literary light and Attila
the Hun," called Jim over to his desk. "Do you know where
the FBI office is in the town?" was the first question.

"No," said Murray.

"Do you know where police headquarters is in this town?"

"No," Murray kept answering.

Richardson leaned back in his swivel chair and said, "You don't
know anything, do you? . . . Can you *write*?"

"Oh, yes," said Murray. "I can write like a son-of-a-bitch."

Richardson told Jim he could start the following morning. "But
the next thing I said, which endeared me to him," said Murray,
"was 'Can I have an advance?' "

This was a point in time when Jim considered Los Angeles
a wildly exciting place. The shipyards were humming; there were
troop movements going to every point of the compass. There
were so many murders the city was running neck-and-neck with
the South Pacific. Life was the only thing the OPA couldn't keep
the lid on.

The moments were never dull, and if they were, the front page of the *Examiner* never admitted it. Its shrill calamitous presence was felt from Lincoln Heights Jail to the hibiscus-studded mansions of Beverly Hills. To Jim, Los Angeles made his native Connecticut seem like a monastery with a state House.

Jim was on general assignment a short time before it became evident to Richardson that he *could* write like a son-of-a-bitch. When I arrived on the scene three months later, he was already a member of the rewrite battery.

With little ready cash and no credit, Jim found it difficult to get around the strange spread out city of Los Angeles. He needed transportation to free him from the streetcar routes, so he went to a place where salesmen accommodated newspaper reporters. There he bought a large black four door box which was referred to as a Pierce Arrow automobile. Its headlights emanated from the fenders and there was a statue of an Indian with bow-and-arrow which was called a radiator cap, and Murray said the old four-wheeler was "the last of that run on the assembly line." It looked more like the last of its breed.

"I had to save my ration stamps for two weeks if I wanted to drive to the beach," he said. "Then I could only get enough gas at one station to make it to the next."

After signing up to make monthly payments for his classic car, a mutual pal called Jim to get over to the Five Seventy Five Club and "meet that pretty girl you said your heart's been melting for. You know, the gal who plays the piano. She wants to meet you."

Jim met Geraldine "Gerry" Brown, and that was the last time he dated another woman.

After I got to know all the guys in editorial, my father got a yen to be among newspapermen and some of us got together to do the town. The group consisted of Pop, Jim, Gus Newman, night editor Pat Hogan and police beatman Bill Zelinsky.

The downtown nightclub we hit was so *declasse* that the bartender was pouring its cheapest flit into Seagram's Five Crown

bottles. You could get high on the marijuana smoke filling the
sour air. The constabulary had not yet classified the weed as
a dangerous drug.

Zelinsky, moonlighting as the dive's master of ceremonies,
grabbed the microphone and began to inform the dingy drunks
that "Gene Fowler, the famous author is with us . . ." Among
them, no one ever read a book and had not a clue as to who
Gene Fowler was.

Before heading back to the city room we stopped off at the
county morgue. Lined up on gurneys were the bodies of an old
woman and a child cradled between her legs. The tag on the
woman's right great toe identified her as an "unwed female," and
Pop said, "Wouldn't it be interesting if we have her an old maid
who always wished to have a child . . . and now, in death, her
wish had finally been granted her?" Then a young man's body
was rolled in. He had been knifed. And at that time, Murray was
saving up to buy a pair of shoes. Pat Hogan looked at the shiny
patent leather shoes on the dead man and began removing them.
"Take these, Murray," said Hogan. "He won't be needing them
any longer." The morgue attendant did put a stop to this.

Late that spring, Jim and I crossed the street from the
Examiner and visited LeRoy's Jewelers, which shared space in
Sam's Cigar Shop, and picked out an engagement ring for Gerry
Brown.

Word got around the city room where we'd been and Walter
Naughton, the taffy-pull kid, asked to look at the solitaire. He
and Jim went out onto the veranda where Naughton held the ring
up to the light to study the diamond's sparkle.

"Jesus Christ," Naughton said. "This is the worst god-damned
stone I ever saw. Why, I wouldn't give this to my worst enemy."
With that, he threw the ring across the veranda and onto the
street below.

Frantic, Jim yelled, "Jesus Christ, Walter! What the hell are
you doing?" He didn't realize Sid Hughes was playing one of
his practical jokes. Sid had substituted a hunk of glass from the
five-and-dime store for the real thing.

At the October wedding, Jim said, "I was afraid Hughes was going to pull some sort of stunt, so I drank practically nothing."

The couple planned to stay a week at San Francisco's St. Francis Hotel, but ran out of money and had to come home a day early.

Jim wasn't writing sports yet, but he went to every sporting event he could. In 1946, we were first time spectators to a national golf tournament. It was the Los Angeles Open with Jug McSpaden beating Ben Hogan for the championship. Sammy Schnitzer, while fingering his Kansas City bankroll in front of the group of girls, had promised that free passes would be waiting for us. They weren't and we had to put up $40 (two-thirds of a week's salary) for us to get in with our wives.

The Murrays had settled in an apartment complex spread over many acres in West Hollywood nearby Gilmore Field and Third and Fairfax. Here, Bob Cobb's[18] Hollywood Stars played Triple A baseball. The major leagues had not yet franchised Los Angeles. Next door, the Goodyear blimp roosted at night in Gilmore Stadium.

During a crosstown series with the Los Angeles Angels, Chuck Wells and I sat outside the apartment waiting for Jim to arrive home. Dinner was planned for seven o'clock but Jim showed up a half-hour late.

Gerry opened the door and Chuck and I became witness to a woman thrashing her husband for being late for her home-cooked dinner. And I could see that right hand coming at me by way of Santa Monica and I was too late for me to duck. As it landed, I heard Gerry cry: "And as for you, Will Fowler! . . ."

Chuck and I ran downstairs to wait, too intimidated to return for the meal.

---

[18]Bob Cobb was the creator of the acclaimed Cobb Salad and Brown Derby proprietor.

In July of 1946, Jim rushed Gerry to Good Samaritan Hospital where she gave birth to their first child, a son they named Theodore. This happened at the same time millionaire Howard Hughes crashed his hot experimental pursuit plane into a Beverly Hills mansion. In critical condition, Hughes was rushed to St. Vincent's Hospital just a few blocks from where Teddy was to make his debut. I was assigned to St. Vincent's to cover the Hughes death watch. However, Hughes' executives had cordoned of an entire floor on the hospital and restricted reporters. This became a challenge for me to get in for an interview, so I slipped into the doctors' locker room on the floor below and confiscated and intern's smock and stethoscope. Then I climbed the stairs and entered Hughes' room. Trying to look like a physician, I studied the chart at the foot of his bed and began asking questions about the crash. Hughes was hard of hearing and I had to talk very loud. This aroused the millionaire playboy's guards and the doctor on the floor, who said: "This man is an imposter." Two gorillas tossed me out, but I did get the semblance of an interview.

The following morning, Hughes was removed from the critical list and I found time to visit a flower stand and buy four dozen red roses in celebration of Teddy's birth.

By this time, Jim was consistently winning the *Examiner* awards for the best written story of the week and the month.

One slow afternoon Jim was having a difficult time writing a story about some unknown bum who'd killed himself. "I kept writing this damned thing, and it was nothing," said Jim. "He'd hanged himself in a skid-row flea bag . . . so? . . .

"First I wrote it straight and when I handed it over, Richardson said, 'No, we need something with a little more human interest to it.' "

Murray said, as though Richardson was kidding, "Come on, come on." Richardson glared, so Jim thought, "What the hell. I'll give him what he asked for." Then he wrote:

William Wonderfield, 68, at the Barkley Street Hotel yesterday knotted a light cord around his neck . . . and stepped off a chair into eternity . . .

Richardson looked at it, laughed, threw it in the wire basket and said, "Okay, go on down to Gallagher's and have a beer."

This light conflict of personalities inspired rewrite man Johnny Reese—who wasn't doing anything special at the time—to create a poem in dedication. After tapping his fingers on the desk a few times, he started typing and had the thing done in about twenty minutes. He titled it *Jim Richardson's Rewrite Man.*[19] It follows:

Jim Richardson's Rewrite Man

The rewrite man was writing the death
Of a miserable Skid Row whore,
From the after effects of a drinking bout
Some two or three week before.

The facts were simple and dull and brief,
And he had it almost done
When suddenly came the raucous voice
Of James H. Richardson.

"On that murder case," the Great Man said,
"You can give it lots of play.
"Go into the mystery angle, too,
"For we're short of news today."

The rewrite man gave a startled cry
At the mention of mystery.
And round-eyed, turned to the desk and said:
"Were you addressing ME?"

"Of course," said the Man, and his voice grew thick,
"Some merciless sadist slew
"This innocent child of East Fifth Street
"Tho' he probably loved her, too.

"Get into your lead that a ghastly smile
"Was pitiful on her face;
"And in saying how she was slain, hark back
"To the Peete and the Denton case.

---

[19]This poem appeared in a Press Club annual later, under the by line of Charles Amador. It was Amador who handed the piece to an overworked editor. He was not the Bard as both Murray and I watched Reese write it.

"And somewhere high in your story tell
"Of the marijuana ring
"That made this maid in the seventh grade
"A wretched, besotted thing.

"Oh, yes, in your opening sentence quote
"MacArthur on the Flag,
"Ignoring the coroner calling her
"A syphilitic bag.

"Write wistfully of the cocktail glass
"That broke as her body fell.
"The artist will alter the photograph
"Of the gallon of muscatel.

"Mention a wilted yellow rose
"To tincture it with romance,
"And refer somewhere to an evening gown,
"Forgetting she wore no pants.

"The barroom bum she was living with,
"We'll call her mystery man.
"And try to mention the Japanese
"And the Communists, if you can.

"Get excited about the drama here
"Of passion and crime and greed.
"Write a good, objective story, and
"Get all of this in your lead.

"Give me a take as soon as you can;
"I want to give it a look.
"But don't start in till you've got the facts.
"... And hold it to half a book."

The rewrite man, with a ghastly leer
That the Great Man didn't see,
Started again, and finished at last
At twenty-five after three.

The climax came the following week.
He was gratified to get
The prize for the finest writing to
Appear in the overset.

It served the bastard right, of course,
As philosophers will note,
For being a rewrite man at all
When he could have slit his throat.

Murray had long before concurred with the rest of us that Richardson was a monster. "He'd send you out to steal pictures and if you didn't get them, you'd probably get fired."

Richardson was an SOB, but an interesting SOB ... He did so many weird things ... He was a monster until ten after three, our first deadline ... Then he'd pretend to skate about the city room. He had actually been a real ice skater and came down from Winnipeg and he and his first wife would put on skating exhibitions in nightclubs on little sheets of artificial ice. So every-once-in-awhile when the first edition was put to bed, Richardson would place his hands behind his back and skate around the city room: *"Humm, dumm, de, dumm,"* he hummed the Skater's Waltz ... And everyone would pretend to applaud.

But if it was ten *of* three, Richardson would jump up and he'd screw himself into the ceiling and he'd howl and make unnecessary flap. One time he leaped up and ran the length of the city room, cursing. Reporter Jack Massard looked up from the story he was writing and remarked: "There he goes, looking for someone to blame."

Years later I told Jim that Richardson had gotten livid at me over the paper's new two-way radio car phone. "Do you know about the Overell case?" he asked.

"No, Jim, I don't," I said.

Well, Richardson cursed over the radio phone and the monitor cut him off for using foul language over the airwaves.

"You," I said to Murray, "were the one to tell him, How the hell could Fowler know about the Overell case. He was on another story."

"But I'll tell you something more ... Something I learned: Never say 'no' to Richardson. Or, never say 'no,' you didn't read the paper."

On the day the Overell story broke, Richardson turned to Murray and said, "Do you know about the Overell case down in Santa Ana; where this boat blew up?"

Murray didn't, because it happened over the weekend and he rarely read the Sunday *Examiner*. "Oh, yeah," said Murray, "but I don't know any more about it than you, Will. I wasn't as honest as you, and also, I could see he was already mad."

It was late in the afternoon and Richardson told Jim to get photog Al Monteverde and go on down to Santa Ana and cover the story.

Photo department head Sam Sansone told Jim that Monteverde was down at Gallagher's having a sandwich.

"Come on, Al," Jim said to Monteverde, "we've got to go down to Santa Ana. There's a murder." And Jim is trying to figure a way to get back in the city room to look at the clips without Richardson catching him.

"I'm off in a half-hour," said Monteverde, "and I want to go home."

"Monte," said Jim, "I don't think you'd better. Now, if you don't want to go to Santa Ana, that's up to you. But I think it very advisable that you go. I would just *not* go up and tell Richardson, 'I'm off in a half-hour, and I want to go home.' By this time, he thinks we're already halfway there."

So Jim went to Santa Ana. "It was Monday, March 17, and I never got off that damned case until October 6, nearly seven months later."

She was a juvenile. Her parents were wealthy and their estate was situated in the affluent Flintridge district of Pasadena. She was a spoiled and only child. Her bedroom was filled with dolls and Teddy bears. She had taken private tennis, riding and swimming lessons. Her French governess had taught her the subtleties of etiquette. And on March 15, 1947, nine months before her 18th birthday, Beulah Louise Overell allegedly helped her 21-year-old lover, Bud, beat her parents' skulls in with a ball peen hammer before blowing them to kingdom come on their family yacht.

It was eleven o'clock on a leisurely Saturday night when the tall, hazel-haired and blue-eyed Louise and George "Bud" Gollum sneaked ashore from her parents' cruiser docked at Newport Beach in Santa Ana.

Forty-five minutes later, the concussion of a thunderous explosion rocked the pier and the *Mary E* began to sink by the stern at her mooring.

Louise and husky six-footer Bud—a pre-med student at Los Angeles City College—had "gone out to buy some hamburgers." They reappeared fifteen minutes following the explosion. The Coast Guard had arrived as the *Mary E* slipped beneath sixteen feet of water.

Following a preliminary investigation, local police released Louise and her bespectacled boyfriend. They wished to spare this anguished, teary-eyed girl the agony of viewing the bodies of her parents, Walter and Beulah Anne, as they were being raised from the water.

After their release, Bud and Louise motored north to the Overell estate where they spent the remainder of the night.

Late Monday, Jim and Monteverde had located a Santa Ana hotel room. And the following day, they were with police and sheriff's detectives when 31 sticks of unexploded dynamite were discovered in the *Mary E's* galley. This was the second of two charges, but a bulkhead separating the two prevented the large one from going off. The initial charge had worked well enough to kill Mr. and Mrs. Overell, but not efficiently enough to cover up the damaging evidence it left behind.

That afternoon, there was a knock at the Overell mansion's front door. It was the police with a warrant for murder.

On March 20, Newport Beach Police Chief R.R. Hodgkinson told Jim Murray that "the wires and tape found attached to a clock time-bomb aboard the Overall yacht is identical to those found in Gollum's car glove compartment."

Bud had been living with his mother, Wilhilmina, and stepfather, Dr. Joseph Stomel, where Bud volunteered his evenings as an assistant scout master for the neighborhood's Troop 21.

Chief Hodgkinson informed the press that the time-clock which detonated the dynamite had been "attached to the minute hand, and would have to have been set within one hour of the explosion." He also told Murray that Gollum, who served as a Navy Radio Man 1st Class during World War II, had the technical skills required to rig such a bomb.

Up until this time, no one had come up with a picture of Walter Overell, the dead father who had accumulated his wealth as a land developer and president of a large finance corporation, so Richardson sent George O'Day and me out to hunt for one.

On a hunch, I checked with one of my contacts. He was itinerate mortician Laverne Twiford. Twiford and I had become acquainted the first day I went out looking for stories. Twiford said he had a fellow embalmer friend who was presently the custodian to Walter Overell's body.

Armed with a bottle of booze, O'Day and I headed for Twiford's friend's funeral parlor in Costa Mesa and after the bourbon made him more affable, I posed my problem to the mortician. "It seems the only way we can get a photo of Mr. Overell," I said, "would be to take a picture of the body itself."

"But his extremities have been blown clean away," said the mortician.

"We don't want a picture of his arms and legs," I said. "Just the face."

"Well, I guess that'll be all right. But he looks awfully dead," he said.

"You won't know him when you see his picture in the *Examiner*," I reassured him.

The gentleman took us to the double refrigerator in the rear, and without any qualms, slid out his body.

We propped Overell's trunk up against a wall and O'Day shot the picture. "Do you think I could have a copy?" came to the mortician's mind.

"You've got it," I said. Things seemed to go along nice and easy in those days.

Back at the paper, artist Ray Schuman painted a coat, collar and striped necktie on the photo print of Mr. Overell and the *Examiner* ended up being the only paper to have Walter Overell's picture—although it looked about five downgrading points from the photos of "most wanted" criminals seen on post office bulletin boards.

A post-mortem on the bodies and psychological tests for Louise were ordered. And as the young suspects languished in custody, their attorneys petitioned Orange County Superior Court for a writ of *Habeas corpus* to obtain their releases.

Police Chemist Ray Pinker, with whom I had become well acquainted with two months earlier while covering the Black Dahlia murder, eventually announced that spectagraph analyses matched Gollum's paraphernalia with that found on the yacht. Autopsy surgeon John Montanus, M.D., concluded that the victims had been killed with a blunt instrument prior to the explosion ... It must be explained, however, that many successive autopsy surgeons came up with several different opinions regarding the time of Mr. and Mrs. Overell's deaths, and where each had occurred.

Murray interviewed Captain Thomas McGaff of the Orange County Sheriff's Identification Bureau, who said, "... fractures were an exact fit to the bloodied ball-peen hammer taken from the scene and is now in custody of the Department."

On March 24, Sheriff Musick announced that he had identified the explosion timer as being a clock belonging to Louise, and a recent gift from Bud.

With this amount of overpowering incriminating evidence piling up before him, District Attorney James L. Davis for some unknown reason was still hesitant to file a formal murder charge. Murray said: "Although Musick was convinced the victims were killed prior to the explosion, Davis' reluctance came because there was a political rivalry between former USC football star Musick and himself ... as how to approach the investigation and indictments. At the time, their public exchanges got quite biting."

As more enterprising reporters do, Jim departed the company of press members crowded around the police station who were waiting for updated news bulletins. Instead, Jim followed a tip of his own. "A reliable source"—as it's bandied by television news reporters today—informed him that the young lovers might have purchased the dynamite the day before the Newport Beach explosion, in the San Fernando Valley. He passed this on to Richardson and I was sent out to locate the desert store. I located the place in Chatsworth. It was the Trojan Powder Company. There, I asked the proprietor if a young couple had purchased explosives from him recently. He said he did remember a young man fitting Bud's description. "And there was a young lady sitting in his car outside. A Pontiac coupe, I believe."

Bud had signed the receipt with an alias. It was dated March 14, the day before Walter and Beulah Anne met their deaths.

On April 2, one of the nation's leading holographic experts, J. Clark Sellers, stated that the bogus signature on the dynamite receipt supplied him by the *Examiner* was positively identified to be Gollum's handwriting. And when Ray Pinker identified blood found on Bud's effects matched that of Louise's mother and father, District Attorney Davis filed his indictment.

Fighting for a judicial decision before Louise turned 18 on April 30 (the date she and Bud had set for their wedding), her attorney, Otto Jacobs, had a consideration: If dealt with as an adult, Louise could receive a life sentence. But if tried as a juvenile, her imposed sentence would be effective only until Louise reached the age of 21.

On April 4, Jacobs convinced Superior Judge Franklin G. West to release Louise on $50,000 bail on the grounds she was a juvenile and evidence against her was "insufficient." But she remained in her Santa Ana jail cell purportedly for the convenience of her attorneys to be able to keep in close touch with her.

Gollum's group of attorney's did not ask that bail be posted for him, and the trial was set for May 26.

By this time, Murray wanted some respite from the ongoing investigation. Richardson was nagging him. The city editor had heard that letters were being passed between Bud and Louise, and he wanted Murray to find out more about it.

"The letters were reported to be so sensual in nature," said Murray, "tyat they would make the Marquis de Sade blush."

"Richardson knew I didn't have time to steal any letters," Jim went on, "and one night while I was drinking with Maury Godchaux of the *Times*, and feeling lonely for my family, I phoned Richardson and asked him to let me go home, and he said, 'Okay, if you don't want to cover the biggest story in the country, then you can come home and I'll get you a nice job writing the weather report ...' I wanted to kill him before I got off the story ... Gerry and I had a new son. Tony was a brand new baby, and there I was in that ratty Santa Ana hotel room."

By this time had the ensuing case come up in a civil action suit instead of a criminal court procedure, defense attorneys for both Louise and Bud would have been satisfied to plead *nolo contendre* and accept the court's judgement ... the evidence being so overwhelming against them.

Time between indictment and the court's convening, however, was never considered *limbo* to Richardson. This was when he became more merciless and unreasonable with this reporters. And he wanted copies of those damned letters.

Bud's were often outright scatological. Louise's were reluctant; a little more embarrassed. Murray later said: "They were better than *Fanny Hill*. You could have made an Italian movie out of them."

Because of this leak, California State Attorney General Fred N. Howser eventually relieved Orange County District Attorney Davis, and substituted his own prosecutor, veteran Eugene D. Williams, who had never lost one of the 28 cases his tried.

"And with the Attorney General had come his familiar factotum," said Murray, "a derby-wearing, cigar-smoking Irishman named George Gallagher, and George knew everything that went on in the State."

"Those kids are passing notes and the jailer is photo-stattin' them," George told Murray, and Murray alone, in the corridor.

Jim would remember that day as as long as he lived, in which "bells went off in my mind and a light blazed as I tried to look unconcerned sidling toward a telephone to flash the city desk this extraordinary news tip."

With this explosive information, Richardson phoned the attorney general. "Old pal," said Richardson, "how would you like to make a lifelong friend out of the biggest newspaper in Los Angeles and slip us those letters?"

"I don't know how Richardson got them," said Murray. "I was not only kept in ignorance by Attorney General Howser, but Richardson didn't *tell* me he got them."

Lloyd Emerson, the *Examiner's* dean of the DA beat was secretly dispatched to make the vital letter pickup.

"The night Emmy made the big grab," said Murray, "the night the biggest scoop I had ever heard of—a 22-column scoop from Page One clear back to Page Three—22 columns of news the opposition didn't even know existed, Emmy called me aside and told me exactly what his assignment had been."

Murray had actually acted as a smoke screen for Emerson's activities during this time, so the opposition—naturally—immediately figured they had in Jim Murray the greatest news bloodhound in history. Instead of hanging out at the police station, reporters began following Jim around. One night he discovered a reporter hiding under his hotel room bed. His phone was tapped and some of his notes strangely disappeared from his room.

"Attorney General Howser came roaring down in a five-car caravan with a police escort to make a show of it, pretending to 'investigate the leak' in his office," said Jim. Richardson had made a deal with Howser, probably promising him the paper's endorsement for any office he chose to run.

The attorney general dramatically pointed to a wall safe. "The *Examiner* reporter must have rifled it," Howser told the opposition, in order to keep his political skirts clean.

"You mean, Murray?" asked the incredulous Maury Godchaux.

"Yes, Murray," said Howser.

Jim said he could have kissed him. "In fact," he said, "it wasn't too many days before I began to believe it myself."

"I might even have bragged at home to my wife how, in the best traditions of Hildy Johnson, Lee Tracy and Richard Harding

Davis, I had skulked into the state office and picked the safe lock—but Gerry would have laughed."

Were the young lovers found guilty and sent to jail for life? Had all this overpowering, unquestionable incriminating evidence spelled their doom even before the case went to the jury?

No!

After a nineteen week trial, during which 90 witnesses were called by the prosecution and 30 by the defense, and a million words of testimony and legal arguments were transcribed, a jury of six men and six women—in less than two days—had bought the defense's axiom that Louise and Bud were "victims of circumstance" ... and *"the accident of suicidal tampering with dynamite by Walter Overell."*

Santa Ana citizens were surprised, but joyous over the verdict and thousands of townspeople filled the street outside the red stone courthouse to cheer and get a glimpse at the victorious defendants.

Prosecutor Williams had termed the romance as being "... an illicity, perverted passion, amounting almost to a frenzy ..." and Judge Kenneth E. Morrison had disallowed the 100 lurid letters to be read in court.

Nine months later, a slimmed-down Louise married her jailer, police officer Robert Cannon. Although the marriage lasted only a short time, a son was born to Louise. There was a second marriage in Las Vegas, and in 1965, at the age of 36, Louise was found dead in bed by her husband. The coroner's report showed she had died of acute alcoholism.

Gollum had traveled east and was also married twice, during which time he served two years in a federal prison for transporting a stolen car over state lines. He has not been publicly heard from since.

"I finally got to go home," said Murray, "and returned to the rewrite desk where I belonged."

Befriending Jim Murray in my youth was not the most difficult task. Educated in parochial schools where the nuns nailed students to the wall if they didn't learn their lessons well, Jim was the most informed man my age I ever met. He was filled with fascinating historical knowledge and yearned to be a foreign correspondent during the war. He never knew it, but Jim became my role model and eventually, my confidante.

For nearly 15 years while our kids were growing up, our families gathered following Easter Sunday mass to celebrate the end of Lent. The first year I owned a swimming pool, Jim slipped into a bathing suit and removed his glasses to head outside. But a well-polished glass sliding door abruptly stopped him. It shattered and severely lacerated his leg. We rushed him to the nearest emergency hospital where it took eleven stitches to arrest the bleeding. When we returned and propped up Jim's sore limb on a pillow, I said: "Well, I guess this ruins our celebrating." "You've got to be kidding," said this Irishman just coming off 40 days of abstinence.

Shortly before Jim joined the staff of *Time* magazine in February 1948, we gathered with Pop, Jack Dempsey, Rube Goldberg and the Dean of sports writers, Grantland Rice at Romanoff's in Beverly Hills. Jim was in awe of this revered columnist who had graduated *cum laude* from Vanderbilt University in 1899, and had created such sobriquets known colloquially today as "The Galloping Ghost," "The Four Horsemen," "The Manassas Mauler," "The Georgia Peach" and "All America."

When he joined the *Time* staff, Jim said he didn't feel intimidated as do most newcomers. He learned to write their style. *Time* had a greater respect for the truth of an assertion, but Jim said he was allowed to be as humorous as he liked so long as the research was right.

When Jim started interviewing Hollywood cover story personalities, he became known by figures in the entertainment business. When he dined at Chasens with Marilyn Monroe, guests also knew who the guy was with her. When Humphrey Bogart was failing and his wife Lauren Bacall allowed him only one drink a day, Bogey used to wait for Murray to arrive and have it with him.

He golfed with Bing Crosby, played poker with John Wayne ("he was lousy") and kibitzed with Groucho Marx. When he interviewed Marlon Brando, Jim said, "I knocked on his door, and I knocked . . . for a hell-of-a-long time and he'd never answer. But as soon as I walked away, he'd fling the door open and cackle like a rooster."

With a feeling of greater security Jim decided to purchase a house. He was an Easterner and preferred being near the sea, so the Murrays moved to Pacific Palisades. It was a roomy white house with a walled backyard and you could smell the Pacific salt air blowing in from a mile away. Their daughter, Pamela, and my godson, Eric ("Rick") were born there.

In 1953, Chairman of the Board Henry R. Luce decided *Time, Inc.*, was ready to enter into the sports magazine world. Rather than merely reporting major events, it was Luce's theory that the public was also interested in an in-depth look at the game and its champions and participants. Putting it together, the magazine's masthead was *The Sport*, which eventually became *Sports Illustrated*. And because of his proclivity for sports was so strong, Jim Murray was called upon to help crank it up.

It was fascinating to be witness to the magazine's gestation period. In this case, it happened to be the Fourth of July of sports magazine publications. Among the enthusiastic followers listening to Murray tell how the magazine's makeup was coming along was my father. He and Hearst editor Walter Howey had created the *New York Daily Mirror* tabloid in 1925 as competition to the *Daily News*.

Jim showed us the sample run covers in full, corrected color. The first displayed a sea of people reacting in various ways to the progress of a sporting event. The second, and far more dramatic to me, showed a lonely figure launching his ball from one of golf's most beautiful but demanding holes. It was the 16th at Cypress, California, with a carry over thrashing Pacific Ocean waves. If you didn't land on the green for a par three, you usually ended up with a *twelve*.

When the first edition was readying to roll from the presses, Mr. Luce personally typed a letter still framed on Jim's wall:

Dear Jim:

This is the day after Christmas, and the quiet in the office gives me a chance to go over some of the copy for The Sport Magazine.

I have read your "Footloose Sportsman" for the Los Angeles area. It's just fine, and I also appreciate the fact that you had to do it in practically no time at all. I want to congratulate you on this piece. And even more, apropos of this, on all the work you have done in the last few months.

Fingers must always be crossed about futures, but it does indeed look as if we have a good magazine coming up. Anyway, it's a lot of fun as well as work.

Although Murray did go back to *Time* for awhile, he eventually returned to *Sports Illustrated* and remained its West Coast correspondent until 1961.

In 1956, the Murray clan moved to a larger home where the four children would have more room to expand their lungs in clean air. It was on a promontory overlooking the Pacific in North Malibu. "The drives to the office and local sporting events were hideously long," said Jim, "but the view and the peace was worth the time it took to get there."

My father had been dead about four months when the Murrays and the Fowlers gathered to celebrate Thanksgiving Day in 1960. Jim said he had two jobs offered him and would have to decide whether he wanted to move back East to take on the position as SI's Editor-in-Chief or become the *Los Angeles Times* premiere sports columnist.

"I never gave it much thought," said Jim, "but what the hell *is* a sports columnist's routine?"

"You just keep hoping the next guy you talk to will give you an idea for a column," I said. "If he just says 'Come on over to the house for a drink' and nothing else, avoid him."

An authority on the miseries of surviving an eastern winter, Jim said, "I'm really fed up with galoshes . . . and with four kids now . . ."

Jim chose to remain in the West and his first column appeared on the *Times'* Sports Section front page Feb. 12, 1961. In it, he had a collection of fresh phrases; a new approach of how to view the sports scene, whether with a sense of humor or a tug at the heartstrings:

- "I am against the bunt in baseball . . . The last time a bunt won a game, Frank Chance was a rookie."
- And, "I'm glad the Rams traded Billy Wade . . . He bumped into more people than a New York pickpocket . . . The play usually ended up with some mastodon of a defensive end holding Billy upside down by the heels and shaking him, like a father with a kid who's just swallowed a quarter. Billy gave up more ground, faster than Mussolini at the end of the war . . ."
- And, "I'd like once more to see Elroy Hirsch and Tommy Fears going out on a pass pattern and looking back for a Bob Waterfield pass. Throw in Jimmy David on defense and I'll pay double. David was the only guy I ever saw who could maim a guy while pretending to help him up."
- And, "I don't think anyone should be surprised at the disappointing showing of our Olympians in the '60 games. There is an old adage, 'When in Rome, do as the Romans do.' So our boys did. The coaches didn't like it, but the girls did."

He ended the column with a modest reference to himself; about when, as a child, he played baseball with a "dime rocket" ball wrapped in thick friction tape.

Jim's success with *Times* readers was instantaneous. It was the first time in town, too, when housewives began following a sports column *en masse*. When meeting him for the first time, one Saturday afternoon football widow said, "I love your column, Mr. Murray . . . I don't know what you're writing about, but I just love it."

The column ran six times a week and during the years he won the *National Sports Writer of the Year* award fourteen times out of sixteen.

His column circulated in more than 150 newspapers throughout the United States and Canada.

Many of his one-liners were shocking. Things like at the Indy 500: "Gentlemen, start your coffins . . ." or, "Rick Henderson has a strike zone the size of Hitler's heart ..." or, "Frank Howard is so big, he wasn't born, he was founded ..."

His word picture of Paavo Nurmi, the greatest of Finnish long distance runners of the 1920s is remembered: "He had the pulse rate of a fish, the suspicious nature of a Paris cop. He was as severe as the Finnish winter, as bleak as an icicle, as gloomy as the second act of an Ibsen play."

Jim became so prolific at knocking cities that he was either a pariah or invited to tear a town apart with his acid observations.

"The first city I knocked was Cincinnati." Jim told me. "We were on the road with the Dodgers and were losers ten straight when we hit Cincinnati in the rain."

There was nothing to write about. You can never find ball players to interview when it's raining. So Jim looked out the window in Cincinnati and took apart the city.

"I remember I wrote things like, 'They stand around watching haircuts' and 'An evening's excitement is going downtown to watch them wind the clock.'

"But the thing that got to them most was when they were building the new Riverfront Stadium right outside Crosley Field. They hadn't done a thing on it in a year and I wrote, 'I guess it was Kentucky's turn to use the cement mixer.' But actually it was a period of time, as President Nixon put it, when the cities were in terrible shape."

When the monstrous *Entrance to the West* arch in St. Louis, Missouri, was completed Jim referred to it as "the world's largest croquet wicket." He said he couldn't help it. "I thought they could have built something more utilitarian."

Adversely, people from Spokane, Washington, begged Jim to write about their city. Someone would come to him and say, "I want to tell you about Spokane ... There's nothing to do after 10 o'clock ... in the morning ... " and, "the railroad station is built across two highways."

His mail got so raunchy that Jim stopped allowing his secretary to open it, especially the packages that most often contained unmentionable and filthy items.

After the first Cincinnati column, Jim said "I wrote it and never gave it another thought. But you have to give it thought because L.A. is a place full of people from someplace else . . . like Willow Creek, Iowa. The way I remember about Willow Creek is because Andy Williams comes from there. Just 286 people live in this town. I wrote something about it, and sure enough, a couple of people send the column back to Willow Creek, and they say, 'Who the hell does this guy Murray think he is?' "

Some of his columns literally come from "out of left field." Once while covering the 1962 World Series in Yankee Stadium, there was a seat mix-up and Murray ended up sitting directly behind a steel post. But this didn't ruin the afternoon for Murray. He wrote about the *post*.

We went to the new Los Angeles Sports Arena together early on in his column when Jim covered the first *Los Angeles Times Indoor Track Meet*. I had expected this would be a sort of sacred cow piece, and was taken aback when I read it the following day. It was all about my claiming to have poor eyesight, but falling in love with the visage of sprinter Wilma Rudolph and her beautiful legs . . . all the way across the stadium floor.

When we went to the Cassius Clay-Archie Moore fight, Jim cautioned me to be careful about using offensive language. He explained that in public, "I always have to preserve the image of neutrality. Particularly being syndicated. I don't root. If you root, you're going to be a basket case at the end of the year. You get too involved."

He explained that some of his friends have embarrassed him at sporting events. "Six months after something like this happens," he said, "the subject will come up and someone might say, 'You should have heard that foul language Jim Murray used,' and it wasn't me at all."

He said once at a basketball game a friend started rooting against Wilt Chamberlain, "and Chamberlain would see this. He wouldn't know exactly who it was who was rooting against him . . . sometimes thinking it was me."

When someone is closely associated with a man of national fame, and the two happen to have been friends for an appreciable number of years before this celebrity struck, there are

responsibilities and confidences which must run constant when
in earshot of an inquisitive stranger. In other words, one must
be careful not to blow the whistle, if there is a whistle that should
not be blown.

In the case of Jim Murray he had become famous to my way
of thinking by the time we ordered our fourth drink at Betty's
Broadway Circle back in 1944. So it wasn't necessary for me
to attend any school of diplomacy when it came to discussing
Jim with strangers. To start with, I never had anything bad to
hide about him. And to this day, I've never known anything corrupt or wicked about Jim.

The first of three books with exclusive collections of Jim's
columns, *The Best of Jim Murray*, was published by Doubleday
in 1965. I'm forever interested in dedications and Jim's fit me
because none of my four kids ever read any of my books. It read:

*To my three sons, Ted, Tony and Ricky, who have never read
my columns and doubtless won't read this book, and my
daughter, Pammy, who won't either. To their mother, Gerry,
who not only read, but, bless her, laughed at all the jokes.*

The long Malibu commute finally got to Jim and in 1973, he
and Gerry moved nearer to town, to Bel Air. There was warmth
in the house, and when they gave parties, real people showed
up. I first met my tennis idol Jack Kramer at the Murray's.

It was during these years when Jim badgered the segregated
Masters often enough that they changed the Caucasians-only
status after Jim wrote:

"It would be nice to have a black American at Augusta in something other than a coverall . . ."

After Jim wrote, "Either let him in the front of the Hall—or
move the damn thing to Mississippi," famed black pitcher Satchel
Paige was inducted into the Baseball Hall of fame.

Then, on July 1, 1979, Jim wrote a column he never thought
he would have to write:

I lost an old friend the other day. He was blue-eyes,
impish, he cried a lot with me, laughed a lot with me,
saw a great many things with me . . .

He had a pretty exciting life. He saw Babe Ruth hit
a home run when we were both 12-years-old. He saw
Willie Mays steal second base ... He saw Rocky
Marciano get up ... You see, the friend I lost was
my eye ...

It had happened in Miami a few days before the 1979 Super
Bowl football game. "Funny how dusty the air is in Miami," he'd
said to Dallas Cowboys linebacker Thomas "Hollywood"
Henderson.

"It's as clear as a bell, Jim," said Henderson.

But it wasn't to Jim. The retina in his good left eye had become
detached. (He was already growing a cataract in the right one,
which only afforded him peripheral vision). Now both eyes were
in trouble. Five surgeries over the following year failed to save
one.

Now, Jim was legally blind. He nearly quit writing, but his spirit
kept him going. He had a special driver to chauffeur him to events
he could hardly see.

During this crisis, Jim phoned me. I could tell he had a problem.
He said he was going blind in the eye with the cataract—the one
surgeons were afraid to operate on. He needed me "right away"
to drive him across town to the Doheny Eye clinic near General
Hospital in East Los Angeles. It took us three hours to get there
in the dense busy Friday afternoon traffic.

Fortunately, the doctors handled the problem and his eye was
saved.

When the cataract was to be removed, there was only a 50-50
chance that Jim would not go completely blind. But he put off
the surgery "until I could see my first grandchild," Pammy's
daughter.

Of the four children, Ricky was the most affectionate. He was
the communicator who shared laughs with his father. Following
in Gerry's footsteps, he also played the piano "like a dream."
But this dream came to a halt on June 6, 1982, when Jim and
Gerry returned home from a golf tournament. There was a business card sticking from the front door. It was from the County

Coroner and listed a phone number for them to contact regarding Case No. 82-7139. The case number was Ricky's. He had died from an overdose of drugs.

Fingering the worn card he carries in his wallet to this day, Jim is still self-recriminating. "I don't know what happened," he said. "Dedication is hard on the marriage, hard on the family life. Maybe it was all of it . . . I spent long hours with my family . . . God knows they were never neglected . . . I think about Rick every day."

I was a pall bearer at my godson's funeral that bright, warm, sunny day at Holy Cross Cemetery. It was the kind of day kids like to raise hell in. A good day for the beach. A good day for practically anything else.

A few weeks later, I packed up and moved to Phoenix, Arizona. Following a divorce after 38 years of marriage, I thought I could sort my life back to some way of reasoning. During that time, Jim's life was placed in great danger when he underwent open-heart surgery to replace the faulty valve that had restricted him from enlisting in the service in World War II.

During my self-imposed year of exile, Gerry found time to write, to keep me up on the family happenings. But the letters eventually stopped and Jim told me Gerry had become seriously ill. Because of this, I returned to Southern California to take up residence in Sherman Oaks on March 1, 1984. And a month to the day later—on my daughter Jenny's birthday—Gerry died after a very long bout with cancer.

I was quietly bitter as I made the same sad trip to Holy Cross, once again a pall bearer carrying someone I loved so very much. I had never seen Jim so crushed and seemingly helpless. At the end of the requiem mass, when I put my hand on his shoulder, Jim looked at me and said: "What am I going to do?"

On the day of the funeral, Jim's farewell to Gerry was published in the form of an open letter next to a portrait of his wife on the front page of the sports section. He wrote:

> I lost my lovely Gerry the other day. I lost the sunshine and roses, all right, the laughter in the other room. I lost the smile that lit up my life.

God loved Gerry. Everybody loved Gerry. She never went 40 seconds without smiling in her life. She smiled when she was dying. She smiled at life and all the people in it. When you thought of Gerry, you smiled ... She never grew old and now, she never will ... If there was a Hall of Fame for people, she would be No. 1. She was a champion at living.

She never told a lie in her life. And she didn't think anyone else did. Deceit puzzled her. Dishonesty dismayed her ...

She played Galway Bay on the piano every St. Patrick's day for a maudlin husband who wept over a moonrise he'd never seen or a sunset that existed only in a glass and an ice cube. She was fun ...

We would have been married 39 years this year and we thought that was just the natural order of things. I had my speech all ready. I was going to look into her brown eyes and tell her something I should have long ago. I was going to tell her: "It was a privilege just to have known you."

"I never got to say it. But it was too true."

When we first met, the only thing Jim had to hang on the wall in a Santa Monica hotel room was a pair of freshly washed socks, if there was a nail there. After spending the money he had hidden in his left shoe, he subsisted on peanut butter sandwiches.

He has since become the most celebrated sports writer of our generation.

A few years back, Jim phoned to say he was traveling east to visit with his Gerry's relatives "just to have some fun and laughs about old times," he said. He didn't mention that he was stopping off on the way to be inducted into the *Sports Writers' Hall of Fame* in Cooperstown.

Until April 12, 1990, I had been on the soap box for several years, claiming the Pulitzer Prize committee had blind vision, a carrot in its ear, in that Murray hadn't won our nation's highest literary honor. The only other sports columnists who had, had been coted in the environs of the *New York Times* (Red Smith, Dave Anderson and Arthur Daley).

On that date, it was finally all done, put together, when Jim won the Pulitzer. But only in his way did he do so. Not for sports writing, but in the higher international category of communicated understanding: *Commentary*.

Approaching the half-century mark in friendship, Jim and I are only in contact about five or six times a year now. But most important is that we have gone through the rite of passage together in the newspaper business which has given us an unshackling bond.

"I don't have time to see my old friends any more," Jim recently told me. "All I talk to these days are second basemen."

No matter how he handles this dilemma, Murray has ultimately become a bondsman to his fans. As opposed to the obscure, the celebrity, in his case, must constantly relinquish his visa to privacy.

Regarding Jim Richardson:*

Former Hearst reporter and now a special news director and producer at KABC-TV in Hollywood, John Babcock told me about the retirement party for Jim.

It was a bang-up affair thrown at the downtown Statler Hotel on October 14, 1954. The most noteworthy civic, state and Hollywood personalities crammed into the festive dining hall to get their pictures taken with the now aged firebrand making his debut among the ancients.

Much detail was given to make it a celebration to be remembered. The party trappings were many and expensive. The *Examiner* even had a dummy front page printed beneath its masthead. Famous by-liners and national and Hollywood columnists contributed electric copy reviewing Richardson's professional past and poking fun at his ungodly temper and unreasonable character.

Having quit Jim four times, I had no affection for the bastard. This was public knowledge in the newspaper business. Therefore, I didn't attend the gathering.

I wish I had, though, because of what John Babcock reported to me.

"Richardson, now in a wheel chair, came late to the dinner honoring his long years of service with the Hearst organization," said John.

Some of the Hearst boys were there, including George, Jr.

"Two things caused surprise," said Babcock. "One was that so many people would show up to honor the son-of-a-bitch, and two that he'd even show himself."

Both questions were answered when it was Richardson's turn to speak. He said:

"I know that all of you hated my guts ... and I want you to know it's mutual ... I only came tonight to see how many hypocrites would show up and to tell you that in all my years with the Hearst organization I got my 20 pieces of silver and I got my pound of flesh ... Good night!"

With that, James Somerset Richardson wheeled into history and obscurity.

PULITZER PRIZE WINNER JIM MURRAY (left) interviews suspected parenticide murderers Beulah Louise Overell and George Rector "Bud" Gollum at sensational 1947 front page trial in Southern California. Internationally-famous sports columnist Murray was a 27-year-old rewrite reporter for the *Los Angeles Examiner* at the time ... Gollum's mother, Mrs. Wilhilmina Gollum Stomel, is at right.

THE FIVE WISE MEN—(l to r)
W.C. Fields, Gene Fowler, John
Barrymore, John Carradine, Jack
LaRue and John Decker making
merry at the 1941 opening of John
Murray Anderson's Hollywood
nightclub.

BEFORE THE MUTINY—Motion picture
idol Errol Flynn with young bride Nora
Eddington aboard Mexico-bound yacht *Zaca*
from which Artist John Decker and others
would jump ship a week later.

THEATER'S FIRST LADY—Ending long
absence from pictures, premiere actress
Helen Hayes is interviewed by reporter
Fowler on her return to star in *My Son
John*. *Daily News* reporter is at center.

X

Anatomy of a Scoop

To most people, the word "scoop" is something that has to do with ice cream. But when it was coined in the vernacular of the Fourth Estate in 1890, it took on the meaning of "news obtained (and published) in advance of a rival newspaper."

In order for a reporter to get a scoop, he had to be crafty, creative, alert and unusually lucky. Getting a scoop was the main game in newspapering, a device that often turned drudgery into delight.

There were several ways to obtain a scoop. A reporter could walk away from his opposition and develop an angle of his own. He could pretend to "blow" a story along with his rivals and return to the scene later to talk reluctant subjects into an interview along with giving him photos of a person or persons (if missing).

He could opt the simple approach often ignored: Look up a sought after suspect's address and number in the phone book. He could also get a day ahead of the police on a lead by out-maneuvering them with his own private investigation.

Then there was the art of misdirecting the opposition. The reporter could also blackmail the constabulary when covering a story out of town. (This was never done in one's own backyard where the reporter worked with local authorities on a regular basis). But many miles away from home, it was free game to supply the already corrupt with anything from booze to women.

Then, the reporter could become a housebreaker in search of clues or photos. But today this type of approach would land one's ass in jail.

But the way a reporter most often got his scoop was to be just damned serendipity-doo-dah lucky: trip over a flat clue when he wasn't even looking for it.

I have had my own good fortune pursuing exclusives. My first sizeable one turned into an international scoop back in 1946 when Irish war bride Bridget Waters shot her husband dead in Las Vegas while holding their 16-month-old son in his arms. This story had all the ingredients of an international front page story.

It was early evening when my photog Ferde Olmo and I flew into this sleepy gambling town. Gangster Bugsie Siegel's casino establishment, The Flamingo Hotel, was just being created by his architects when the Strip was still a stretch of desert sand.

After registering at bandleader Horace Height's small hotel, I learned that Bridget Waters was being held incommunicado in the town's four-celled jail. I sought out Las Vegas's chief official honcho, with whom I proceeded to drink whiskey. I gave him money to gamble with and supplied him with a whore so high-priced he couldn't turn her down.

I visited the small jail the following morning and when I was refused an interview with the murderess, I phoned my honcho friend; I explained that I had forgotten to mention I was a reporter from the *Los Angeles Examiner*, and that I was not being allowed an interview with Waters.

This was what is referred to today as being "between a rock and a hard place." Honcho was a good family man with children. He didn't want it to be found out at home that he was an erring husband, so he had no recourse but to allow me my exclusive interview including pictures of Waters behind bars.

But a reporterless Associated Press photog followed Olmo and me into the jail and got a grab shot of Bridget. Now I had to figure a way to remedy this in order to keep the story exclusive. I did this by breaking into a curio shop where AP had a wire photo-sending setup (the only one in Las Vegas) in the back room and made it inoperable by shorting some wires and un-vacuuming a few vacuum tubes.

Olmo was unable to get a picture through the front door peep-hole of "the other woman's house"—she being the reason in the first place that Bridget had done her husband in—so I suggested to Assistant Coroner James Young (who was running the inquest, that the other woman, Miss Lucille Griffith, should be present during the proceedings.

Never having presided over a case of this proportion, Coroner Young agreed and called for Miss Griffith to sit in with the audience of locals jamming the small courtroom. And when Ferde Olmo grabbed Lucille's picture and the opposition asked who it was he had just photographed Olmo pointed to a completely different woman in the audience, one who had absolutely nothing to do with the murder inquest at all.

Finally, Ferde and I approached a wealthy gentleman who owned an airplane, plied him with hooch, and convinced him it would be great fun to fly us to Los Angeles with the exclusive negatives and get his name in the paper. I tried not to appear anxious, but there was no scheduled flight to L.A. for four more hours. By this time, the AP photog could have driven back with his negatives.

Sometimes side-bars came the hard way when looking for an angle the opposition wouldn't suspect. It was a different one for me after a high school girl had been gang raped by several senior boys. She had died from a combination of an overdose of drugs and internal bleeding. I was still smarting when covering her funeral because Tom Towers of the *Examiner* had beaten me by stealing the right photo of the dead girl from a stack of pictures at the death scene. (I was working on the *Herald-Express* then).

I was looking for anything different to pursue over-and-above the usual funeral when I noticed a teenager who appeared to be manufacturing some tears. I took him aside after the funeral and asked him if he knew the dead girl. He said he had met her a few times and thought she was beautiful.

After pumping the young man for more quotes, I had my photog Tom Courtney shoot a picture depicting the lad bowing his head over the casket.

I wrote the "love from afar" side-bar which was given a lot of picture space on page three.

Shortly after the paper hit the street, the "love from afar" kid phoned the paper. He was very upset; said he'd been humiliated; said his pals were joshing him and that the *Her-Ex* had better do something about it.

There was nothing to do *post partem* except for me to visit the young man with a few six-packs of beer. I finally convinced him that his pals were envious because he'd gotten *his* name and picture in the paper and not them. He finally agreed with this view and we parted friends.

Then there came the time to appear outwardly honest. This happened while covering a murder-suicide; a man had blown a hole in his wife's chest with a shotgun before turning it on himself. When I arrived, one plainclothesman in particular was busy expediting various items such as expensive fishing gear and camera equipment. All I said to him was: "You keep the camera and give me the film." This made sense and the *Examiner* picture beat the other papers with exclusive shots of the couple during happier times. (Note: I was never a thief as a reporter or private citizen. I do not believe in stealing things mainly because I always thought it would be damned embarrassing if I was ever caught at it.)

One time in the San Fernando Valley—Van Nuys, to be specific—my photographer and I had our lives threatened by a group of tough cement workers while we were trying to hold on to a scoop.

The story had to do with a construction worker who had beaten his wife's head in with a hammer. Police had phoned his house to locate the whereabouts of the missing suspect. Communication with the Spanish-speaking baby sitter was impossible, so detectives gave up until another time.

In any event, I later made my own call after looking up the suspect's number in the phone book. I was lucky and connected with one of the suspect's children who happened to be exceptionally bright and who told me her father was presently screeting cement for a new gas station only four blocks from the Van Nuys City Hall. (The City Hall in those days contained a hive of city offices, the courthouse and fire and police departments all under one roof.)

My photog Phil Glickman and I arrived on the scene and spotted the suspect at work. He knew what we were there for when Glickman shot his picture. The suspect's fellow workers ganged together with their pickaxes and other lethal weapons and asked the suspect, Bill Acherman, "You want we beat the shit out of 'em, Billy?"

Glickman and I were ready to make a run for it with the negative plates when Ackerman said, "I don't think you better." Then I told Glickman I'd give him an hour's start before phoning the cops to tell them where Ackerman was. But I only held out about 50 minutes when Ackerman's friends again started mouthing some pretty hard threats.

When I phoned the detectives, a collection of the opposition was sitting around with feet up on the desks, waiting for the next lead to develop. And within minutes after I hung up the public phone receiver, I could hear the whine of sirens approaching four blocks away.

By that time, Glickman's negatives had probably already been selected by picture editor Don Goodinow and were on their way to makeup.

It turned out later that Billy Ackerman had been an exemplary father who sat home nights with his kids, cooking dinner and helping them with their homework while his wife—a full-blown alcoholic—was out picking up men at the local piano bar for a romp in the hay.

Good father Ackerman was never drawn further into the case after the Coroner's jury came in with a verdict of "justifiable homicide," and District Attorney Ernie Roll refused to file against Billy for murder, first or second degree.

The irony here that never made the papers came when the freed wife-killer returned to the Van Nuys police department and asked for his hammer back.

Gus Newman had a beat so dynamic that it developed by chance only after he had written the initial piece about a World War II veteran's homecoming.

After writing the routine picture story showing Marine Sergeant Douglas W. Bogue, 26, having a home-cooked meal, sacking in on a soft bed and sharing a Zombie cocktail with the 24-year-old girlfriend who had waited for him, Betty Wearing, Newman recalled a wire story out of Washington, D.C., mentioning that the Pentagon suspected atrocities had been committed on U.S. prisoners of war. "I recalled Bogue telling me he was sitting on a big Pentagon secret," said Newman, "but I couldn't get out of him what it was."

Newman checked back on the wire story he'd spiked earlier on his spindle. It said the Pentagon would shortly release a story about these suspected atrocities following escaped Japanese prisoners of war interrogations.

"It was an outside chance that Bogue might be connected with the Pentagon story," said Newman. So he returned to Bogue's house and after much talk, Bogue finally broke his silence.

He gave Gus searing details of the wholesale murder of 150 American Marines, soldiers and sailors by their Japanese captors in a prison camp on the island of Palawan in the South Pacific, and how he had managed to escape the bloody slaughter.

Bogue said the Japanese believed an approaching convoy was going to attack them. "In a fanatical frenzy," said Bogue, "they herded prisoners into air raid trenches and butchered and burned them."

Bogue said he'd been working in the fields near his prison camp one afternoon "... when we were ordered back early. We were told to get into air raid trenches that held about 50 men each."

Fortunately, Bogue said he and two others ducked into fox holes just five feet inside the barbed wire fence and away from the shelters.

The Marine said he heard a dull, muffled boom—and then machine gun and rifle fire.

"Those screaming bastards were pouring gasoline in A Company's shelter and tossing flaming torches on them ... Then there were all those prisoners running out, all on fire, and they were mowed down by machine gun fire while running into each other."

Bogue and the other two prisoners lurched out from the fox holes and dived through the barbed wire fence, shouting, "We can make it!"

But they didn't. Not the other two.

"How those machine gun bullets missed me, I'll never know." Bogue told Gus. Then Bogue said he lept into the water and ducked several times in order to miss the gun fire.

Bogue was able to work his way around a point where he ran into three Japanese sailors with a Lewis machine gun trained on him.

"In a flash, I saw the actuator wasn't back," he said. "The gun couldn't fire until it was back. That's all the time I needed."

Bogue piled on top of all three, punching and choking them so fiercely that two of the Japanese sailors started running away.

"I wrenched the gun from the third," he said, "and I started shooting ... All three of them fell."

After that, it took Bogue two weeks of escaping into the jungle where, after being bitten by wild bees, his feet swelled so that his toes didn't touch the sand when he walked. And if he hadn't gathered rain water caught in tree hollows and eaten raw snails from the beaches, he would have died before he was rescued by a Philippine native from an isolated tuberculosis colony.

And if it hadn't been for Gus Newman remembering the spindled Pentagon future alert, this story would never have come to light.

There was one scoop which might have been classified as being unilateral on the part of the *Examiner, Herald-Examiner, Times* and *Daily News* which was unintentionally perpetrated against the city and county of Los Angeles executive offices. It occurred when officials and elected representatives were caught flat-footed when the President of the United States accepted an invitation from the newly formed Greater Los Angeles Press Club to speak in the City of Angels while on his 1948 re-election campaign train tour.

Attending a First Anniversary meeting and wondering what could be done to focus national attention on the still very young club, beatman Bevo Means drained his glass, tilted back on his chair and said: "Why the hell don't we invite Harry Truman to come speak?"

The boardroom in the Cabrillo Hotel became silent. None chanced an instant opinion as they considered if Bevo had had too much to drink, or if it was a good idea.

The next day, Bevo's suggestion was so well received that several board members began taking credit for the idea. A letter of invitation was composed and went out to President Truman before the weekend arrived.

Expecting a polite refusal, club officials remained outwardly noncommittal. Los Angeles officials, including Mayor Fletcher Bowron, were still unaware of the invitation because local newspapers remained poised, awaiting a White House decision.

J. Howard McGrath, Charlie Ross and Clark Clifford sat across from President Harry Truman in the Oval Office at 1600 Pennsylvania Avenue. "Read it again," the President said to McGrath.

"... Chicago ... Omaha ... Seattle ... Portland ... Berkeley ... San Francisco ... Los Angeles on June 14. Luncheon with the Greater Los Angeles Press Club ... then swing back East ..."

Truman had been concentrating on the West where he thought the Democratic Party was weakest. Nodding approval, the President pressed a button and the "word" echoed through the nation's wire services and newspapers that Los Angeles, a heretofore whistle stop, had been included in Truman's agenda.

When Los Angeles administrators heard the word, most were so confused at the news it seemed they didn't know who to blame for not being informed of the Press Club's correspondence, much less the invitation.

Walter Ames of the *Times* was the Press Club's chairman and received President Truman's telegraphic reply:

> The President has asked me to tell you that he can accept invitation of Greater Los Angeles Press Club to be guest speaker at their anniversary luncheon Monday, June 14. We will appreciate it if you will furnish us with details such as time the President is expected and luncheon program as soon as possible.
>
> Regards,
> Matthew J. Connelly, Secretary to the President.

Looking back, Maury Godchaux wrote: "The President's acceptance had thrown all the Los Angeles politicians for a row of broken platforms. Smoke came out of one corner of the Democratic camp where some of the Bourbons muttered darkly that they had been ignored—or at least bypassed. Everybody, it seemed, had wanted the President, but the Press Club got him."

Walter Ames followed up Truman's acceptance with a detailed wire assuring the White House that the Press Club would have the valued assistance and advice of sound local Democratic figures. Unfortunately, there wasn't enough money in the Press Club's coffers to cover the cost of the lengthy telegram, so it was necessary for the hotel bellboys to take up a collection to pay for it in advance before it was dispatched.

Overnight, the Press Club—brawling young, brash and still in swaddling clothes—matured and became seasoned. Politicians, bearing gifts, with hats in hand, scrambled for tickets to the affair.

On the day the President's private train rolled into Union Station, kinks in planning seemed to have smoothed out and disappeared. All anyone really cared about was that President Harry, Mrs. Truman and their daughter Margaret would make it safely to the Ambassador Hotel for the appointed luncheon.

Along the parade route, spectators clinged to the roofs of buildings, jammed windows and fire escapes and crowded five-deep along the sidewalks—a million Angelinos bidding the President welcome.

Arriving at the Ambassador, two veteran Secret Servicemen arrived to put finishing touches on the niceties of Presidential protocol.

Participating Press Club executives' wives retained their imperturbable poise and were charming to Bess and Margaret.

Prior to the luncheon at the hotel, the President served as bartender for Ames. The large group of Democratic officials and hotel manager J.W. Benton took it all in with amazement when he heard Truman shout: "This is the best god-damned welcome I've been given! It tops anything, anywhere, before!" The Ambassador's newest tradition now was: "President Truman stayed here," and the bellboys from then on announced Truman's as being the "Presidential Suite."

"By this time, there were three network and three more local TV stations settling in the Los Angeles area," said Stan Chambers who had just joined Klaus Landsberg at KTLA. "But having entered the infant medium's news and entertainment arena earlier than the rest, KTLA was ahead by far with viewer ratings." And this day, they were set up in the Coconut Grove to transmit President Truman's luncheon address. This time though, the big, cumbersome electronic camera sported the KTLA logo in place of W6XYZ.

There were 1,054 guests of varying political stripe assembled and *Time* magazine suggested that perhaps two-thirds of them were Republican.

The occasion avoided the pitfalls of introductory speakers and their bland remarks. Walter Ames and Gene Sherman met their moments suavely and the President stood to offer his address that was billed to be non-political, which it was not.

Rather, the Chief Executive gave a lightning-and-thunder address calling for the Democratic Party to join together and fight for his election. And in the best of Truman tradition, he lambasted his foes and defended his friends.

"President Truman," wrote Carl Greenberg, "gave the GOP-controlled 80th Congress a new whipping, in Los Angeles, for inaction on eight major recommendations."

Not having had previous political experience in throwing a bash of national proportion, press club officials respectfully withdrew from the field.

Two-and-a half hours and hundreds of handshakes later, the President looked at his watch, nodded, and Secret Service wheels started to turn again. Margaret and Mrs. Truman selected a few orchids to take with them and the machinery of the Chief Executive's transcontinental tour again geared into motion.

The limousines didn't linger this time. Swiftly, the party moved back to Union Station to board the Presidential special. The goodbyes were said, press club collars were loosened, and a summer night was closing in as the engineer tooted his whistle and the train slipped eastward.

With President Truman's visit, the Greater Los Angeles Press Club had gained national stature. It had achieved its goal because Bevo Means had casually suggested: "Why the hell don't we ask Harry Truman to come speak?"

MAKING A POINT WITH UMPIRES—Fowler and Bob Hope discuss a close call with umps in 1948 baseball exhibition game to raise funds for VA Hospital bleachers in West Los Angeles.

FLIRTING ON PICKET LINE—First postwar studio strike was called by Herb Sorrell's Painter's Union on Dec. 16, 1946. Related unions sympathized. Here, reporter Fowler (left) fraternizes at Warner Bros. Studios with picket and daughter of actor Barton McLain. Peace ended next day when studio guard was shot. The picket line was gassed and there were many injuries.

ESTHER WILLIAMS INTER-VIEW—Interviewing actress Esther Williams underwater in her specially-constructed tank at MGM Studios in 1951 was one of Fowler's happier assignments ... Williams could hold her breath 45 seconds; Fowler, three minutes, having gained great lung capacity playing the tuba in high school.

XI

Television News
Makes History

The initial media invasion of the Fourth Estate came with the advent of commercial radio in 1920. It quickly became network-controlled with all its station letters east of the Mississippi beginning with "W" and those to the west of our longest river with a "K." News was mainly the milieu of adult males, women's fare were shows like "The Easy Aces" and "Abie's Irish Rose," and kids took to afternoon serials the likes of Tarzan and listening to actor Paul Douglas shouting into the microphone: *"Buck ... Rogers ... in the Twenty-fifth CEN ... tu ... ree!"* And following the 1929 Wall Street crash, radio became the temporary escape from the terrible fact that the country was flat broke.

News inroads were being made by several weekly programs such as "The March of Time." But movie house receipts substantially fell off on Sunday evenings when columnist Walter Winchell came on the air with his staccato voice declaring: "Good evening Mr. and Mrs. North and South America ... and all the ships at sea ... Let's go to press!"

The motion picture theater's remedy for this lapse in attendance was to switch off the movie and pipe in Winchell's broadcast along with the popular "Amos and Andy" show.

During radio's infancy, news departments had staffs of three or less, with budgets as small. Announcers did a lot of "cribbing," getting stories from metropolitan newspapers. Many became expert in lifting the first paragraph from a hot story and reading it over the airwaves, fleshing it out with telephone interviews.

But when Adolf Hitler's dirigible *Hindenberg* went down in flames over Lakehurst, New Jersey, in 1937, and announcer Herb Morrison lost his composure describing the scene, crying out, "... all this humanity ... this is the most terrible tragedy," listeners' minds seized on the fact that on-the-spot remote news coverage was the most electrifying act performed by radio. This was the real thing where listeners could live what was going on along with the victor or the victim.

The late Clete Roberts was broadcasting news on the CBS network at that time. During these innovative years, Roberts said: "We taught ourselves the skills of 'talking writing,' that is, putting words together in such a way that they sounded better when read on the air. We honed our 'verbal writing,' the technique of extemporaneously describing a scene in such a way as to present a lucid word picture for our listeners who were 'viewing' what we saw with only their auditory sense."

Roberts said the radio newsman's biggest problem was to be accepted at press conferences by both the printed press and by those who had called the session. "To put it bluntly," said Roberts, "we were something less than second-class citizens at press conferences."

Once Los Angeles *Times'* veteran newsman Tim Turner threatened to walk out of a press conference unless broadcast reporters were banned from the meeting.

World War II elevated radio newsmen's status to that of first-class citizens. The intensive style of Ed Murrow helped speed that image along.

During radio new's return to the peaceful life during the spell from 1945 to 1947, there was no friction between the two mediums. But this was also the period where the end of experimentation was being carried out on perfecting the image-orthicon tube—the breakthrough that made television practical for commercial marketing.

The year 1947 presented television with a game wherein the rules hadn't been written, and the techniques hadn't been invented. As it was done in the first days of radio, TV set about developing an entire new craft. The news borrowed much from radio—too much at first. Roberts said: "The early television reports were little more than a series of radio bulletins with occasional still pictures.''

The use of newsfilm and the development of a visual report for the networks didn't come overnight. The KTLA remote coverage was still on a local signal level. For some reason, networks were slow to expand into the news film business. When Clete Roberts first took his Auricon news camera abroad—along with his trademark tan trench coat—it was difficult to locate network television correspondents or stringers in key cities.

(Even as late as 1960, when I was News Director for Los Angeles' television station KTTV where dynamic newsman George Putnam abounded—garnering the highest newscasting salary in the entire industry for his two local 15-minute shows— much was lacking in overseas news film communication. In May of that year, Soviet Secretary Nikita Khrushchev announced the capture of a U.S. reconnaissance aircraft over Russia. In a pique of anger, Khrushchev removed his shoe and banged it on his desk. I had a stringer who got that exclusive and now historic picture on film and expedited it through Customs. When KTTV's short-sighted president Richard Moore received a $100 invoice, he told me I was not to spend ''these exorbitant sums'' before consulting him.)

Within two years after television went commercial, the public went wild over this newest post-war electronic gadget and bought up all the seven-inch tube sets available. This was a status symbol and most people wanted to be first on their block to own one.

Invited to a friend's house for dinner, I was unable to carry on a conversation as they preferred to stare at actor Bill Boyd galloping about on his horse *Topper* and shooting up the bad guys in his ''Hopalong Cassidy'' movies.

As the art of American conversation began to erode and take a back seat in favor of looking at a television set, people were already trying to outdo their neighbors by purchasing larger sets. Radio networks were battling for TV franchises from New York to California.

By April 18, 1949, television sales had burgeoned and now nearly five million U.S. homes were equipped with TV sets. This was the date, the April Friday afternoon, when a three-year-old girl child named Kathy Fiscus had been playing in a San Marino field in South Pasadena. The field was freshly green following a nourishing rain that made the grass tall. The ground was no longer muddy and it was a good place to play where rocks and discarded trash were no longer visible. Neither was an open abandoned water well.

Kathy's five-year-old cousin began to miss her. Then he heard her cry, "Mommie, Mommie! ... Come help me, Mommie!" When he discovered that her voice was coming from the hole in the ground, he ran for help.

Two apprehensive women arrived and called down the shaft, "Kathy, are you all right?"

"Yes ... yes," Kathy replied.

The San Marino and Pasadena fire departments were dispatched and neighbors began to gather.

Herald-Express veteran photographer Ben White, who used to recite the poems of Robert W. Service while on the way to stories, was having coffee at Moran's Bar when a young reporter entered. "Come on, Ben," he said. "We have a little girl stuck down an abandoned well shaft in South Pasadena. Let's go!"

Ben swallowed his coffee and said: "Kid, you're about to cover the most important story of your life."

By the time Ben and his tyro arrived on the scene, it had already taken on the character of a major rescue effort. About 200 spectators had gathered as police began cordoning off the area.

Initial fire department rescue attempts failed and mining and oil well drilling experts were called in. And as Kathy Fiscus's predicament was swiftly becoming a personal interest to the locals, Los Angeles wire services began feeding bulletins out to the nation.

The story was flashed overseas by radio. Newspapers in Paris, Rome and London began holding back normal deadlines to include the latest news from this California suburban town. Although not directly linked up with Los Angeles TV, out-of-town-and-state television began interrupting scheduled programs to update the news about "the little girl caught in a well shaft."

Chicago, New York, Dallas and other major city newspapers reported they were unable to handle the calls which were glutting their switchboards. A *Salt Lake City Tribune* operator said: "I haven't seen anything like this since the end of World War II. Even tiny children, almost too young to talk, are calling for news about Kathy."

Because of the confinement of the narrow abandoned shaft's opening, circus thin men, contortionists and even midgets were volunteering to be lowered into the hole to try to free Kathy. Retired sandhogs and plumbers were also offering their services.

Rescue efforts had continued all that Friday night and into Saturday morning. An air hose had been lowered so Kathy could breathe more comfortably and a shaft adjacent to the abandoned one had begun to be dug. All were apprehensive because no one had heard Kathy's voice since she cried out to the ladies who were there the day before.

Those at the scene, listening to the radio and reading the latest newspaper accounts, began to feel as though they, too, were emotionally involved with the ongoing dilemma.

Ironically, David Fiscus, Kathy's father, had just returned from testifying at the State Capital, pushing legislation to require cementing up and covering all open wells. He was an official of the water company that 40 years earlier had sunk the well in which Kathy was now prisoner.

Early Saturday morning, Klaus Landsberg decided to close down all his KTLA programming and send a remote crew out to the San Marino field which overnight had become the focus of the world's interest.

The KTLA remote setup was cumbersome. Besides the truck that had to hookup to a permanent supply of electrical power before its limited battery supply was dissipated, cameras weighing hundreds of pounds had to be put in place on tripods. They were not as easily transportable as are today's light transistorized television tape cameras which are carried on the shoulder and capable of directly transmitting an image to its station. In other words, TV news was incapable of covering on-the-spot stories that were over with in a short space of time. For TV to be successful at this, the stories—such as this one—had to be ongoing.

For nearly 28 hours, KTLA sent out its non-stop signal with reporters Stan Chambers and Bill Welsh spelling one-another on camera.

Raymond Hill, a close friend of Kathy's parents, David and Alice, was an experienced engineer and took late charge of the rescue operation. His plan was to dig yet another hole with a circular drilling machine. He would bore deeper; below the base of the abandoned shaft and tunnel up to rescue the child.

While all this went on through Sunday morning, sleepless Los Angeles TV set owners listened and watched with neighbors as Welsh and Chambers continued trading off while endlessly describing what was happening on and off camera.

Along with the newspapers, there were newsreel and other cameramen who would fly action film from the scene to television stations hundreds of miles away from and outside the direct beams[20] emanating from Los Angeles' Mt. Wilson.

Engineers Bill Yancy, Herb Harple, Whitey Blickensderfer and others discovered they had become overnight folk heroes.

Tension built and prayers were being offered for Kathy at church services everywhere. Nerves were frayed and officials became grim and testy as the microphone down in the well casing was turned off.

Then there was quick conferences and the family physician, Dr. Robert McCullock, was lowered into the shaft by means of a parachute harness.

After a short time, grim-faced Dr. McCullock reemerged from the well to tell Sheriff Biscailuz that Kathy was dead.

Because his face was familiar now to local television viewers, Sheriff Biscailuz suggested Bill Welsh break the news to the family.

---

[20]While radio waves curve around the earth, television beams can only be cast in a straight line.

Shortly afterwards, another family physician, Dr. A. Hansen, picked up a public address microphone and spoke to the large, quiet crowd:

"Ladies and gentlemen, Kathy is dead . . . and had been dead for a long time . . . The family wishes to thank one and all for your heroic efforts . . . to try to save our child . . ."

Strong men wept.

This was the first time that the cathode tube had out-and-out scooped the newspapers. There was no argument. Not even a rebuttal. But along the way, TV had done it in such a shocking, yet sophisticated manner that news coverage would never be the same again. Both sight and sound had ultimately been simultaneously served on the spot for a news-hungry public. The radio was still capable of flashing the news to a person in his car, but in a short time to come, when he arrived home, he would turn on his television set to get the complete picture. Nor would it be long before the morning newspapers—the ones that survived—would have lost some of their glamor.

Commercial television was in its infancy in 1949, so to join in I began writing, producing and directing fifteen-minute dramatic segments filmed for Proctor & Gamble's "Fireside Theatre." My problem was that I was only earning $100 for each package and was unable to grind out enough scenarios in volume to support a large family. So I decided if I couldn't make a living producing TV, I would do it by selling the damned sets.

A crazy Chicago used car salesman named Earl "Madman" Muntz migrated to Southern California and branched out into retailing television sets. I was doing exceptionally well as a floor salesman in Muntz's Hollywood location, but when the store manager ordered me to sweep up the display room, I tried to explain to him that I was a salesman and not a janitor. And when he insisted again that I sweep, I told him to stick the broom up his ass and walked out. My independent years as a reporter had made me a free soul and I refused to be intimidated by anyone.

From the sales floor, I took a job in Paramount Studio's publicity department across the street from KTLA. At Paramount, I wrote exaggerated copy about more exaggerated movies and actors. But now, even the picture studios were beginning to feel the financial squeeze as the public continued more-and-more to sit home enjoying free entertainment. The usual Hollywood panic set in and studio personnel was either drastically cut or departments were eliminated wherever possible. The lack of seniority led me early to the chopping block and somehow, I sensed a feeling of relief.

So I departed this land of shanty-bred hacks and half-baked hams and returned to reality where factory and office workers, streetcar conductors, pickpockets, felons and politicians frantically survived from one day to the next.

I phoned Aggie Underwood to ask if the *Her-Ex* had an opening. The editorial roster was filled and she said, "I'll call you right back." She did, and she said: "You're hired. Come in on Monday. Six o'clock. In the morning, that is."

SO LONG, AGGIE—Hired as one of Red Skelton's three TV writers, Fowler resigned from *Herald-Express* and newspaper business in 1952. So irate was managing editor John B.T. Campbell, he had edict posted refusing Fowler access to the paper's city room. Celebrating Fowler's good fortune (?) are (l to r) Skelton, the great city editor Agness "Aggie" Underwood, Skelton's second wife, Georgia and balding Fowler.

XII

Enter *Her-Ex*

When I joined the *Herald-Express*, Hearst papers had editorially ceased fighting with the Los Angeles kitchen cabinet running the city from behind the scenes. Again, crime, sex and scandal sullied our pages.

During my overall tenure as a reporter—described as the "post World War II era," our city boasted four daily newspapers all in fierce competition ... the morning *Examiner* and Hearst's afternoon *Herald-Express* (which we affectionately referred to as the *Her-Ex*), the *Mirror* and the *Daily News*. This excluded the *Times* which remained respectably distant and refused to wallow in disreputable news stories.

Had I not been stuck with a name-brand such as was mine, and if conditions had been different, I really wanted to work for the *Daily News*. Its staffers had the opportunity to be exposed to several facets of the city room operation. Instead of just ventilating on one job, a reporter could function as an assignment editor, makeup editor, headline writer, copy reader sitting in the slot, a rewrite man, and even take his turn writing editorials.

The *News*, which was a favorite of the city's Pacific Electric (streetcar) system commuters, was independently-owned by eccentric liberal millionaire and physical culture nut Bernarr MacFadden, who took his first parachute jump in celebration of his 80th birthday. The paper was so popular with the Red Car straphangers that it managed to make money putting out around the clock editions—sometimes as many as eight in one day.

It was the *News's* profit-making that interested conservative *Times* publisher Norman Chandler, so in 1948, he started the

Mirror in competition. Disregarding how the yet-to-be constructed freeway system would alter Los Angeles commuter travel habits, Chandler probably thought blue-collar workers would continue reading their tabloid as they traveled to and from their jobs, and that nothing in principal would change. No one at the time had an inkling that the streetcar was becoming a thing of the past.

Early on, the *Mirror's* front page was actually printed sideways for better newsstand display. Please understand this: when you stared at it on the rack, it looked like a normal newspaper, but when you opened it up, you turned it around to read.

The *Mirror's* style seemed strangely like the format underground newspapers would use a generation later—the kind of newspapers kids would sneak into the house and read under the covers or behind a locked bathroom door. This was especially apparent in the personal classified pages with their risque (for that time) double entendre ads. The *Mirror* was planned to be the tabloid to end all tabloids. It intensified the usual editorial battles against organized crime and for improved rapid transit. To these were added crusades against black-market baby adoptions, loan sharks and for better housing, along with cleaning up the city which had become frayed at the gutters, and that the presumption that alcoholism was a crime.

Just west of Figueroa along the north side of Pico Street lay two dilapidated city blocks which were considered by miserable locals and purlieuists to contain a uniquely volatile personality. Often, when a mute fog settled in during the early hours, an out-of-town stranger would arrive to walk these two blocks with a feeling of immunity from harm. This was an acute mistake in judgment.

Conveniently located just a block north of Georgia Street Receiving Hospital and nearby the *Her-Ex's* circulation department's loading docks, this district was called "Pico Street" was a common ring of fierce unscheduled knife fights. Simple skirmishes were hardly paid attention to. These set-tos were quickly broken up in The Continental by bartender George Banker. A fiercely powerful man, Banker's Pico Street campaign ribbons consisted of a broken kneecap, a blinded left eye and a whiskey voice in the range of a Russian basso.

Murder along this two block stretch of our downtown society's back pocket rarely made the papers. Because of their character—the unchanging pattern of a drunken fight over nothing in particular and a knifing—they were considered too insipid for a short paragraph. These killings usually averaged out at about 50 or so a year.

By this period in his life, Cappy Marek had definitely seen better days. His only reward now was that he had lived long enough to receive his severance pay and monthly Social Security benefits. This, plus a modest salary for editing a weekly retirement newspaper, kept his head above the poverty waterline.

Cappy lived on the floor above the Continental. Of the ten rooms, his was the only one not rented out to a whore. When business was slow—usually on holidays when guilt-ridden husbands went home early—the girls would sit with Cappy and listen to him philosophize and talk to them about the old days. He liked being appreciated. It had been two years since managing editor John Campbell fired Cappy from his job as city editor on the *Her-Ex* for drinking.

By this time, Cappy was thin and frail. He dressed as neat as a buttercup even though he always wore the same habiliments: a gray vest with the bottom button missing. His maroon Paisley cravat was accentuated by a cultured pearl stick pin and his single-breasted blue waistcoat had black bone buttons—three on one sleeve and four on the other. He wore striped light gray cuffless trousers held up with black silk suspenders displaying an alien monogram on the right strap. He also sported spats, and his painful limp was eased by a sterling silver-handled Mallaca cane. The charcoal-colored Tyrolean hat he wore at an angle had also seen better days. Frayed, like Cappy himself, it had a corded band with brush and silver clip. With the exception of the absence of velvet clothing and silk stockings, Cappy made me sense the presence of Oscar Wilde incarnate.

While not counseling his covey of strumpets or editing his paper for senior citizens, Cappy spent most of his time at Moran's Bar.

He would graciously accept a few glasses of white wine from a newcomer intently listening to his tale of when he was in Juarez, Mexico, with Harry Morgan and Jack Stevens. In his oft-told tale of 1920, Marek included that he had not been as fortunate as his American journalist friends "in that I was not being held hostage in a whore house."

Cappy's stories varied in embellishment, according to his mood and how much he had to drink. But they contained the same elements in that he had been stuck at the border, high-and-dry without booze.

"I was thinking how I might agitate a band of contented Mexicans on the south side of the cyclone fence," he used to say, launching into his descriptions after the manner of W.C. Fields in painful recollection. "They were leisurely playing their guitars . . . while beautiful *senoritas* . . . squirmed on the soldiers' laps . . . sipping tequila."

He went on that the galvanized fence dividing two countries eliminated any derisive action wherein he might confiscate some distilled cactus juice.

"My thirst was killing me . . . and drove me to come upon an idea . . . I would form two lines of men . . . in abbreviated platoon . . . And at my command . . . the mercenaries at the fore began throwing rocks . . . and tossing epithets Mexicans do not like to hear . . . The reaction was immediate!" he would cry, predicting victory. "The Mexicans began mortaring anything they could put their hands on . . . In this case . . . their half-filled tequila bottles!"

The tale ended, Cappy would settle back to his stool and condescendingly accept another glass of wine.

After friends left for home, Cappy and I found ourselves sitting at opposite ends of the bar. I studied his face as he quietly mulled over things. Here I was at the tail end of my 20s and only into my seventh year of reporting. And as Cappy beckoned for me to come over, I wondered just how long I'd be able to keep the world on a string.

When I sat next to him, Cappy was complaining that Curly was going to put in a television set over the bar. "I swear," he said, "if this happens, I shall take my business elsewhere."

Not really caring if anyone was listening, Cappy drifted into one of his black soliloquies:

"One of the worst things about your second 30 years is the burgeoning conviction that you can't be very bright. Else your inadequacies long since would have shamed you into swearing off printers' ink and going about seeking some other business ... When I was a young reporter, I got to go everywhere; talk with everyone and see everything, and I hadn't a doubt in the world that my perception was perfect.

"But today, while editing this old sheet for old people, I only talk with reporters, not go out with them to cover a story ... And if not here at Moran's, it's usual that I talk with them on the telephone. And it's now that I realize that our minds seldom meet; that the flashes of comprehension coming when they do, chiefly serve to illuminate the lack of any real communication among humans.

"The flashes can dazzle, but they make little news copy. Either you can't capture them at all in 65 screen, or—like the devastating things you should have said—they occur to you far too late ..."

Moran's Bar was on the north side of Pico Street between Georgia and Trenton streets, right in the middle of the gauntlet and across the street from a bank of brown-colored wino joints, buildings that looked like a collection of forgotten chocolate cakes.

Moran's existence for the most part depended on *Herald-Express* trade from reporters, pressmen and ex-pugs employed in the circulation department. One, named Spike, was the cause of Cappy's anger regarding Curly putting in a TV set over the bar. Stolen, naturally, Spike was furnishing the set in order to pay up his long-standing bar bill.

Moran's had ten stools with plenty of standing room between the bar and two imitation leather booths that had been marked by wear-and-tear. There was a kitchen in the rear which was never used, but was required by the sanitation department or by some factotum to be there. Also at the back were the "Gents" and "Ladies" restrooms that stank. It was a draw if they smelled more of urine of disinfectant. And when things got a little drunk,

no one really cared which sex used either can to relieve themselves.

This was the place where Sheriff's beatman Bevo Means began
his day. Shortly before night photographer Frank Rutherford
would drive him north to the Hall of Justice at six o'clock, Bevo
would pick up a case of beer from Moran's back entrance. The
24 bottles were his ration for the day's watch. He was getting
too old to heave the wooden crate around so he dragged it across
the *Her-Ex* parking lot by a stout rope. The amplified scraping
noise along the tar surface proclaimed that the day had begun.
Rutherford—who actually weighed so much that he had to use
the freight elevator to get the the city room on the third floor—
would drive off with Bevo and his beer. Rutherford's at least
600 pounds so drastically weighed down his side of the car that
when it rounded the corner, the car listed like a sailboat leaning
20 degrees across a strong wind.

Moran's was a sort of embassy for *Her-Ex* reporters in that
we were on safe territory and were known by all the local mob-
sters, whores, bookies and con men.

Curly—who was curly—opened up at six A.M. and turned over his
watch to Johnny at 4 P.M. Johnny was tall, had a thin red moustache, was slim and was continually looking over his shoulder.

Beside Cappy and local bookmaker "Cocky" Lou Gregorius,
other regulars certified as being characters.

There was Any Time Annie. She was eking out her final days
as a prostitute. Practically burned out in her early 40s, Any Time
was five-and-a-half feet tall. She had a lousy platinum blonde dye
job and wore a tight red silk dress accentuating her fat folds,
axe-handle hips and generous ass. Her pendulous breasts hung
far out and we were constantly waiting for one or both to flop
out. But like most middle-aged women who no longer go to
beauty parlors, Any Time powdered her face too chalky-white,
over-blackened her eyelashes and made up her lips so thick that
she looked like a child's painting.

Annie's prices varied according to her needs. She would take
on a well-dressed dude whose alcohol-glazed eyesight misinter-
preted her faded charms, for five dollars. This would be for an

hour of half-and-half or whatever he wanted that wasn't too back-breaking, in her room upstairs over the Continental. When she was flush enough to buy a bottle of gin or a couple of envelopes of cocaine, Any Time got lazy and would only cede of her services in the back alley for five minutes to give one of her regulars a blow job for one-or-two dollars ... whatever he had.

Taxi Bill, like most who had disappeared and was hiding from society or the police of another county or state, didn't have a surname either.

Whatever his age, Taxi Bill looked ten years older than that. He was squat and had a three-day beard that never seemed to grow longer. At the end of World War II, he had been propositioned by two soldiers and a sailor in Manhattan's Grand Central Station to drive them all the way out to their families in Southern California. A deal was made and the four—along with Bill's Brooklyn accent—made it to Los Angeles in five days. Shortly after arriving in his now hot company cab, Bill painted it black, sold it to a used car dealer and took up quarters in the Pico Street area. A handy man or small-time burglar, Bill survived doing odd jobs or locating slightly used small appliances at a good price.

In return for a warm place to sleep in the back, Blind Virginia cleaned the barroom and toilets before opening and after closing at Moran's.

Virginia was small, slight and very quiet. She was in her 50s and wore dark glasses. Sightless for the past 20 years, she developed a talent to recognize regulars by the sound of their step and their voices. When she was in her 30s, Virginia had been a popular neighborhood whore. But one night she took a soft-spoken man with a limp to her hotel room. There, the smooth talk turned to shouting, and when Virginia had refused to have sex, he raped her, then gouged out both her eyes so she wouldn't be able to identify him if he was ever taken in by police. Ever since, Virginia had been listening for this stranger's limp and soft voice. Beneath her blouse, she always carried a barber's straight razor.

Dirty Marie lived up to her name. She had an untamed mouth and could outswear anyone. She was probably in her late 50s, but one never knew. Dirty Marie would start out quiet and non-responsive while drinking her 15-cent glass of muscatel. But when she reached a certain plateau, the language became animated and Navy-blue. Her hair was stringy and she chewed her nails. She had a modest income, most of which she spent at Moran's.

The only time Curly grew uneasy about her language was when a reporter brought in a "high class" for a drink. He was bothered with Marie when I brought Red Skelton in for a visit. This was when the comedian's show was number one in the national television ratings.

Marie refused to believe he really was Red Skelton. "Someone's tryin' t' put somethin' over on me," she growled. And the more we tried to convince her it really *was* Skelton, the madder Marie got. She vocalized the best of her bawdy lexicon, pacing the length of the bar, spouting her "sons-o'-bitches" and the rest.

What Curly couldn't understand was that Red was getting a kick out of Marie's searing invectives. In any event, while Marie was giving out with her best, Curly slipped a Mickey Finn (a few drops of potent croton oil) into her wine glass.

Marie drank down her muscatel then slowly went mute. Beads of sweat began breaking out on her forehead, and when she got stomach cramps, she realized what had been done to her.

Resolutely now, Dirty Marie stood up between the bar and the booths. "All right, you lousy bastard," she grimaced, "you done it to me, an' now you're gonna have t' clean it up!" At this, Marie hiked up her skirt, squatted and let everything go from both ends.

Curly slammed his sawed-off shotgun on the bar and threatened to split Marie in half. Skelton stopped laughing when he saw the gun and came up with a folded piece of currency. And when Curly spied a "100" on a corner of the bill, he put the double-barreled weapon away. Then he closed down for an hour and Blind Virginia helped him mop up.

This was part of the tattered and treacherous atmosphere I had returned to following a time away from the vocation I loved.

During the interim, I had purchased an acre of Encino land in the San Fernando Valley. I built a fine home of my own design, shingled the roof and worked along with the carpenter rough crew. We moved in after I finished building the wardrobes, kitchen cabinets and hanging twenty-one doors.

Except for a short stretch of highway laid down in the Hollywood area, there were no freeways yet. In order to arrive at the *Her-Ex* at six, I had to roll out of bed at 4:30. The advantage I had going was that only the milkman and a sprinkling of drunks shared the roads.

I showed up at the paper on Trenton Street the morning of August 7, 1950, wondering why the hell I'd agreed upon this limbo time of day. It took a lot of getting accustomed to, arriving in the dark while normal people were still sleeping. For some reason I couldn't explain, it made me feel like I was partaking in something evil.

The *Her-Ex* building's front entrance was still locked, so I walked around to the rear and found the freight elevator that would lift me to the city room on the third floor. Inside the truck delivery bay, it was as dark, cold, silent and as unfriendly as the back room of a funeral parlor. Then the silence was pleasantly tampered with by the sound of the metal corners of Bevo's case of beer being dragged across the parking lot.

"Willie," came Bevo's voice. "I thought you were still in Hollywood. Why the hell're you back for a second dose of this newspapering crap?"

"I got lonely," I said. "Nuts belong around nuts."

Night photographer half-ton Rutherford pulled his beat-up station wagon to a stop, nodded at me and waited for Bevo to lift his 24-bottle treasure into the rear. "God-damned hernia's gettin' worse every day," he groaned. I picked up the beer and Bevo continued in *sotto voce*: "You know that poor son-of-a-bitch has to sleep sittin' up? He weighs so much, he'll strangle if he falls asleep layin' down."

"Why the hell doesn't the beached whale lose a couple-hundred pounds?" I asked, closing the car gate.

"Says he's got some kind of gland problem."

"Did anyone ever spot a fat man in a concentration camp?"

"See you at Moran's after work," Bevo cried out from the car window as Rutherford tacked around the corner.

The freight elevator gave a grunt as it started upward. When I pulled the rope to open its gate, I stepped into a large composing room. But for about 50 yellow firefly lights hanging over each hulky Lineotype printing machine, it was gray dark. With their four banks of different style type keyboards, the Linotypes reminded me of the big console organs I first saw as a boy in New York's Radio City Music Hall. To the right of each Linotype, and hanging like a Christmas goose, was a large shiny bar of lead being slowly fed into an elevated melting pot. Instead of typewriter foolscap paper, these talented Linotype operators with green celluloid eyeshades used hot lead for copying the stories in pica lengths. Their craft was meticulously unforgiving as they wandered from one machine to the other, selecting *agate*, *elite*, *italic*, *brevier* and other type-styles needed to be reproduced. And for all its bulk, the Linotype in operation sounded like a delicate glass Chinese wind bell flirting with a soft wind.

As I approached the double swinging doors that led into the city room, I paused as an alien sensation—like the sexual desire welling up in the flanks—invaded me. I felt the urge that I wanted this feeling to either come to orgasm, or abate. The first day I reported to the *Examiner*, I had experienced a blush of impetuous elan, the kind when an apprentice is stricken with awe. But this was different, intense. I was a journeyman now, a veteran.

Herman Melville's chapter about the Pacific in *Moby Dick* came to mind somehow. There seemed to be a meaningful correlation with my returning to the city room I so missed during the time I was away. The Pacific chapter was only two pages long, but it was the first tract of literature I had put to memory in my youth. Melville reported his essay in Ishmael's mind as *"The Sea of His Adoption:"*

> *When gliding by the Bashee isles we emerged at*
> *last upon the great South Sea; were it not for other*
> *things, I could have greeted my dear Pacific with*
> *uncounted thanks, for now the long supplication of*
> *my youth was answered ...*

The double doors to the city room had two look-through windows the shape of a ship's round portholes. They were padded for good reason. During deadlines, doors did havoc to editors, reporters and composing room jockeys colliding with sticksful of loose type.

When I did open the doors, the quiet of the oncoming dawn was cracked by noise and chaos. It was something I'd forgotten that existed in the city room of an afternoon paper. Rewrite men were shouting: "Boy! ... Oh, boy! ... Copyboy!"

Deftly, people were dodging one another, rushing about on the pallet of a worn wooden floor. An assignment editor called for a reporter to find a photographer with: "... and get the hell over to Georgia Street Juvenile. Some kid just shot his father ..."

A hungover sob-sister who hadn't finished last night's column was fighting to concentrate in the din. She shook her head from side-to-side and began talking to herself.

With a cigarette hanging from his lip, a rewrite man was being assaulted by a copygirl who was ripping short takes from his typewriter and rushing the copy—still hanging by a participle—to the city desk. Masterfully, he rolled in a three-carboned book and continued without a pause.

The sob-sister futilely cupped her ears with her hands and with a great crescendo, shrieked: "Ooohhh ... *shh iitttt !!*"

This caused a transient pause in the confusion until Aggie Underwood said: "Take a rest in the lady's room, Mary." Then, "I have a little something in my purse if you need a drink."

Then Aggie spotted me. "Fowler," she said, "pick up a head set and take some dictation, or whatever the hell Jimmy Shambra's phoning in about from the police beat."

Shambra gave me notes about an overnight suicide that I would have to write about. It was now that I realized Jim Richardson's Jericho wall had fallen. I would be writing stories from now on.

When the 7:15 deadline arrived, a group gathered around
another newcomer that day. It was an orange colored porcelain-
painted machine the size and shape of a refrigerator. It was a
juice dispenser and photog Perry Fowler, who had been Aggie's
assignment sidekick before she historically became the first
female city editor on an American metropolitan newspaper, was
grousing as he studied the contraption and its coin slot. "I'll be
damned if *I'm* gonna pay fif ... teen ... cents for a Dixiecupful
of watered-down orange juice," he said "Not unless it has something more substantial in it."

A chain smoker, Perry had enlisted with the Canadian
paratroopers before the United States entered into the war. During an early drop over German-occupied territory, he was taken
prisoner of war and spent the rest of the conflict in a prison cell
in Nuremberg[21] communicating with his comrades through toilet
facility pipelines. After his long incarceration, it was hard for Perry
to get too serious about anything. "You think if we used our
own cups," Fowler reasoned, "they'd give us a shot of orange
juice for a dime?"

As most of the city room people broke for breakfast, Perry,
still complaining about the 15 cent price, mumbled: "I'm definitely
going to do something about this."

It was now that Aggie found time to hand me an assignment
to cover.

For the past six years, Aggie and I had been in tender opposition ... meaning that she worked on the Hearst afternoon paper
and I, on the morning *Examiner*. Therefore, there was no competition. If the *Her-Ex* missed a key local news photo the wires
didn't carry, it could always be picked up from the *Examiner*
for use the next day along with a followup story. This went vice
versa, but Jim Richardson's professional vanity wouldn't allow
him to accept a picture from the *Her-Ex* unless he was under
duress to do so by orders from Van Ettish.

---

[21]Goring, Speer, Ribbentrop and most of the other Nazi leaders were captured
and subsequently tried by the Allies as war criminals in Nuremberg.

The primary difference between an afternoon and morning paper was that the afternoon paper pointed at feasting its readers with the feeling of urgency. Its news stories told that whatever it was, it happened "today." This treat of exigency, however, has since been dulled since television news finally evolved into the greatest source of immediate information ever known. Thus, the death of most afternoon newspapers.

The morning newspaper was just that, as it remains today: Porched at the front door in the early morning, it offers something to be read in more depth, over a leisurely cup of breakfast coffee. It was understood that the reader was familiar with a major story break, and therefore, these stories were—and are today— still referred to as having occurred "yesterday."

It was here at the *Her-Ex* that I ran into two gentlemen on the rewrite desk who shocked me from my tunnel vision opinion that there were no scribes of my generation—or near it— capable of turning a newspaper phrase as picturesquely as my father. I found I had been doting up the wrong tree when meeting Jack C. Smith and Richard V. O'Connor.

Of Smith, O'Connor once wrote: "Much of a man's character can be determined by his attitude when caught in a moment of history in the making." He was referring to when Smith was a teenage Honolulu reporter making his way home one morning following an all-night party in 1941 when the Japanese struck Pearl Harbor. After experiencing several violent concussions and watching diving Zero attack planes, Jack raised a weary eyebrow and announced to no one in particular: "I guess I'll grab a little sleep before thinking about all this."

While fleetingly employed by the *Daily News* after the war, Smith was assigned to critique a classical musical recital he did not wish to attend. His piece turned out to be so hilariously out of place that it never made the paper. But not wishing for it to go to waste, he pinned it up in the city room and emerged as the bulletin board maven around town. It was more a takeoff on musical criticism than on the recital itself. It read:

> Music lovers who heard the delibitating if somewhat roguish debut of Pianist Honeysuckle Glotz last evening

in the Paganini Palace came away with the feeling that
while Miss Glotz undoubtedly has taken a lot of lessons and sits a stool as well as the next artist, she has
a long way to go before her incisive if rather pedestrian technical verisimilitude is eclectic enough to meet
the vast sweep, power, niaveté, and insouciant con-
cupiscence of Glugenhoffer's Opus No. 1 for fife and
yazurka.

Still, despite her painfully evident inability to
approach the dizzying penchants Abbleheimen's First
Stanza in C Sharp Flat for kettledrum and pogostick,
it must be admitted that Miss Glotz was delightful,
particularly—to select a specific case—when she stumbled over a bravura and plunged into the pits, her
organdie concert dress puffing up about her shimmer-
ing limbs like an inverted mushroom.

There were moments when the promising but by
no means arrived young artist seemed to sacrifice
sparkle for sheer meticulousity, such as in Org Gizzle-
waite's giddy, generous, and delightfully sarcastic Russ
Nausea in Patres Tres for Heartstrings and Viscera.

My first cover-and-write story for the *Her-E*x came a month
after I joined the paper. It was a modern version of Samson and
Delilah, starring a svelte 97-pound lady and a 270-pound professional wrestler and operatic student.

It seemed that Orbie Cleghorn couldn't do anything right that
September night when he and Evalyn Ruth Sloann were parked
in his convertible in the Windsor Hills. Overcome by the beauty
of a full moon and sparkling stars in a still clear Los Angeles sky,
Orbie was taken with *amores et hae deliciae quac vocantur* and
threw his girth upon the petit redhead.

But Evalyn Ruth strenuously objected to being smothered. She
leaped from the car. Later, she said: "Orbie kicked me in the
stomach and tried to choke me, so I decided I'd better start
defending myself."

Therefore, Evalyn Ruth kicked the singing wrestler in the groin
which could speed up his reaching high C.

I spoke to Orbie later. He wore his hair pageboy style that covered his cauliflower ears. Orbie, whose wrestling fans billed him as the "Pagliacci of the mat," fondled his two pet cats and denied both beating up or being beaten up by the fiery redhead. But Evalyn Ruth ultimately informed investigating deputy sheriffs that she had fended off Orbie, not by clipping his pageboy bob ala Delilah, but by more practical methods: *Judo*.

Orbie had failed his homework lesson to learn that Evalyn Ruth was employed as a private investigator and held many awards in the art of self-defense. Nevertheless, Evalyn Ruth insisted she was going to prosecute Orbie "for conduct unbecoming a gentleman in a parked car."

This was the year when 22-year-old Shirley Temple had divorced actor John Agar and announced her marriage to movie producer Charles Black, to whom she had now been happily married for the past forty years.

Just a few weeks prior to the marriage of the be-dimpled little girl we recall singing and dancing and stealing America's hearts, Elizabeth Taylor fled from her first husband, hotel heir Conrad "Nicky" Hilton, and went back to her mother.

The striking 18-year-old actress shed tears before us and said: "Nicky treated me like a beautiful plaything when all I want to be is a wife."

And a wife she was. Eight times, I think.

Television was not yet into covering funerals and it was still a few years off until the three network and three locally-owned stations would begin coverage using 16 millimeter Filmo cameras. This would take them to the step when any hard news story would be shot and within 20 minutes after it reached the station, the film would be ready to flash on the tube with voice over descriptions of the action and quotes.

The funeral I covered (without looking over my shoulder to see if TV news was with us) was that of Al Jolson. It attracted the attendance of the greatest number of entertainers to that date.

Dick O'Connor, who had written the story about the 64-year-old super star's unexpected death on October 24, by-lined three front page pieces about Jolson.

Offering subscribers what they wanted in high-pitched style, O'Connor wrote:

> The humble and the mighty gathered by the thousands today for the funeral of Al Jolson, honoring the man who gave 50 years of his life to show business, and his last physical resources to entertaining American troops in the front lines in Korea.

Among 57 honorary pallbearers at Temple Israel in Hollywood were such celebrated figures as Jack Benny, Edgar Bergen, Bing Crosby, Eddie Cantor, Louis B. Mayer, Groucho Marx, Darryl F. Zanuck, Joseph Schenck, Harry and Jack Warner, Harry Brand, Bob Hope, Cecil B. DeMille and William Paley, president of ABC Television.

It took fifty uniformed policemen to keep the traffic moving past the temple on Hollywood Boulevard where hoards of spectators squeezed and gawked.

We reporters often came up with times of stress while covering a story; when we got in fights with the opposition, or even when we got miffed with our own people. In regard to the second instance, only one exacerbation comes to mind; when I felt justified to kill my photographer with my bare hands. This was when Al Jolson's young widow, Erle, visited Forest Lawn Memorial Park. Word had gotten out that she had a quarter-of-a-million dollars to spend on the *Mammy* singer's edifice.

My photographer, slow-moving and heavy-set Howard Ballou, awaited the widow's arrival. Forest Lawn's impressive Glendale gate was fashioned after London's Buckingham Palace with filigree and vertical iron shafts crowned with gold-plated herldic *fleur-de-lis*.

The attractive Mrs. Jolson arrived in her chauffeur-driven limousine and was greeted by an establishment representative (salesman) dressed to the nines, trying to disguise his eagerness to serve.

There was a lightning-bug effect as news photogs flashed their cameras. Everyone seemed satisfied with what they got and were anxious to get their pictures back to the paper.

But when the group filtered, I noticed paunchy Ballou chasing after widow Erle and the salesman who were on their way to the front office. He was bouncing his cellulite and garbling: "Just-a-minute, just-a-minute."

"My god!" it hit me, "Ballou didn't get his picture," as Mrs. Jolson glared at the salesman whose thoughts were mainly on his potential bonanza commission.

"We'll have no more of *that*," the vexed Erle spat at the salesman.

Now it was necessary to wait for Erle to emerge from the office building so my bungling photographer could have another chance at a grab shot. But worse, deadline time was wearing thin.

"For Christ's sake," I warned Ballou, "set your damned focus at eight feet and just squeeze one off."

I must have referred to my watch about twenty times before Erle emerged from the office building a half-hour later.

At once, Ballou leaped forward to block her, but started focusing his camera all over again. Then missing, he trailed her babbling: "Just-a-minute. Just-a-minute." He was really deep into that focus compulsion.

A now *very* mad Erle disappeared into her limousine and drove off.

I was incensed. "Damn it," I growled and kicked Ballou right in his fat ass, "you didn't even *shoot* the god-damned picture!"

This time after taking the wheel of Ballou's car, I speeded violently around the convoluted roads that were marked with words such as "Peace," "Heavenly" and "Holy." The one marked "Passionate" seemed to suit my mood at the time.

After breaking through a line of cars following a hearse to a gravesite, I finally located Mrs. Jolson's limousine parked near a bluff overlooking the city. It seemed to be a resplendent site in which to rest the remains of the great singer who was known and loved throughout the world.

This time I hid Ballou behind a red berried hedge with rude thorns. I set the camera's focus myself and said: "Now, when she comes out this time, just shoot the picture . . . And don't you . . . dare . . . screw around with the focus . . . We are blowing a deadline this very minute . . . and I'm not about to go back to the paper without a fucking *picture!*"

Again, Erle emerged. This time from a mausoleum. But, as if he was riding point in an army cavalry movie, the now highly nervous salesman—protecting a commission tantamount to two-years' work—cautiously peeked out to see if the two were alone.

Ballou leaped from behind his prickly camouflage and began focusing his camera!

"That's it!" the young widow shouted at the salesman. *"I'll not have my husband buried in this thoroughfare!"*

I wrenched the Speed Graphic from Ballou, and the only way I could think of to shock Erle into turning my way and glaring at me was to yell: *"Hey, asshole!"* She never returned to Forest Lawn.

Several months went by before Howard Ballou felt safe in my presence. Erle reallocated her $250,000 and had the prominent, sought-after and high-priced black architect Paul Williams create a solemn Greek white marble-domed edifice where Jolson's body lays today. It is in the Jewish cemetery, Hillside Memorial Park in Inglewood.

Each time I pass through Inglewood on the way to the airport these days, I never fail to point out Jolson's monument that can be seen through the smog from the freeway. I tell my out-of-town friends: "I know the man who was actually responsible for Al Jolson being buried there . . . His name was Howard Ballou, and once when Howard and I were . . ."

XIII

"Aggie"

The *Herald-Express* city room setup was much the same as that of the *Examiner's*. The managing editor's fish bowl office, however, was at the far end of the bull pen from the city desk. The slot where the paper was made up was directly to the west of the city desk. To arrive at the slot, it was necessary for John B.T. Campbell to walk the length of the bull pen from his office. When he did, Campbell had a way about him that made me think of his right wing political views. That is, he held his head jutted forward and he stared neither left or right. Unwavering, his eyes squinted straight ahead as though pointed at his prey. His nose reminded me of an American bald eagle just about to take off to perch in the middle of the Seal of the President of the United States. When he headed toward the slot following a good slug of whiskey, he spoke with no one. At the makeup table, Campbell personally created the front page each day. He was good and he was fast, but old-timers had a way of telling how much their managing editor had had to drink by the sometimes bizarre setup and words he used in his headline, such as when Jimmy Doolittle took off from an aircraft carrier in World War II and bombed Tokyo. Campbell's headline read:

DOOLITTLE DOOD IT!

While we were making small talk between deadlines, Jimmy Shambra phoned Agness Underwood from the police beat. He said detectives were on their way to check out a dead body reported in East Los Angeles. Aggie told me to take photog Ed Phillips. "Just something easy," she said. "Something to get you back into the rhythm of covering a story."

When Phillips and I arrived, an old man's body had already been removed. His modest square white stucco house had thick prison bars anchored in each window. The dead man was later identified as a recluse with no known source of income. His name was Charles Babonet.

While looking around for photos of Babonet, I removed some books from a generous shelf which told me he'd been a reader. Four banded and marked bundles of currency dropped to the floor. I called a detective over. "I haven't touched this," I said. The bands on the bundles represented $20,000. Then a lot more money was found around the house as we reporters were escorted from the place. A quick judgment told me there must have been hundreds-of-thousands of dollars there.

With no photos of the old man, we did what I'd done in the Overell investigation I covered for the *Examiner*. We went to the private funeral parlor where Babonet's body was being held and photographed it. This time, already neatly dressed.

Pieces of information were eventually put together about how Babonet had come into a vast amount of money. Sight unseen, he'd purchased two small Huntington Beach lots in 1914 for $125 each. He had lived in Aurora, Indiana. Oil was discovered on the property and the Reliance Oil Company leased it and paid Babonet a generous royalty. Over the years, he received in excess of half-a-million dollars. Never quite trusting banks following the 1929 stock market crash, Babonet kept all his money in the house. Hence, the bars on the windows. There was a discrepancy regarding the amount of money which was supposed to be in the house. Police reported there was only slightly more than $100,000.

When his will was probated, it was learned that Babonet has settled several large sums on a group of people he hardly knew. One day some of them had treated the lonely old fellow to a pleasant day at the beach. In the will, he wrote: "If I ever live to be a thousand, I'll never forget that day." Neither did the bequestees, especially a "little girl named Sue who was so kind to me." He left Sue the modes sum of $10,000. Through leads given by people mentioned in the testament, the court located the girl. By then, Sue had become a 42-year-old nun, Sister Suegnia Bogart, who taught at St. Stephen's School in New Orleans. Because of her vow of poverty, the endowment was channelled to be used for her school's charitable pursuits.

I phoned Aggie from the mortuary and she told me to drop by the East Los Angeles Municipal Court. She said: "Some guy is being arraigned for molesting his daughter."

Municipal Judge Charles W. Hartmann was a kindly old hard-of-hearing gentleman who had passed his prime and was giving the court system a hard time because they were trying to ease him into retirement. He had been passed over four times for a seat on the Superior Court.

I checked with the judge to see if he could move the molestation case up on the docket so I could make a deadline. He so ordered.

I identified the paternal sex offender to His Honor. "Now, when he comes before you," I said, "give the son-of-a-bitch holy hell for his sins against the law and the Old Testament."

"No need to tell me what to say, son," said the magistrate.

When court came to order, I alerted Phillips to be ready for a good shot of the judge blowing up.

A man appearing cowed approached the bench. And before the bailiff could call the case, Judge Hartmann launched into a tirade. "You terrible man," he said, rising from his seat and leaning forward. "You base piece of humanity ... allowed to walk this earth! God will never forgive the sin you have committed!"

At this, the bailiff and I frantically waved at Judge Hartmann while Phillips was getting some exceptional pictures. Ignoring us, Judge Hartmann continued mercilessly to tear into this man.

"This is one of the most reprehensible, frightful and odious sins against the Ten Commandments ... I don't know which one it falls under, but you have committed it!"

The bailiff and I gave up signalling. The defendant had been verbally drawn-and-quartered. But the judge continued: "You have taken to bed a frail, innocent girl-child of your own seed and proceeded to commit adultery with her. This is *incest*, sir in it's worst form!'' Sitting down again to take control of himself, Hartmann asked: ''Before I hold you without bail for a preliminary hearing, have you anything to say in your defense?''

At last finding his voice, the battered defendant said: ''But, your honor ... I'm only here for a traffic violation.''

It seems the elderly jurist had accidentally shuffled his court papers and the accused molester was yet to come before him. His Honor began showing signs of oncoming apoplexy and the court was recessed.

After finishing my two stories, nothing seemed to be breaking from the beats so Aggie sent a few of us home early. She didn't want Campbell to notice too many reporters sitting around doing nothing.

But for us who stayed, there seemed to be a sort of festive atmosphere in the city room. Employees from other departments were flocking around the orange drink dispenser. Perry Fowler had finally broken into the machine's reservoir and dumped a gallon of vodka in it.

With a head of steam on, thanks to Perry, some of us retired to Moran's where Art Voigt, a skinny animated reporter came in from covering a story in Hollywood. A movie bit player had been despondent over the lack of work and she had locked herself in her apartment bathroom and turned on the gas.

''She said she was going to commit suicide,'' said Voigt. ''Her husband stood outside pleading for her to come out. She was crying up a storm and sucking on a bottle of bourbon and breathing in all that gas ... Some friends came over to help and she told them to all go screw themselves,'' Voigt went on. ''And when she stopped screaming, the gal decided to have a cigarette ... And, WHAM! ... Christ, the blast killed her old man, too.''

It was getting late, so Aggie and a few of us went up to Chinatown with the intention of having dinner. But wherever we went there was someone who wanted to buy us a drink.

By midnight, we'd drunk our way to Charley Foy's Supper Club in the valley. Then Aggie and I went on to my house for some sleep.

Aggie had to be on the desk by five a.m., so after about two hours sleep, we headed back downtown. I didn't feel at all bad because I was still a bit stewed.

It was a fast-moving news morning. Aggie called for me to take some quotes over the phone and write the obit of some important man who'd died overnight. As I adjusted the head-set, my hangover struck.

Fitting quotes into an on-going story being ripped from your typewriter in short takes was hard enough, but with a hangover, it was a feat. What made it worse was the man I was interviewing got hostile. "What the hell are you asking those questions for?" he said.

"Just answer the questions, sir," I said. "I'm on a deadline."

He still refused to be cooperative as I pounded out the story, trying to remember what my last line had been before a copygirl yanked the book on me. "What the hell you ask me *that* for," the man shouted again as I rolled in a new book.

"Now, the background of youth," I went on.

At the end, he continued objecting to questions I had asked.

The 7:15 deadline passed and Aggie told me to go down to Moran's for a cold beer.

By the time the paper hit the street, I was feeling human again as a copyboy came down to tell me Aggie wanted to see me "right away." Figuring it was an assignment, I hurried up to the desk. But it was quiet when Aggie said: "You know the obit you wrote?"

"Naturally," I said.

"Well," said Aggie, "it seems you didn't write it about the man who died. You wrote it about the guy who phoned it in."

"Oh, shit," I said. Then: "Have you any suggestions?"

"I have your informant on the line now," she said. "He says he's already talked with his lawyers, and that by nightfall, Mr. Hearst will no longer own the *Herald-Express*."

"Well," I said, if that meant anything.

Aggie pulled a five dollar bill from her purse and said: "Take this, go down and buy the best bottle of whiskey you can find ... and let's hope the son-of-a-bitch drinks."

Now, that's class Jim Richardson would never attain.

I bought a fine bottle of Haig & Haig scotch and drove to the irate man's house. When he opened the door, I discovered I had run into a volcano erupting from a wheelchair. He was a polio victim.

Two hours later—over our last glass of scotch—I had finally talked him out of suing the paper when the phone rang. It was Aggie and she said: "Well, does Mr. Hearst still own the Herald?"

"Everything's fine now," I said. "Our friend is holding back his tears and I just sent out for another bottle."

"That's good," said Aggie. "Now what?"

"Just one thing," I said.

"What's that?" Aggie asked.

"Well, our friend loves the piece and he made me promise when he dies that we'll update the story and publish it."

"That's a promise," said Aggie.

"He also wants me to buy a frame so he can put the front page story above him mantelpiece."

"Buy the frame," said Aggie.

Agness Underwood was born in San Francisco four years before the 1906 earthquake and fire. She lost her parents when she was very young. She quit high school and left her strict foster parents to travel alone to Los Angeles. There, the 17-year-old girl met and married an auto salesman named Harry Underwood. To supplement his income, Aggie took the job as a waitress at $11 a week and resumed her education at night at a business college.

Her marriage lasted 20 years during which time she gave birth to two children: Mary Evelyn (now wife of retired Air Force

Colonel William Weed of Phoenix) and engineer George Underwood of Greeley, Colorado.

One day in 1926 while window-shopping for things she couldn't afford, Aggie had the desire to own a pair of real silk stockings, so she took a moonlighting job as a telephone operator at the old *Los Angeles Record* to be able to buy them.

A big story broke one day and the *Record's* only two reporters were out on other stories. Aggie left her post, ran over to the *Daily News* and took down the murder story as it came over the wire, something the *Record* did not have. Aggie did so well by her gutsy initiative she inadvertently was introduced to a career in the newspaper business.

Throughout ten years of fierce competition, bucking male reporters, Aggie became a proficient newspaperwoman. And after scooping the *Herald-Express* with five consecutive Grand Jury stories in 1935, the *Herald* had no alternative but to hire Aggie and give her a $2.50 raise.

One of Aggie's early *Her-Ex* stories of consequence came when she covered the mysterious death of the ravishing "ice cream blonde" actress Thelma Todd. The body of the voluptuous and popular foil for Laurel and Hardy, the Marx Brothers and Buster Keaton, was found in the garage of her Malibu dining establishment.

Aggie learned that Thelma had met and talked with Mafioso Lucky Luciano; that he was trying to encourage Thelma to transform her place into a nightclub which would be a base for him to dispense narcotics. "Thelma didn't want any part of it," Aggie told me after I went to work at the *Herald*. "At the time, I was going on the theory of murder, considering the initial Luciano connection. There still remains an enigma today about the youthful comedienne's death that hasn't been dispelled to my satisfaction." Then she mentioned that according to the wishes of powerful studio executives, "authorities and the coroner listed Thelma's death as 'accidental,' caused by carbon monoxide poisoning."

Aggie covered Thelma's post mortem in the Hall of Justice basement. It was her first and she was warned it would be better if she didn't witness it. But after the autopsy was finished and Aggie remained upright, she looked around at the bodies of dead men covered by white sheets and quipped: "Can you imagine what any of these guys would have given to be under a sheet with Thelma Todd?"

Reporters often helped police solve crimes. It wasn't our point to play detective. We were only interested in getting a story.

Aggie had a keen eye when picking up on hidden gestures revealed by suspects. This happened on the story she covered about a meek church organist named Samuel Whittaker after he claimed a burglar had shot his wife to death.

The middle-aged Whittaker had taken his wife to dinner in celebration of their wedding anniversary. And after the couple had returned to their hotel across from Westlake (now MacArthur) Park, two gun shots rang out.

Police arrived to find Whittaker sitting on the edge of his bed weeping over his wife's body. He pointed to an opened window and said a burglar had broken in and shot her. A second detective crew located a wounded man hiding on the hotel roof. He was a transient named Harry Culvert. They arrested him and took him to the station for booking on a charge of attempted burglary and first degree murder.

Later, Aggie wanted to get a picture of the church organist pointing an accusing finger at Culvert, saying: "This man killed my wife." She set it up with police Lt. Thad Brown. But when Culvert was confronted by Whittaker in the general Hospital prison ward, the latter would only point his cane. This made for bad composition because there would be a mile of open space between the two.

However, when Aggie took Lt. Brown to the side, she said: "You know, Thad, I saw something no one else did. When Whittaker was pointing his cane, he *winked* at Culvert. I thought he had a tic or something, but when I set it up at closer range, I saw him wink again ... Why don't you go ask Culvert: '*Why* did Whittaker wink at you? ... not: *Did* Whittaker wink at you?' "

Taking Aggie's suggestion, Brown worked on Culvert who immediately broke down and confessed that Whittaker had seen him on a park bench with his legs crossed and a hole in his shoe, and that Whittaker said: "I'll buy you a new pair of shoes if you help me stage a phony holdup to cure my wife of leaving her jewelry laying around."

Not expecting to do more than frighten Mrs. Whittaker in order to earn a new pair of shoes, Culvert hopped through the hotel window. Whittaker drew a gun, wounded him, then shot his wife.

Wrapping up this strange story, Aggie said: "When Whittaker was sentenced to life in prison, he tore into the judge, shouting: 'If you or anybody else think I killed my wife, *may god strike him dead!*' "

When he was being processed at San Quentin Prison, God struck Whittaker dead. He died on the spot of a heart attack.

An example of Aggie's persistence to work all angles of a murder case came when another middle-aged man, William Morgan from Portland, Oregon, reported that his car went down a steep embankment near Mt. Washington early one morning. It happened a few days following a flash rain. Morgan said he had called for aid during the night to help rescue his wife and three children in the wreckage.

"I was on the scene when Morgan was telling Captain Norris Stanisland he'd been up-and-down the steep, wet hill three-or-four times trying to rig something so he could save his family." Aggie told me this when we were recording our final tapes together in 1983. I'd flown to visit her at her home in Greeley.

"After Morgan was taken to the sheriff's substation for more questioning, Captain Standsland let me sit outside his office so I could get some quotes. And when they were through, Standsland said to me: 'That poor devil sure went through an awful lot during the night, didn't he?' And I said: 'I think he's as guilty as a son-of-a-bitch. How the hell could he have been climbing up-and-down that damp hill all night without getting his pants and coat all dirtied with mud?' "

With that, Standsland held Morgan for 24 hours while he had deputies investigate the wreckage more thoroughly.

Going over the scene again, a deputy found and opened the back of a small portable radio located in the car. In it he discovered a list noting double-indemnity life insurance policies Morgan had recently taken out on his wife and three children.

With no way out, Morgan confessed to beating his wife and children to death with a hammer. He was given a life sentence and was later killed by an inmate.

Aggie was assigned to cover her first court trial in 1937. This was when Campbell discovered she had learned speed-writing in business school.

"There was this man named Paul Wright," Aggie said on our 1983 tape. "He'd gone to an aviator's get-together in Hollywood with his wife, Evelyn, and his best friend, a pilot named John Kimmel.

"The three ended up at Wright's Glendale home and had some drinks. Then Wright excused himself to go to bed ... About four A.M., he got up to investigate a strange noise."

Aggie said Wright had found his wife and Kimmel making love on the piano bench in the living room and that he ran to the bedroom for his gun and came out firing. Then, in an hysterical condition, he phoned Glendale police and said: "I've just murdered my wife and my best friend. You'll find me waiting in my home when you get here!"

When a police prowl car arrived, Wright grabbed one of the cops, Harry Reed, and pulled him into the living room where his wife and Kimmel were still alive. Kimmel occasionally thrashed and coughed up blood. The two were pronounced dead when they arrived at the Glendale Emergency Hospital.

A phone call summoned attorney Jerry Giesler to the Glendale jail later that morning. He learned Wright had confessed a second time to investigating officers. So when they went to court, Wright was charged with two counts of first-degree murder, and with the prosecution asking for the death penalty, Giesler entered a twofold plea: *Not guilty*, and *not guilty by reason of insanity*.

"When the *Herald* came out the same day, November 9," Aggie said, "the rewrite man had a hell-of-a-time describing the unorthodox kind of sex Paul and Evelyn were having." He wasn't allowed to use the Latin, *in flagrante delicto* because Mr. Campbell was afraid some ancient language scholar would cancel his subscription. So my rewrite man, Don Ryan, did his best to put across to the reader exactly *what* they were doing on the piano bench. He wrote that Evelyn and John were fully dressed and facing one-another. He mentioned that Mrs. Wright was lying back on the floor as though she had been on her knees when she was shot. He also wrote that Kimmel was shot in the chest, and Evelyn had three bullet holes which had entered her back.

"What the paper couldn't print was that Kimmel's fly was open and his penis was hanging out ... But Ryan pretty well put it across that Mrs. Wright was going down on her husband's best friend when he caught them."

Not only was the Paul Wright case Aggie's introduction to trial reporting, but the defense lawyer, Jerry Giesler, would go on to be known to the press as the "Hollywood star's attorney." This was before Giesler would defend personalities Charles Chaplin, Busby Berkely, Ruth Etting, Errol Flynn and Robert Mitchum.

Prosecuting attorney at the Wright case was S. Ernest Roll, who went on to become L.A.'s District Attorney. Judge Ingall W. Bull presided over the case.

"When Giesler put Wright on the witness stand," Aggie said, "the veins in his forehead were standing out so, I thought he was going to have a stroke.

"The first thing Wright said was: 'When I saw my wife making love to John, a white flame exploded in my brain.' Right away, I knew we'd found a name for the case: *The White Flame Murder.*"

The second morning of the trial, Giesler came in court limping. During recess, Aggie asked him what had happened, and Giesler told her he'd studied the coroner's photos of the two bodies. He said—off the record—that he didn't know how Kimmel's right leg had been twisted behind him on the piano keyboard. "My wife and I tried to act it out," he said. "I played the role of Kimmel and my wife was Mrs. Wright. Well, last night when we were trying it out on our living room piano, I fell off the keyboard and hurt my hip."

"Just how far did you and Mrs. Giesler go?" Aggie asked, with a smile.

The following day, Giesler showed up with a copy of the Holy Bible under his arm. He wanted to appeal to the jury's moralistic values by reading extracts from the Old Testament as well as a chapter from The Book of Matthew. He dwelled upon the point that God thought that grievous sin was punishable by death.

"The big mistake Ernie Roll made," Aggie told Don Ryan "was when he picked up the Bible and, shaking it in the jury's faces, said: 'Mr. Giesler brought this book into the courtroom and has read sections of it to you to prove that Mr. Wright is innocent. I won't take any more of your valuable time going into this ... *Mr. Wright is as innocent as Satan!*' "

Then Roll pounded the Bible on the table and it slid two feet, nearly falling to the floor.

After deliberating three hours, the jury found Wright guilty on two counts of manslaughter. This relieved Giesler who was afraid Wright might get the murder verdict. Instead, it was decided that he had killed the couple in the heat of passion induced by jealous rage.

Directly after Aggie phoned in her story, she returned to question any juror she could find regarding their reaction to Roll's theatrics with the Bible. She found a lady who told her: "All of us were offended at the cavalier treatment he'd given the book representing the Word of God ... including the way he threw it on the table. We found it most offensive and immediately, we began feeling more sympathetic toward Mr. Wright."

Because Giesler had entered not guilty along with not guilty because of insanity, the same jury would have to hear the second part of the case that would draw one-to-ten years in prison. If Wright was found sane at the time of the crime, he could draw from two-to-twenty if he would serve the sentences consecutively.

When the trial resumed the following Monday, the jury had had only one day off since they found Wright guilty of manslaugher. It had lasted a month and jury members were tired. Now they had to decide Wright's absolute fate.

Four psychiatrists were brought in and Aggie said: "I didn't know if Giesler was putting something over on the prosecution, but something strange went on in the judges chambers."

It seems Giesler had convinced Judge Bull—because the defense attorney had the burden of proof—that he had the right in the second half of the trial to present his final argument after the prosecution's. In this manner, Giesler was allowed to answer all questions previously put to Wright by the prosecution without the district attorney being allowed a rebuttal. With this specific procedure, Giesler had set a precedent in California law.

Exhausted jury members returned after three days of deliberation, and keen-eyed Underwood caught one of the jurors smiling at Wright. She knew Giesler had won.

Wright was found "not guilty because of insanity," and he was then remanded to the Los Angeles General Hospital for examination by a new set of psychiatrists designated by the County Lunacy Commission.[22]

Four days later, in the court of Superior Judge Ben Lindsay,[23] it was decreed that Wright was presently sane, therefore, he walked away a free man.

The fact that Los Angeles had a franchise on sensational court trials might have been forgotten during 1942-43 because war news monopolized newspaper front pages. Then along came the dashing Irishman Errol Flynn who temporarily reclaimed the headlines when two teenage girls accused him of statutory rape.

---

[22]A harsh title such as this would be disallowed in today's times of minimizing and perfuming the distasteful.

[23]Judge Ben Lindsay was the first high magistrate to publicly encourage "trial marriage;" a man and woman living together before wedding. For this provoking opinion, Lindsay was kicked out of Denver and settled in California to resume his revolutionary ideas.

This gay blade (I'm using the archaic definition) who appeared in a number of Warner Bros. buccaneer motion pictures, also enjoyed hide-the-epee off screen with young girls.

Just as consenting female bed-partners under the age of 18 were considered illegal "jail-bait," so were vulnerable male movie stars lured by ambitious lassies in a rush to appear on the silver screen. Woe to the celebrity male adults who failed to keep their promises made them while in heat.

Like a tree standing in the wrong place, lightning struck poor Errol Flynn twice ... at the same time.

In 1942, a 17-year-old Nebraska farm girl named Betty Hansen had been picked up by the Santa Monica police on suspicion of pandering. They also came across Flynn's unlisted telephone number in Betty's phone book. Betty forthwith claimed Flynn raped her. But in October, the grand jury failed to return an indictment against the actor because of Betty's tainted past.

During the Santa Monica district attorney's investigation of the Hansen case, they found the name of a 15-year-old girl named Peggy LaRue Satterlee. Peggy's parents had also visited the sheriff's office complaining that Flynn had *twice* seduced their daughter on his yacht, *Sirocco*, as it lay at anchor in Avalon Bay off Catalina Island. The Hansen and Saterlee charges were combined in a single complaint and a preliminary hearing was set for November 2 before Los Angeles Municipal Judge Byron J. Walters.

Jerry Giesler was retained. And looking back, Aggie said: "Jerry and I had become friends during the times I covered his defense trials of Alexander Pantages, Chaplin, Bugsey Siegel, Lili St. Cyr and Mitchum.

"Because of my track record of being fair, Jerry trusted me."

So when Aggie asked for an exclusive interview with Flynn, he allowed her to talk freely with his client before and during the trial.

"When Jerry gave me carte blanche, this surprised Flynn," said Aggie, "but being the rogue he was, Errol went along with it."

As a result, Aggie believed her pre-trial stories helped Flynn; at the time, a predispositioned public was dead set on Flynn being sent to jail. Aggie said she even heard one woman say he should be shot. And another called the actor a "draft-dodger" because Flynn was born in Tasmania and turned U.S. citizen in 1942.

Aggie said during an interview with Flynn that "there were a lot of things he told me I could have used to nail him to a journalistic wall. As examples, he said, 'Every girl who went out with me was doing so at her own risk.' And, 'I could lay a girl at the drop of a hat, but I always remembered who she was when it was over.' "

After the trial got under way, Deputy District Attorney Thomas W. Cochran representing the prosecution called Betty Hansen to the stand. He established she was 17 when she went to a party at Flynn's Bel Air home, and subsequently went upstairs to his master bedroom where the two had sex. Cochran was trying to establish that Betty went upstairs with Flynn only to "take a nap."

"But when Giesler got to Betty," Aggie said, "he turned to the matter of her motives of going to the party. That she had in mind Flynn would help her get a job in the movies. She said her escort, Armand Knapp, told her to 'play up to Flynn.' "

Giesler went directly to Betty's earlier testimony to the Grand Jury:

> Q. *[Giesler reading]* Did he say anything to you about going to introduce you to Errol Flynn?
> A. He said how I should act and play up to him.
> Q. Tell us about that.
> A. He said play up to him and drink with him.
> Q. Do you remember so testifying?
> A. No. I don't.
> Q. *[Reading again]* Did Mr. Knapp tell you to have intercourse with Flynn?
> A. He said to be sociable and do anything he asked me to do.
> Q. This is true?
> A. Yes.

Q. Pointing out line one, she says she doesn't remember this, where she says, "Even have intercourse with him." She does not remember that. You might have gotten that wrong, you might have said that?
A. Yes.

After reading further where he got Betty to admit she knew what she was going upstairs for and that she had undressed herself, Aggie said: "Jerry thought he was through making his point regarding Betty's inconsistencies and wanted to move on to examining the other under-aged girl, Peggy Satterlee."

Aggie got a second shot at an interview with Flynn and at the end, asked him: "If you get acquitted, will you come over to my place where I can cook a spaghetti dinner for you and some of the reporters covering the trial?"

"I solemnly promise," said Flynn.

The weekend with Peggy Satterlee at Catalina Island began on the night of Friday, August 1, 1941. Flynn, his friend Buster Wiles, Peggy, another girl and a crew of three were aboard. They had spent Saturday night ashore. And on Sunday morning, before photographer Peter Stackpole arrived to shoot a picture layout, Peggy said she had been raped by Flynn in his cabin.

Aggie's Q. and A.:

Q. Did you, during the time he was trying to rape you, as you have told us today—did you at any time feel embarrassed to the extent you did not want to call out to protect your honor?
A. Yes, sir.
Q. The three reasons why you did not scream out: the first is because it might embarrass you, the second because of the crew and third because they were friends of his. Those reasons did not prevent you from resisting him and fighting him to the very bitter end, as far as you were concerned, did they?
A. No, sir.

The deeper Giesler drew Peggy into cross-examination, the more unconvincing her testimony became. After they had

watched the start of the annual aquaplane races she said Flynn
had lured her below that evening to see what the moon looked
like through a porthole.

Aggie said this was the most incriminating testimony in Flynn's
favor. Aggie went on with her Q. and A. about when the *Sirocco*
was sailing home Sunday evening, after Flynn had "violated"
Peggy a second time:

Q. So you followed him in the cabin and looked at the moon?
A. Yes, sir.
Q. Did you look through the porthole?
A. Yes, sir.
Q. Which side was it?
A. The right side.
Q. The right side as you came toward San Pedro [harbor]?
A. As they came toward the dock.
Q. On the right side?
A. Yes, sir.
Q Could you see the moon?
A. Yes, sir.
Q. Where was the moon? Was it up above the boat, or
where was it?
A. I don't know. Naturally I guess it was that way, because
I saw it.

As a follow-up, Giesler went to a chalk and blackboard demonstration, pointing out to the jury exactly where certain celestial
bodies should have been in relation to the *Sirocco* on the night
in question.

Then, before resting the defense, Giesler summoned the harbor master and two local sea captains to the stand. They all
agreed that Peggy would have had to look through the ship's
steel bulkheads to see the moon because it was on the opposite
side. But the most damaging evidence of all was that *the moon
wasn't even visible* in the sky that cloudy night.

On February 6, 1943, jurors acquitted Flynn and the judge,
upon releasing them, said: "I think you have arrived at a proper
verdict."

Giesler's comment to Aggie was: "Considering he had gone into that trial with the dice of public opinion loaded against him, Mr. Flynn was vindicated both by the jury *and* the press."

The following night, Sunday, February 7, and as promised, Flynn showed up at Aggie's place armed with two cases of booze. "And some of my reporter friend's who'd covered the trial," said Aggie, "ate my spaghetti, got smashed and Flynn enjoyed watching the mock trial we held with Perry Fowler and Coy Watson dressed in my clothes, playing the parts of the rape victims."

John B.T. Campbell deserved credit for his foresight in hiring Aggie Underwood as the nation's premiere female city editor on a metropolitan newspaper. He was aware that residually, this decision would eventually open the doors of the Fourth Estate for other women to follow in that job, plus obtain other executive positions of responsibility in the profession.

Of her first day on the desk in 1947, Aggie said: "I was as nervous as a cat and scared to death until old-timer Fred Wiegel walked up from the bull pen and said, 'We've got a deadline coming up, Aggie. You'd better get busy and give us something to do.' Well, this cracked the ice, and everything went well from then on."

Following a congratulatory letter to Aggie, my father also wrote a note to Campbell:

> Aggie's topped us all in one respect—she bore children, reared them, did her housework, and became a city editor. Isn't this some kind of violation of union rules?

Wiegel knew Aggie was fond of lobster, and at the end of the first week, he bought a live 20-pounder that disturbed the routine by thrashing about on the top of her desk. This seemed to set the mutual manner Aggie and her staff shared.

She eventually acquired a baseball fungo bat with which to threaten over-zealous Hollywood press agents. And when it became too quiet in the city room, she'd fire off a blank pistol and cry out: "Don't let this paper die on us today!" And when the inside temperature hit the 100 degree mark, she would send a copyboy down to Moran's and have Curly dispatch a case of cold beer for the men on the copy desk.

Aggie was hard-driving and tough-talking. Jack Smith, Dick O'Connor, Wally Rawles, Don Ryan, budding Edy Jo Bernal and I were all there when she was in full flower. Smith said: "She was at the peak of her awesome energies and stunning intuitions, and in autocratic command of a cityside staff of oddballs, some of them gifted, and most of them as loyal to Aggie and as steadfast under fire as soldiers in the old British square."

The *Her-Ex* city room was a circus. Yet we got out a paper every day, and on time. Reporters and rewrite men kept in mind that every big story had to be topped with a new lead every edition—whether there was anything new or not. And when the final edition went down about three in the afternoon, we hurried to Moran's or home to our wives and children, depending on which of our devils was driving us that day.

Jack Smith showed up on the *Her-Ex* about a year before I arrived to join this insane sideshow of literary humanity. I asked him how Aggie happened to hire him. He said: "I have never told the story before because it isn't exactly an example for the young. But, on the other hand, it's true."

He said he had left the *Daily News* for another paper which soon folded. "On a Friday, naturally," he said. "So in keeping with tradition, I went to the press club to celebrate."

Assistant city editor Art McCarroll had been phoning around for Jack to come to work at the *Her-Ex*. The two had met when they were in the Marine Corps during the war.

"But I wasn't ready to go back to work," said Smith. "My paper had just folded and I was supposed to celebrate."

"Aggie wants to talk to you," said McCarroll after locating Smith.

"Tell her I'm drunk," said Smith.

Jack heard Art speaking away from the phone. "Aggie, Smith says he's drunk." A second later, McCarroll was back to Smith. "Aggie wants to know when you'll be able to start work."

"Monday," said Smith. And he showed up sober on Monday.

Aggie was hard on the staff, but she was harder on herself. She arrived on the job at four a.m., and on a normal day, headed for home 11 hours later. And she never left her desk for a lunch break.

"I can't forget how hard I worked you guys," she said. "But I always gave it back. When things were slow, I'd send you home early, or to wherever the hell you went. None of us ever worked the eight-hour day anyway." Backing this up, she recalled hiring a not-too-bright young reporter.

"He phoned the desk in the middle of covering a fast-breaking story to say, 'I'm off in 15 minutes. What am I supposed to do?' "

Aggie yelled back: "God damn it, go home, and *stay* there!" That was his first and last day working for Aggie.

What she missed most about her job on the desk was not being able to get out on the street to cover stories, just like Cappy Marek had complained before her.

I mentioned to Aggie that in a single day she had me covering exactly *eleven* stories. "And I never got into the office from the time you shagged me out of bed at four A.M. to cover the first one ... until we both signed off at eight that night."

This was around the time in the early 1950s when the gathering and reporting of television news began to rankle Aggie. Although there were few big stories TV could beat the newspapers on—such as the Kathy Fiscus story, the 1948 election returns, an atom bomb being exploded in Nevada and the Rose Parade—Aggie was nettled with the thought of her newspaper being beat by the new medium. Therefore, she was unkind, but most-often right, when she referred to the newcomers invading the medium to which she had been so devoted. And if one cared to arouse Aggie's passionate displeasure in her later years, all he had to do was mention the phrase "investigative reporting."

"Jesus!" she'd cry, "we were *all* investigative reporters in our time. If we weren't, we'd get fired! Today, they have a week-or-so to get their stories, then have little pieces and bits of information fed out over a period of a week by some parrot who never had anything at all to do physically in covering the god-damned story . . . This son-of-a-bitch would be a clean, pretty guy or gal wearing the latest in attire . . . the price of which they could deduct from their income tax . . . and read about some poor bastard being brutally murdered . . . And none of these ass-holes probably ever smelled a dead body, climbed a mountain to cover a plane wreck, ducked bullets aimed at someone else, or held a grieving mother in their arms after her baby was torn apart by some maniac!''

When Aggie and I talked in 1983, she admitted that ''a few network people we see at the top are craftsmen, but you have to remember they have what Cecil B. DeMille had in the movies . . . a cast of thousands . . . backing them up. But I do resent their bending and editing the news to their advantage. They deny they do it, but that's a lot of bull. Take the three networks: They're Democrats on CBS, and on NBC, they lean toward being Republican. The closest to the middle that I can see in ABC. But the independently owned local stations . . . I never know what the hell they are and I don't know half the time when they're reporting the news . . . what with their mispronouncing names of national figures . . . to their cute little bonmots and Joe Miller Joke Book quips . . . I think their 'anchor persons' are half-assed. They're half-actor and half-reader . . . They say they're jour-nalists . . . I don't know. None of them have any savvy or drive . . . or have the pride we had.''

When the *Herald-Express* merged with the *Examiner* in 1964 to become the only afternoon metro in the Southwest, the *Her-Ex* gang moved from Tenton Street over to the *Examiner* building at 11th and Broadway. Aggie was kicked upstairs, and before she was appointed assistant managing editor of the *Herald-Examiner*, publisher George Hearst told her he had considered naming her managing editor of the new paper. However, others around the country with their fingers in the Hearst Corporation executive pie vetoed George's consideration. This was a bad decision for several reasons, mainly because Aggie was well-equipped to handle the job. In addition, it would have made news all over the world and increased circulation for the Hearst papers. Unfortunately, in the case of young Hearst not standing up for her, Aggie sluffed it off with: "Some people become faint when the opportunity comes around."

By the time Aggie started her new position, she had won scores of honors. She held two honorary degrees; a Master of Business Demonstration from Woodbury College and a Doctor of Laws. Over the years, she received more tributes than any other woman in journalism. They ranged from *Most Outstanding Woman in Journalism* awarded by the National Federation of Press Women, to the Theta Sigma Phi national sorority naming her National Headliner. She was named in the first edition of *Who's Who of America Women* in 1959, and Ralph Edwards featured Aggie on his national TV show, "This Is Your Life."

With public adulation going for her when she took over at the *Herald-Examiner*, it was easy to understand that a touch of envy would emerge.

"My managing editor, Don Goodenow, gave me so little to do," Aggie said. "I nearly went crazy sitting in that god-damned little office. And when old friends dropped by, Goodenow and Tom Caton—who I'd treated well over the years, and was city editor now—steered people away from my office."

And to make things worse between herself and Goodenow "while I was wandering around like a half-assed executive, the thermometer was also rising." It was Aggie's first summer in the antiquated, poorly air-conditioned *Examiner* building.

A voice from the city room filtered through: "Aggie, it's 100 degrees." It was one of her pals on the copy desk. The voice echoed like old times and Aggie summoned a copyboy to fetch a case of cold beer for her sub rosa friends.

About ten minutes later, Goodenow phoned Aggie. "Get into my office," he ordered.

When she arrived, Goodenow said, "Are they drinking beer out there on the copy desk?"

"Yes, they are," said Aggie.

"Well, go tell them to stop it."

"You go tell them yourself, you son-of-a-bitch," said Aggie. "I bought it for them."

"But the icing on the cake regarding quiet resentment came when I received a telegram at home notifying me I'd just been selected as *Los Angeles Times* first *Woman of the Year* in the profession of journalism," said Aggie.

Coming from an opposition paper, Aggie said she thought it was a "gag." So she phoned publisher George Hearst and asked if he knew anything about it. He did, and Aggie asked what he thought she should do about it. "Use your own judgment," said young George.

"I was hurt by his sophomoric decision," said Aggie. "I'd given my entire life to the Hearst Corporation, and with the exception of Mr. Campbell taking a chance on me, I can't recall one Hearst executive ever saying 'nice work' over a story I'd covered . . . or even buying me an ice cream cone on my birthday. So help me," she decided, "I think George Hearst found himself in a spot that embarrassed him and was too stupid to realize what an honor his paper was being given, over-and-above what it meant to me."

The *Woman of the Year* honors were bestowed at the home of *Times* publisher Norman Chandler. And when it came Aggie's turn to be presented, Mrs. Chandler said: "I would like to break a precedent and give this award to Mrs. Underwood myself. It's about time for a woman in our own profession to receive this award. And Agness Underwood was the only choice we could make."

For a woman who used to return early from vacations to get back to work, the inactivity was too much for her. So Aggie went to George Hearst's office to notify him she would resign on January 13, 1968, exactly 33 years to the day when she started working for the Hearst papers.

Jo Mosher, wife of journalist-author Al Stump, was new on the paper and considered it an honor to be assigned to write Aggie's retirement story. "But after I'd sent it over and gotten it back from Goodenow," Jo said, "he'd cut the story down like hell." Then Jo went to Goodenow and said: "Why are you doing this? This is our Aggie I'm writing about." Then Jo said the managing editor seemed to be "in complete frustrated anger when he said: 'How would you like it if you had an ogre sitting outside your office?' "

In a personal handwritten letter Richard M. Nixon sent to me in 1982, the former President mentioned he hadn't seen Aggie in some time. He added:

> Please give my best to Agness when you see her. We need her kind of editor today.

The Hollywood Palladium publicized that it could hold one thousand couples on its dance floor when it opened in the late 1930s. High school kids used to go there to hear the big bands like those of Benny Goodman, Gene Krupa, Tommy and Jimmy Dorsey, Harry James and Glen Miller. On the night of Aggie's retirement party, the Palladium was overflowing. And for those who couldn't make it, wires came in from mayors, senators, governors and the President of the United States. Bob Hope emceed.

Aggie was 81 when she died of a heart attack on July 2, 1984.

These days I find myself going to more funerals than I used to. And I notice that frequency is growing. If I could only figure a way how to keep from attending my own obsequies, I would be satisfied.

Funerals are vulgar low-key circuses where grieving relatives are compelled to listen to a eulogist overstate the morality of the deceased. And among those in attendance, there is always a sprinkling of frauds kneeling in the pews and those who never liked the dead guy in the first place.

I saw a few of these at Aggie's funeral in St. John's Episcopal Church in Los Angeles on July 8. They were sitting in the rear, hoping not to be noticed.

Eschewing coffin-side discourses, as I so acidly have remarked, when it came my turn, I read a short love letter to Aggie so quietly no one beyond the third pew could hear me, then sat down.

Aggie's children, Mary Evelyn and George, Coy and Harry Watson, Jack and Denny Smith, Edy Jo Bernal and Ruth Harvey, Bill Ryan and the rest stood about the church's entrance following the services. There, I pointed to a place a block away on Wilshire and remarked: "First time I met Aggie was over there. It was a bus accident back in 1944."

There's still something uniquely electrifying when older newspaper people get together to catch the lightning. I enjoyed this most when I flew out to see Aggie in Greeley the last time. We talked the night through in her house across the street from her son's place.

Here we reminisced about when two-time murderess Louise Peete wanted to come live with Aggie . . . And when I wrote the obituary about the guy who phone it in . . . And when Aggie told a sheriff's captain it wasn't Culvert who killed the organist.

Then we laughed about how Aggie used to shoot off her pistol in the city room, and threaten press agents with her baseball bat . . . and when she fired the tyro reporter when he wanted to go home . . . and when she'd send down to Moran's for beer on hot days.

Then she remarked about how longtime friendships paid off, especially with Mickey Cohen . . . and when reporters put on a mock trial for Errol Flynn. These were the memories that made us happy.

The most memorable anecdote I like to tell about Aggie is when she and Perry Fowler covered the Madam Chang Kai-shek banquet at the Ambassador Hotel in 1947, shortly before Aggie took over the *Her-Ex* city desk.

Madam Chang had traveled to the United States with her diplomatic hand out for money to aid her emperor husband's army to keep Mao Tse-tung's Communist forces from taking over China.

Even though the war had been over some time, good liquor was still hard to come by. And when Aggie and Perry were directed to use the Ambassador pantry entrance off the kitchen to gain access into the big dining room where the shindig was to take place, the two stopped to marvel at the opened and unguarded case of Cuttysark scotch.

With larceny in his mind, Perry said: "Aggie, look what they're handing out to the Chinese Nationalists these days."

"To the freeloading sympathizers," said Aggie.

"What do you think we should do about this?" Perry asked while studying an opened opaque window handy above. "My car's right outside."

"To hell with the Chinese sympathizers," said Aggie, realizing she could pass the case of scarce whiskey through the cream-tinted window, a bottle at a time.

"I'll go outside," said Perry. "And wait for me to reach for it."

Within a minute, Aggie felt the sturdy hand grip the first of the 12 precious bottles.

And just as they had created a sort of rhythm as the last bottle went through the window, Perry reappeared scratching his head. "I just can't seem to find the damned window from out there," he said.

Realizing what had been pulled on them, the two leaped on a table and peered out, just in time to see three shabby-looking men scurrying from the parking lot, carrying the cherished bottles of Cuttysark.

The *Herald-Express* had its shrewd old managing editor in John B.T. Campbell, and a superior news desk under Herb Krauch. But when she was standing over her desk, directing a staff of unpredictable and talented newsmen like a galley master, Agness Underwood represented the spark and the heart of the newspaper.

The last thing I remember Aggie saying to her friends who came to celebrate at her retirement party was: *"Please don't forget me."*

Now, who the hell ever could?

XIV

The Omnibus Beatmen

N ewspaper "beats" were arms attached to the city desk by direct phone lines. Each beat was staffed by the metropolitans and the few independents who wished to be in the ballgame. Their specialists were called "beatmen."

This way, the *Examiner, Herald-Express, Times, Daily News* and the *Mirror* were immediately in touch when a major news story broke in their bailiwicks. When television began operating with the 16mm Filmo cameras in the early 1950s, their photographers were centrally located at the police beat where they covered fast-breaking stories. They were also available to other stories emulating from other beats. In general, at TV's beginning, there was sharp competition when newspaper photogs found themselves pooling together in order to minimize their being beaten by a TV man. What with news airing time having been so drastically reduced over the newspapers, fist fights between the two medium photogs were not uncommon.

Beside the police beat, there were the sheriff, district attorney, superior court, federal, hotel, Pasadena and harbor beats. Eight in all.

The police beat pressroom was the seediest. Most of the reporters didn't wear neckties. They often ate on the run, and were usually in need of a shave. But they were meticulously accurate when it came to getting up-to-date information as quick as the police doled it out.

The sheriff's beat pressroom with its flea-infested cracked leather couch located across the hall from the county morgue was in the basement of the Hall of Justice. This morbid dungeon became our legacy when a county executive appropriated the former sunshiny pressroom on the Hall's ground floor. This was where Bevo Means hung his beer bottle opener.

Together, the police and sheriff's beats kept in touch with what was going on in 16 widely-scattered city police divisions, 12 sheriff's precincts ranging from the desert of Lancaster to Catalina Island, and the California Highway Patrol's domain. Beatmen also monitored crime in 45 major incorporated cities which had their own police departments.

Later, the city desks threw in the Coast Guard, city and county lifeguard services, the County Fire Department and the U.S. Forest Service to cover. Metropolitans, even later, added San Diego, Riverside, Ventura, Orange and San Fernando counties, when their community papers started going under. This was due to television news superceding the possibility of their keeping up.

It was simpler in the '40s and early '50s when assignment reporters and the beatmen used to head out on a hot story. This was when colorful Sheriff Eugene W. Biscailuz made all of us reporters deputy sheriffs; gave us a badge and allowed us to carry firearms. Nervous city and county salaried keepers of the peace were perpetually on guard when newsmen appeared at a stakeout. They would look for the bulge under our coats and hope it was a bottle. Since Biscailuz gave us a licence to carry concealed weapons, there had been reporters who had shot themselves in the foot and even farther up.

The hotel beat had a more cheery atmosphere and its furnishing appointments were fairly anticeptic. It was situated on the mezzanine of the Biltmore Hotel. The world-famous stayed here when visiting Los Angeles.

When former New York Governor Thomas E. Dewey was campaigning on the Republican ticket opposite President Harry Truman the first time, "the little man on the wedding cake" put up at the Biltmore when stumping Southern California. On his first night in town, I covered him with reporters from two other papers. Biltmore Hotel owner Baron Long, as usual, put the press up in a suite adjoining the Governor's. And around midnight, one reporter took a thin-stemmed champagne glass, placed it against the wall and put his ear to it. This acted as a receiver and amplified what was going on in the Governor's suite. It wasn't his intention, but the reporter found himself listening to Gov. Dewey performing the damp-deed-of-darkness with Mrs. Dewey. If veteran hotel beatman Tim Turner had caught the reporter at the end of the glass, he would have had all of us thrown out. Turner, who was highly respected by all in the establishment was a staunch Republican.

The federal beat was considered the plum. During the Christmas holidays, the beatman—if it were his persuasion— could be on the receiving end of a lot of money changing hands under to table. This would be in appreciation of services rendered, such as stories turned in slightly leaning in a lobbyist's favor. The least a beatman could have done was to get his home stocked with vintage wine and bonded whiskey to see him through to the next Yule season.

On a quiet afternoon, one could find a reserved gentleman stripped down to his undershorts, basking beneath a sun lamp, and sipping raw bourbon with alfalfa juice chaser. The latter was a concoction he had bought at his local health food store. This was federal beatman Pat O'Hara, and his reasoning was that the juice built up what the whiskey was tearing down in him. In this way, O'Hara figured he was holding his own.

Along the way, O'Hara repeatedly warned his fellow journalists that one day he would leave the *Daily News*, retire to a remote cabin near San Luis Obispo, write *The Great American Novel*, then hang himself.

Pat—like Tallulah Bankhead—addressed everyone as "dahling" because he couldn't remember names. He had the posture and demeanor of a British officer out of uniform, and lived alone in an incredibly cluttered apartment and was beguiled by a spectrum of things including weight-lifting, wheat germ, psychiatry, murders with a humorous twist, girls and baked sheep's head. Fellow *Daily News* columnist Matt Weinstock once described Pat as a man "who used to delight in shocking people. Essentially he was a scoffer, and had a ruthless approach in getting a story. One might categorize Pat as being a philosophic anarchist."

While baring his wiry chest with its fringe of white hair beneath his sun lamp, and trimming his moustache with his stockinged feet perched on his desk, Pat occasionally chuckled while recalling a nearly forgotten axe killer who had amused him.

"There he was, you know, dahling," he would reminisce, "with this corpse on the floor and the place all bloody, and he carefully put all his cigarette butts in this little ash tray, because he was a neat person, you know, dahling . . ."

O'Hara had started his newspaper career in Chicago, migrating to New York where he lived in Greenwich Village and worked on Hearst's *Journal*. After a shattered marriage, he moved to Los Angeles and worked on the *Daily News* for many years before it submerged. When it folded and employees were figuring how and where they were going to get another job during the Christmas holidays, Pat blithely strolled away to get drunk.

Weinstock remembered that Pat had become shy about asking for a job. Of O'Hara's last days, he said: "Pat just didn't want to grow old. He'd become very conscious of his age—at 55. What he really wanted to do was quietly disappear."

Another close friend, beatman Johnny Arrington (who used to spontaneously direct traffic in his undershorts at Second and Broadway when he was drinking), said: "Pat spent $45 for ten volumes of history by Arnold Toynbee. He was always impressed by Toynbee's writing about the dying days of Rome. If you want my opinion, those ten volumes got hold of him. He decided he'd had it."

None of us ever saw O'Hara alive again after he disappeared to the little cabin he talked about near San Luis Obispo It was a month before his body was found; he had hanged himself to the branch of a lonely tree. And he never did get around to writing his *Great American Novel*.

The district attorney's was the glamour beat; the hottest and swingingest. *People* magazine would have staffed it today.

Following an indictment, obscure murderers would go on trial and become public figures by the newspaper coverage attended them.

There was murderer Caryl Chessman—*The Red Light Bandit*— who evolved into a legal criminal authority while in jail fighting for his life before losing it in the gas chamber nearly 12 years later. There were convicted murderers Dr. Bernard Finch and his young lover, the strikingly beautiful Carole Tregoff. They went up for life for killing his wife. Judged insane by many, killer Stephen Nash stopped off at the D.A. beat while on his way to execution at San Quentin. He had refused to pose for news cameramen unless they paid him. Photogs took up a quick collection and gave it to Nash who posed, then said: "Now, who's crazy?"

There also were the famous who visited the D.A. pressroom. Charlie Chaplin would only stand outside the pressroom when Joan Berry went in to win a paternity suit filed against the silent screen comedian. Singer Ruth Etting had been hauled up for shooting her agent husband, Mo Snyder. And colorful Errol Flynn lavishly entertained D.A. beatmen when indicted on his charge of statutory rape.

There were also stories emanating from the D.A.'s beat which ended up in double entendre headlines. When renowned local private investigator Nick Carter was held up at gunpoint in front of the Town House Hotel—a hostelry noted for registering a plethora of Mr. and Mrs. John Smiths for an overnighter—the *Her-Ex* came out with the bannerline:

BIG DICK STUCK UP IN TOWN HOUSE

When a teenager was arrested and held incommunicado pending questioning by the District Attorney regarding a juvenile murder, the *Her-Ex* struck again. This time the headline read:

POLICE HOLD TONGUE IN SNATCH OF TEENAGER

The Hall of Justice elevator was large. The county regulation notice posted limited it to carrying 40 passengers. And when overloaded during business hours, it often carried several of the 13-story Hall's employees beyond their floor because they were unable to fight their way to the front to get out.

A particular Monday found Jack Stevens caught in such a situation. But he was with photog Maurice "Mitch" Mitchell who had remedied this problem with a surefire solution. Jack was standing in the rear with Mitch, behind a couple dozen riders. Logistically, Mitch planted himself behind a morbidly overweight woman. At his side, he carried his always-ready-with-flashbulb Speed Graphic.

When the elevator stopped at the district attorney offices on the third floor, none of the passengers would budge when Stevens politely said with Texas accent, "Third floor. May I please get out?"

With his remedy, Mitch yelled in panic: "I think I'm going to be sick!"

The passengers hastily made a path, but the fat woman refused to give ground. Mitch then pressed his camera reflector against her caboose and let go with his seering hot flashbulb.

Whoever had been in the way earlier . . . wasn't.

Reporters relieving vacationers also favored the district attorney beat. Lloyd "Emmy" Emerson had been many years in this atmosphere where free booze flowed. The beat reflected a country club attitude, but old timers such as Emmy knew their physical limitations and how to pace themselves. Reporters relieving them, however, fell into the temptation of taking all they could as quick as possible. This happened to Jack Stevens, who should have known better.

Jack had just completed working on one of Hearst's favorite projects: the *Youth for Christ* campaign designed to have *Examiner* readers encourage their children to have religious gatherings and return to church.

It was Jack's practice to go on the wagon and stay on it until his wife Mickey's birthday or the conclusion of the *Youth for Christ* promotion . . . Whichever came first.

Mickey's birthday wasn't due for another month, and Jack had decided to tough it out; not take a drink of hard whiskey until his wife's birthday. But in didn't work out that way.

Between the joy of getting away from Richardson for a few weeks, coupled with the gallons of available free bourbon flowing in the D.A. pressroom, this new situation could have tempted Faust.

News was slow when Jack checked in with a briefcase filled with his personals. Innocently, while shaking hands with old friends, Jack figured he might as well have a few drops.

The following twelve days, up until the second Thursday drew a blank for Stevens.

He awakened from his Van Winkle sleep and cried out: "Where's the dog? Where' the *dog*?!''

Daily *News* beatman Jack Cravens answered Jack. "There's no dog here. What dog are you talking about?"

"The one that shit in my mouth!" said Stevens, painfully sitting up and wetting his parched lips. "What day is this, anyway?"

"Thursday," said Cravens, who went on to become a deputy D.A.

"My God," Jack moaned. "Four days."

"A *week* and four days," said Cravens.

"Jesus ... Kee ... rist," Jack said. He began packing his personals into his briefcase. He was certain he'd been fired, even though he hadn't spotted a reporter to relieve him. After all, twelve days had passed and Jack hadn't once contacted his city desk.

Too hungover to complete his watch, he shuffled from the pressroom when the phone rang.

His heart wasn't in answering it, but Jack's Texas heritage demanded that he did.

From the other end, Richardson's voice registered. He didn't sound any more agitated than usual. He growled: "Stevens? That you, Jack?"

"Yeah, it's me, Jim," said the depressed Stevens.

"Jesus, Jack," Richardson continued, "where the hell have you been? I've been trying to get hold of you for the past twenty *minutes*."

Not having worked a beat for a time, Jack had forgotten that fellow beatmen always covered for one-another. For all these days, they had been writing Jack's stories and phoning them in to his desk while he was in a blackout.

After taking care of whatever Richardson asked him to do, Jack started unpacking his personals again and figured, even with his terrible hangover, he would still be able to last out the final two days covering the D.A. beat.

The Pasadena beat was most always as quiet as a rumor. It was covered by a reserved, modest gentleman named Dave Swaim. But when a front page story broke in the land of little old ladies wearing tennis shoes, it was usually a hum-dinger. Like the time Judge Frank C. Collier presided over the city's only superior courtroom.

Judge Collier sat on the Pasadena bench during the 1930s and 40s. Over the years, he had picked up the nickname "Clipper Collier," the castrating judge.

This stern jurist was hard on felons coming before him if they were charged with sex crimes against children.

Any man found guilty in his court for molesting a child under age 14—girl or boy—was given "Collier's Choice."

When I was still with the *Examiner*, Swaim covered one of these court procedures which was infamous among defendants and their attorneys.

The stately white-haired magistrate would inform a defendant standing before him that he would go to State Prison for the maximum term prescribed by law, or, he would receive a moderate county jail sentence and probation, with one provision of the probation being that:

"You will be transported forthwith to the nearest hospital, where in the presence of the bailiff of this court, you will undergo surgery for complete bilateral castration."

The assigned bailiff most always shuddered because he had been ordered to witness the bloody event whereupon the offender would be rendered a eunuch.

Judge Collier told Swaim he had handed down his sentence about 40 times during his tenure on the bench.

Collier also insisted that years later he received letters from several of his castrated defendants, thanking him for restoring their self-respect and their place again in the community.

I had covered a story in the judge's courtroom when one of these disturbed youths received the sentence by "Clipper" Collier. Upon hearing what was about to be done to him, the young man whipped out his stand-up-proudly and furiously began masturbating, shocking the female jurors.

Another convicted man sentenced to the scalpel in Collier's court was a 63-year-old chaplain of a private school. His victim had been an 11-year-old girl.

Gladys Towles Root, the ostentatious Los Angeles woman attorney who specialized in defending sex offenders, fought Judge Collier long and hard on both legal and medical grounds with this case. Gladys, whose professional trademark was wearing spectacular color mismatched dresses bordering on the vulgar, most always—as she did this one—lost her cases.

Shortly after the Pasadena city council passed an ordinance banning women from wearing hats while court was in session, Gladys showed up in the pressroom dressed to kill, but with no hat.

This so disappointed reporters that Gladys peeled off a wide, flashy sash from her midriff and wrapped it about her head, creating a turban. And wearing the impromptu millenary, Gladys entered the courtroom. Judge Collier didn't even notice it.

After court, I asked Collier what he thought of Gladys' hat. The Judge said: "I don't really care what Gladys Root wears on her head, as long as she has something *in* it."

"Collier was always good for a punch quote," said Swaim. "Once I heard him sentence nine—yes, nine—youths for statutory rape, a real gang-bang, of a 16-year-old girl."

Aware some of the young men had been acting smart-alecky at times during court procedures, Swaim said Judge Collier reprimanded them:

"You may think I'm going to let you scallywags off easy, but I'm not, because all during this trial, I have taken note of your cocky conduct."

Swaim swore Collier was unaware of his accidental double meaning, "but I quoted him direct, and the line went through three editions before some pristine editor caught it."

Years later, after Collier had died in 1948, I had asked
Gladys—who was clad in a puce, gold and red ensemble at the
time—her summation of "The Clipper."

"Collier was the one who should have been castrated," she
growled.

The independent cities of San Pedro and Wilmington were
annexed by Los Angeles in 1906 and were consolidated as the
Harbor District which would soon become one of the largest ports
in the world.

Just west of Harbor Boulevard, an area began to develop which
catered to the desires of seamen who had money to spend without
wandering too far from their ships. Here was a coagulation of
bars, gambling and whore houses available to a wayfarer's dissipation and part him from the lucre burning a hole in his pocket.

Following World War I, every other establishment along this
stretch called Beacon Street was a bar. Intermittently, there were
pawn shops, bail bond offices and tattoo parlors. And the town's
eight seraglios which operated 24 hours a day were usually
located on the second story of buildings with convenient out-
door back entrances when tipped off raids were pulled.

San Pedro began to be of interest to Los Angeles-based papers,
and long after, when Bill Chernus arrived there in 1939, the Los
Angeles branch City Hall had been standing 11 years. It housed
harbor department offices and various branch units of the Los
Angeles municipal government. Dominating the civic center, the
tan-bricked building also included the fire and police departments.
Its top story (the seventh) contained the city jail—dubbed *Seventh
Heaven*—which was mostly filled Sunday mornings with
demimondes of stumbled virtues and wrecked hopes.

Across the street and caticorner from Seventh Heaven was
the Cabrillo Theatre where the harbor pressroom was located.

San Pedro winos hung about Beacon Street between Third and
Seventh during the day. At night, they drifted over to sleep in
Happy Valley, an open area in the town's slums. There, a murder
occurred most every night. None were worth reporting. Life
span of the homeless wino in Happy Valley was about two
months.

The bars along Beacon Street were distinctive in character and name. In an erstwhile bank, old salts and prostitutes straddled stools before white marble counters as the "banker" replenished his stock from the vaults where he kept his liquid assets, often more negotiable than other bonded stuff. The joint was named *The Bank Cafe*.

The *Silver Dollar* saloon featured exotic oriental murals created by a Chinese artist who, upon completion of his work, lay on the hip[24] for three days, then shot himself.

Goodfellows was the large tavern where masculine Scandinavian seamen gathered to solemnly dance with one another to wheezy tunes played on an accordion.

There was Johnny Reno's "longest bar on Beacon Street," Brad Kellogg's *Chateau Gardens*, *The Gay Way* and the *Fern Hotel* bars. But the most colorful and popular of them all was *Shanghai Red's* saloon at Fifth and Beacon.

"When I got there," the quiescent, husky Bill Chernus said, "Robert Ripley had already referred to Beacon Street in his *Believe It Or Not* newspaper strip as 'the toughest four blocks in the world.' Mr. Ripley should have included *Shanghai Red's* as being the roughest bar."

Two pagoda doors led inside where a customer could be poured anything from bathtub gin to Turkish *Rahki*. Red's back room was a miniature Las Vegas—long before the desert town knew what a crap table looked like. Red's two whore houses represented one-quarter of San Pedro's prostitute action. Whatever else there was, Red had a piece of that, too.

"The odd thing about Red," said Chernus, "was that he'd never been in Shanghai, and his hair wasn't even red."

But Red was an imposing and powerful man with the largest hamlike fists I ever saw. He could lift a gallon jug and pour a drink from it with one hand. He also had a big belly made more prominent by the $14,000 diamond mounted in his belt buckle.

---

[24]"... on the hip" is an old expression for lying down on one's side and smoking opium.

Above the bar was a shiny brass ship's bell rung loudly when a fight broke out and a bouncer was summoned to expel an obnoxious person disturbing the normal flow of business.

Red's two bouncers were women: Big and Little Stormy. Big Stormy was more than six-fee-tall with a body constructed of 200 pounds of muscle. Little Stormy was short and had reactions as quick as a mongoose. She was also completely bald, and God help any drunk who tried to play with her blonde wig.

"If Red passed the word around that a particular person or persons were to be *left alone*," said Chernus, "they were never touched by anyone. That's why we reporters covering the harbor were able to navigate Beacon Street with impunity."

Red was tough, but sometimes he wasn't quite honest, even though he poured an honest drink. Often a sailor who just hit the beach would come in and say: "Red, I have $500 and I want you to keep it for me while I get drunk." If Red liked to guy, he'd give him back his money. If he didn't, the sailor would return in a couple of days and ask for his loot. In this case, Red would say, "You drank it all up."

Chernus, who said he was part Indian but didn't know how much, went to UCLA on a football scholarship where he majored in journalism. Following graduation, he worked on the *Santa Monica Topic* and six months later, applied for a job on the *Examiner*. Harry Morgan said: "If you want to work on this paper, you'll have to get some more experience."

To get this experience, Bill went north to work on the *Dunsmuir News* and the *Santa Maria News*. Here Bill said: "I didn't like my editor. I once heard him call the society lady editor a 'bitch' in front of other employees."

Bill visited the local police department to ask the Chief: "What do you get for punching somebody here?"

"Depends on who you want to punch," said the Chief.

"I want to punch my editor."

"Well, it depends if you get caught," said the Chief. "How badly do you want to punch your editor?"

"Real bad," said Bill.

"Well then," said the Chief, "there's a greyhound bus leaving town in about two hours."

Chernus returned to the paper, soundly thrashed his editor, then left for Santa Monica on the Greyhound.

He returned to get his job on the *Examiner*, and because of his being tough, Richardson assigned him to pair up with Bill Gershon, a ruddy faced ambivert. On the *Times*, there were Charlie Crawford and Wayne Cave. Other papers had only one man representing the beat.

Dave and Bill put out a complete daily harbor news page. This was in addition to arrival and departure personality stories and pictures that ran over the local news pages. Every harbor beatman was a *double threat* reporter. He took the story and shot his own pictures.

The harbor was a focal point for international commerce. With the exception of Pan American World Airways, passenger planes were not yet spanning the Pacific on a scheduled basis. Entertainment and ranking world figures enjoyed opulent ocean liner accommodations as large as any luxurious hotel suite, leisurely steaming toward the States. These were the final days of eased comfort before the adverb "posh" was replaced with "expedite."

A harbor pilot manned the helm while guiding large vessels through tricky waters of the basins unfamiliar to ship captains under foreign registry. So, with the opportunity to get a newsworthy story wrapped up by the time passengers disembarked, a harbor reporter's day usually began when he drove out to the two-story Pilot Station at the tip of Pier One that was in full view of outer harbor traffic. Here, he boarded the boat and sped out to the liner hove-to a mile off the breakwater. And when the seas were choppy, many a reporter lost his footing and fell into the Deep Six. But, above all, he never lost his camera.

Through the years, Chernus had interviewed personages the likes of Madam Chang Kai-shek, Eddie Rickenbacker, Zane Grey and Bounty trilogy authors Charles Nordhoff and James Norman

Hall when shuttling to-and-from Hawaii and Tahiti aboard Matson liners *Lurline*, *Monterey* and *Matsonia*. Among the movie personalities he interviewed and photographed were Fred Astaire, Clark Gable, Joan Crawford, Mary Pickford, Bing Crosby, Charlie Chaplin, Marion Davies (*always* Marion Davies), Harry Carey and Anna May Wong.

Also, there were situations which Dave and Bill fell into that drew them from their sumptuous aboard-ship champagne breakfasts and tete-a-tetes with idols of the ilk. Most often, it was in-house emergencies which dragged them from their warm beds. And then, too, they had a night editor named Hicks Coney from whom they never knew what to expect.

Coney could best be described as being slightly off true compass. He was forever having visions of great proportion. His revelation usually struck when things were quiet around town. An intense fellow, Coney always began his late night phone conversations with, "I didn't wake you, did I?"

This kind of intrusion came one very rainy night when he called Chernus. "For Christ sake, Hicks," said Bill, "it's past midnight."

"Sorry," said Coney, "but I got a tip that Point Fermin is going to fall off the side of San Pedro, and I want you to cover it!"

"Now where the hell did you get *that* tip from? *God*?!"

"From a better source than that!" said Coney.

Bill dressed in his foul weather gear and before heading out into the squall, phoned Dave Gershon.

"Did Hicks phone you, too?" Dave asked. "Jesus, does this nut realize Point Fermin's the size of a small city?"

The reporters later met at a public phone booth and after flipping a coin, Chernus made the first call. "Everything seems tight down here," Chernus reported.

"This heavy rain looks bad," said Coney, "so stick on it."

Thirty minutes later, it was Gershon's turn. "Weather's still bad."

"That the same phone booth Chernus called me from?" asked Coney.

"Is Bill on this story, too?"

"Yeah. Have him call me if you see him."

"Oh, I'll do *that* all right," said Gershon. Then after hanging up, to Bill: "Let's get the hell out of this miserable place; go to my house; dry off; have some drinks. If Point Fermin drops, we'll be able to hear the crash from there."

Through the night, Bill and Dave took turns phoning with variation about the possibilities of what might happen if a chunk of the State of California fell into the sea. And all the time, the two had their stockinged feet propped up on Gershon's coffee table among a collection of empty beer bottles.

Dave made his final call just before 8 a.m. as the sun was breaking through thinning storm clouds. Coney's last words were: "Well, if it's not going to happen on my shift, you might as well go home."

The fact that there was a distance of more that 100 miles between William Randolph Hearst's San Simeon castle and the *Los Angeles Examiner* was inconsequential when The Chief wanted something in a hurry. One night—late—I had to speed up to this most expensive house in the world, carrying a package of bitch pads for Marion's dachshund that was in heat.

Bill Chernus got stuck once when he had taken some negative up to the paper for a story follow-up in the home edition.

In ran Hicks Coney while Bill was sitting before a bull pen type-writer making up his weekly expense account. "*Stop everything!*" shouted Coney. "I just got a call from The Chief!"

"What the hell happened?" Bill asked.

"Do you know what *Peptinoids* are?"

"Something for the stomach?"

"I think so," said Coney. "Mr. Hearst wants a bottle of *Peptinoids* immediately. Go on out to an all-night drugstore and get a bottle of *Peptinoids*. How much money you got?"

Bill dug into his pocket and came up with "thirty-five cents ... How much you think it'll cost?"

"Probably very expensive," said Coney who must have been financially better off than the staff knew. He pulled some currency from his wallet and said: "Here's a fifty dollar bill. That should cover it."

Chernus had never held a fifty dollar bill before. "Why the hell didn't Mr. Hearst call the *San Francisco Examiner*?" he asked as he looked up the address of an all-night drugstore. "It's twice as close to San Simeon than here."

"Mr. Hearst doesn't trust the *San Francisco Examiner*," was Coney's illogical answer.

Having located the story, Bill asked the pharmacist if he knew what *Peptinoids* were. He did, and they were for the stomach.

"How much is a bottle?"

"Forty-nine cents."

"I'll take one."

"Do you want it *with* creosote, or *without*?" The pharmacist had thrown Bill a curve.

"Christ, I don't know. Just give me one of each." Then, "Do you have change for a fifty?"

The man in the white smock became suspicious. He took the bill, held it up to a light bulb and studied the engraved portrait of Ulysses S. Grant. "Where did you get this?"

"I'm a reporter on the *Examiner*, and Mr. William Randolph Hearst phoned to say he wanted a bottle of *Peptinoids* right away ... He lives in San Simeon, and when Mr. Hearst wants something ..."

"Are you crazy?" the pharmacist interrupted.

"No, I'm not crazy," said Chernus.

"Then Mr. Hearst must be crazy. He can get *Peptinoids* at his local drugstore."

"Would *you* like to tell that to Mr. Hearst?"

"Now, what if I didn't want to change this fifty dollar bill for Mr. Hearst ... and I didn't let you have the *Peptinoids* ... what would Mr. Hearst do then?"

"Well," said Bill scratching his head, *"you know what he did to Cuba."*

Back at the paper, Bill gave Coney his $49.02 in change and the stomach medicine was handed to a ready cyclist. In turn, the cyclist rushed the pills to the Glendale Airport where a chartered airplane was standing by to fly the package to San Simeon . . . and an hour later, Mr. Hearst taking his *Peptinoids* . . . *with* or *without* creosote.

First woman to break the harbor beat sex barrier was a dark-haired, brown-eyed, tough, but feminine-when-she-wanted-to-be gal named Mary Neiswender. No matter how drastically the elements changed, Mary always wore a dress and high heels while on assignments.

A first-generation Yugoslavian, Mary came to the harbor beat during my last year on the *Her-Ex*. She represented the *Long Beach Press-Telegram*. And alluding to my description of Agness Underwood, a woman had to put out that extra effort to survive in a newspaperman's world. But Mary had one strong advantage over the boys in the pressroom. She was fluent in the tongues spoken by most of the people making a living around the harbor. Having been raised in the area, Mary could speak four languages.

"I'm sure the guys must have groused a lot when they found out I was being assigned to the pressroom on the third floor of the City Hall,[25]" she said. "All-in-all, though, they were real gentlemen, more often real drunk gentlemen."

But reporters went to the trouble to make room. The first day Mary walked in, all waited to greet her . . . including an assortment of detective.

The initial thing to hit Mary's eye was a fake geranium stuffed in a cracked earthen pot on her desk where a quickly devised nameplate stated: MARY NEISWENDER.

---

[25]This was after the Cabrillo Theatre building had been demolished.

From walls to ceiling, the pressroom was filled with blowup pictures of nude women; antecedents to the *Playboy Magazine* centerfolds. However, the walls at the corner that were frizzied up for Mary contained several heroic *male* nudes.

Mary also said her introduction was the last time reporters brought up the subject of her sex, skirt or high heels. She said: "From then on, they fought as hard against me as they did against each other for a story break. And after working the harbor beat, the competition for me elsewhere was a breeze."

A month after Mary checked in, an ambulance and *Code 20* call came over the shortwave radio. Two longshoremen were trapped beneath an overturned barge in the harbor. Rescue workers were in the process of righting the barge when reporters arrived. But in order to get good rescue pictures, they had to climb a tall stack of unstable lumber. This posed a problem for Mary because she was wearing a skirt and high heels. Other reporters refused to help her. But a new-found Italian longshoreman friend recognized that she was having trouble. The forklift operator rolled his rig over, lowered his pallet and Mary hopped on. He raised her as high as the lift would go. As a result, she ended up twice as high as the others and got more dramatic shots of the rescue.

On another occasion Mary was forced to climb a tall ladder in a dry dock yard to get pictures of workers scaling barnacles from a ship's hull. As she preceded Charlie Crawford up the ladder, the *Times* reporter reneged his promise and cried out so everyone could hear: "Jesus, Mary . . . why the hell don't you wear pants?!"

"That moment," said Mary, "I thought every Yugoslavian, Italian and Mexican within earshot could speak English."

Mary learned much from the police, too. "Those were also the days when reporters didn't consider cops *bad*, and vice versa. I'll never forget when detectives were pulling up a woman's body in a gunny sack from the harbor channel," said Mary. "She was a nurse who'd been killed, then dumped in the water about eight days earlier." She said she wanted to follow the lead of Bevo Means and his impeccable stories about the Black Dahlia. "So I wanted to know more about her description, hair color . . . Did she have painted nails?"

Mary didn't take heed when a detective said: "You don't really want to see this, kid." She remembers Chernus raising his eyebrows. Then someone opened the sack and Mary looked in.

"I guess everyone except me pretended to have a good time about it," she said. "The dead nurse's fingernails were red, but I was green. I don't think I ate for a week."

To keep up with the veterans, Mary continued to take advantage of everything and anything she had going for her. "If I didn't know everyone in the harbor, I'd find out the rest were relatives." Her multilingual talents helped her beat the opposition when a major bank robbery occurred. "There was a teller engaged to the daughter of a high-up Mafioso in town," she said. "The teller disappeared shortly after 'cooperating' with the robbers."

The teller's parents spoke no English, so Mary went on with her interview, conversing with the missing clerk's parents in Serbo-Croation. She learned much of the teller's last activity before taking French Leave. Reporters were furious because she wouldn't share the information. This way, Mary had enough leads to go on and keep ahead of the other reporters.

"As the boys in the pressroom bitched," said Mary, "I reminded them they'd told me when I first arrived that they would give me 'no quarter' just because I was a female."

Mary remained in the newspaper business for several years after I left. She had become such a good writer by that time that the Long Beach Press-Telegram had her driving the 25 miles between the harbor and L.A. covering noteworthy trials. They worked her hard, but she thrived on it. The proof of her writing abilities came when the wire services picked up her stories.

What got Mary started on her long commutes was when she covered the murder trial of one of her San Pedro deputy district attorneys named Jack Kirschke.

"Kirschke found out his wife, Elaine, was having a love affair with an airplane pilot named Bill Drankhan," she said. "Kirschke, who was politically readying himself to run for a judgeship, waited in ambush until his wife and Drankhan were going hard at it in his master bedroom. There, he shot them both very dead."

Kirschke was handed down a death sentence, but this was commuted to a term of imprisonment shorter than the press had expected.

"Kirschke had a nasty habit of threatening people," Mary pointed out. "But to start with, I had dug up a lot about him as a D.A. and published it as an expose. He dearly hated me for this and when I was covering the trial, he had access to a phone and he called me and threatened me with no uncertain words that he was going to have me killed.

"And to put an ending to the story," Mary laughed, "when the son-of-a-bitch was released from prison, I was assigned to do the story. I said to my editor: What the hell are you trying to do to me? This crazy guy wants me *dead*." But being the newspaperwoman she was, Mary did the interview. "Either Kirschke had done a good job on prison psychiatrists, or some of his hate had worn thin during his stay," she said, "because he greeted me like an old friend."

Mary won several awards for her exclusive interviews and was twice nominated for the Pulitzer Prize. The first came when she doggedly pursued then California Governor Ronald Reagan with features successfully urging him to keep the state's mental hospitals open.

The second came in 1969 after covering the ghastly murders of film director Roman Polansky's young pregnant wife, Sharon Tate, three jet-setters and the caretaker's friend at Polansky's Benedict Canyon home. The slayings were dubbed "The Charles Manson Murders."

A few months before August 9, Manson had visited movie star-singer Doris Day's son, Larry Melcher. Melcher, a song publisher, had promised to record one of Manson's pieces and Manson visited him in his Beverly Hills home. After that, Melcher avoided Manson, so, in a temper, Manson sent four of his young cult members to the house to kill Melcher.

The unsupervised kids, Susan Atkins, Charles "Tex" Watson, Patricia Krenwikle and Linda Kasabian, arrived to discover the house was no longer being rented by Melcher. This made no matter, though. The youngsters were hopped up with drugs and they lit into Sharon, her companion Voykek Frykowski, coffee-heiress Abigail Folger and hair-stylist Jay Sebring. Knifing and strangling them all, Susan stabbed pregnant Sharon several times and later told Mary she had also tasted Sharon's blood.

Before killing the jet-setters, they knifed the caretaker's friend, Steven Parent.

The killers had reported to Manson that the victims had "screamed like banshees" before being killed. So vexed was Manson that he led his followers to a nondescript home in the Los Feliz area to show them how to kill people quietly. He tied up storekeeper Leon LaBianco and his wife, Rosemary, then commanded his cult members to kill the two.

During the trial, Mary came to know Charles Manson on a personal basis. And when Manson finally decided to tell what the prosecution had not known to date—exactly what had gone on during the murders—he said:

"Mary Neiswender is the only person I'll tell it all to."

For her stirring story of Manson's confession, Mary was nominated this second time for the Pulitzer. She was also elected Newspaperwoman of the Year.

There came a time when Mary said police were covering up the mysterious death of a young black athlete found hanged in a Signal Hill jail cell.

"I just couldn't let it die," she said, "in spite of my paper wanting to steer free from the story after it's initial piece. There'd been previous stories leaked out about racial prejudice in the Signal Hill police department."

The athlete was 22-year-old Ron Settle. He had gone to college on a scholarship and had several pro-football contracts offered him.

"He had a good reputation," said Mary, "and everything to live for." But she said she didn't like the way the paper was handling the story . . . or her.

The *Press-Telegram's* action became so odious that Mary walked into the city room and gave her editor the very same two words I had offered Jim Richardson when I quit him some years earlier. The second was the acceptable "you," and the first was an Anglo-Saxon word that galvanized the personal pronoun.

Because it was tough, Beacon Street took a long time to die. Along with the sailors and 100,000 shipyard workers, San Pedro was a place for thousands more soldiers from the induction center at Fort MacArthur to stroll the live-wire avenue.

In the bars hunched together along Beacon Street, Nat King Cole got his start working from a little white piano in the middle of the dance floor at the Club Del Rio. And there were Andy Russell, black entertainer Nellie Letcher, the Mills Brothers and Billy Eckstein. Also, Spike Jones, Ozzie Nelson and Sammy Kaye, who brought in crowds.

A few years after the war, however, commerce came to a sudden stop. People began to disappear. Gone now were the thousands of soldiers and shipyard workers. The Navy moved to Long Beach, and eventually to San Diego. The canneries, along with the fish, had vanished. The city was beginning to take on the look of a ghost town. Whores, gamblers and con men traveled to places like Las Vegas. But the few who didn't know where to go, or were too old to migrate, stayed on, hoping for yesterday to return.

It was when a project called "urban development" was being launched that Shanghai Red died.

Indian Mae West had finished her time on Beacon Street a few months earlier, worn out at the age of 50. It was when I attended her funeral that I felt the cold finger of perdition finally pointing condemningly at the street.

Indian Mae had closed down her whore house and joined the Salvation Army a few years before her death. Early every Sunday morning, she had shown up a Seventh Heaven to lecture to the prostitutes who had been locked up for the night, awaiting bail. Mae never turned in the money she collected in the bars. Rather, she bought magazines, cigarettes, lipstick, stockings and badly needed soap to distribute to the locked-up girls.

Those who heard it could never forget Indian Mae's fire-and-brimstone sermons delivered while standing on a chair in the holding tank behind prison bars.

"Now, I want all you damned whores to listen to me!" she would cry, smacking her fist in her palm. "I used to be just like you ... Back then, I owned a whore house ... Then I came to see the errors of my ways ... and repented ... Now, I want you to get down on your God-damned knees ... and I want you to pray to the good Lord to forgive you just like he forgave me!"

The girls who went to their knees got the lipstick and stockings and soap. But to those who didn't, and put out their hands for gifts, Indian Mae said: "Go fuck yourself!"

Bill Chernus said he thought the street was beginning to die when he left the *Examiner* in 1959 to take a public relations job with the Harbor Department. Mary Neiswender said it was the day Beacon Street suffered a heart attack when a black wreath was tacked on the pagoda doors of Shanghai Red's.

Hundreds of Red's pals—prostitutes, panderers, seamen, cabbies, hustlers and street people—filed past his casket to say good-bye. Others stood on the curbs crying as the big man's cortage detoured from the usual route to pass by his saloon and the drunks who couldn't make it to the mortuary.

"Then characters like Round the World Whitey, Stormy Weather, the Wandering Jew, Dog-Faced Pat and Sweet and Sour began to disappear," said Mary. "Pawn shops fell like toothpicks. The Fern Hotel was condemned by the Immigration Department for obvious reasons, died a dusty death under the battering of a wrecker's ram. The Alhambra and Anchor hotels were closed by court order—described as 'houses of prostitution.' "

The only legitimate edifice left on the street was a decorative fountain put up by the Women's Christian Temperance Union in case someone happened to want a drink of water. But it was used more often as a leaning post for drunks taking a recess between bars.

Even the once-beautiful WCTU fountain—splattered, chipped and generally abused—went dry on the wettest corner in the world.

WAITING FOR THE SHIP TO COME IN—A 1945 study of *Examiner* harbor reporter Bill Chernus resting dockside between assignments with camera.

FOURTH OF JULY FIZZLE— Famous swimmer Florence Chadwick (wrapped in blanket, center) was kidnapped by Fowler after failing to cross Catalina Channel. Her exclusive interview was radioed to Fowler's paper while his promoted yacht cruised a half-mile off shore. "Tarzan" movie star Johnny Weismuller (white captain's hat) and Fowler (dark captain's hat) assist Chadwick from boat.

Short Takes

When fighting time to get a story in the paper before deadline, a copyboy would stand behind a rewrite man and rip copy from his typewriter—usually at the end of each paragraph—then run it to the city desk. The rewrite man would continue until he finished, or the city editor said, "Cut it off."

In newspaper vernacular, this was known as sending over a story in "short takes."

Another meaning of the expression referred to non-newsy short paragraphs containing a single piece of information. It was separated from other paragraphs with an asterisk.

Another drift of short takes involved stories collected along the way by reporters. And somehow, they seemed to be too good to throw away. Often times, they were copied and passed around to be shared by reporters on other newspapers. Most of the short accounts were not earth-shaking stories, but they were always unique. Some had to do with didoes performed by newsmen on the job in pursuit of getting his story. Some were also too vulgar to make the paper.

The following has to do with the didoes and the vulgar:

I had covered a murder-suicide that lacked the sensational hills and valleys of news interest. It was also closed on the homicide's books. However, I was obsessed with trying to straighten out one aspect of the crime which would put it back on police records as being a double murder.

To back up my theory, I first had to locate a detective friend named Chick. He had been on the case where a husband and wife were found shotgunned to death. My photog had taken a picture of the grizzly scene and his photo showed the husband's index finger on the shotgun's trigger. When he had turned the weapon on himself, the only way the husband could get off a shot would have been to use his *thumb*. This meant that there must have been a third party there after the man's death to place the gun incorrectly in his hand.

If I could get a witness to corroborate this, I'd continue to be a pain in the ass to homicide after reaching one of two conclusions: Either the husband had been murdered, or for some yet unknown reason, a shoddy detective had placed the dead man's hand on the trigger after he was dead.

Chick wasn't answering any of my phone calls, so it took beatman Bill Zelinsky to flush him out for me. Bill told me Chick damned near lost his job and was presently being disciplined for lifting a case of hard liquor from the scene of the crime. After admitting the deed, Chick was placed on probation, but his partner, who owned up to swiping a shotgun from the scene, was kicked off the force. The watch Chick drew was most distasteful. He was assigned for three months to sit in a row of toilet booths in the men's room of the downtown Pacific Electric Red Car trolley station waiting for sex deviates to thrust their joy sticks through the "glory hole" bored between two booths, then make arrests for crime of various sexual nature.

I found where Chick was trolling and sat down on the throne next to his. In these adverse conditions, Chick told me the dead man's thumb, indeed, had been on the shotgun trigger, but his partner had taken a shine to the expensive shotgun and stolen it. He knew there were no bore marks on shotgun pellets, so he replaced the weapon with a cheap model from the wall. In doing so, the new ex-cop had clumsily placed the dead man's index finger on the trigger.

With the first part of my theory blown and the second being unpublishable unless my paper wanted to instigate a feud between itself and the police department, I was about to leave when I heard the lock click shut to a third booth.

Chick and I stopped talking. A few minutes later a stranger tapped on Chick's compartment wall. This was followed by some obscene words and Chick took up the conversation.

When some sort of agreement was reached, the stranger slipped his baton through the hole in the partition. And with a length of strong fishing line already secured to the wash basin, Chick adroitly slipped its noose around the mushroom head and yanked it tight.

Entrapment had not yet been entered into the state's law books at the time, so Chick went around, kicked in the booth door and handcuffed his suspect. Chick also refused to release the tight noose from the greatly-shrunken organ until his prey stopped screaming.

I had blown my theories about the murder-suicide, but what had happened turned out to be a fascinating experience and I could hardly wait to get to Betty's Broadway Circle bar to relate the story there.

Usually, I was assigned a story first thing in the morning and was off with my photog without breakfast. This went on for too long a time and I told Aggie this much. She said she hadn't noticed, so sent me off to the Pantry following the 7:15 deadline.

I'd crawled in a filled car and we were off, but on the way, I noticed a woman in the front seat of a parked car on Ninth Street. Her head was thrown back and she looked very dead.

"Hold it," I said. "I want to look at something." Perry Fowler saw it too, and we both got out while the rest went to break-fast. One reporter promised to call the desk about the woman in the car.

Close-up, Perry and I saw that the woman had shot herself in the chest with a horse pistol. She looked about forty years old and her cheeks were puffed and discolored, obviously from a beating.

I noted the fingers of her right hand had an indelible purple on them. I thought she might be an accountant and the purple came from handling an adding machine.

Then I went through her purse which was laying on the seat while Perry shot his pictures. I took down her home address and read a short note that had been left beside her. It said she had left her husband who was presently serving time in the county jail for burglary. She had grown tired of his beatings.

When detectives arrived, I handed one the note and the other gave Perry and me a lift back to the paper.

Perry handed his negs to the inside man and we headed for the Hall of Justice where the dead woman's husband was locked up on the 13th floor.

Wearing a white short-sleeved skivvy shirt, he entered the room where I waited. He was tattooed from the neck down to the cufflines on his wrists.

Instead of showing any kind of grief when I told him his wife was dead—and how she got that way—the guy broke into a rage and it took two jailers to subdue him.

After he was under control, I learned his wife had been a well-known tattoo artist along Main Street. So expert that he'd married her. (It was the ink from an electric tattoo needle that had discolored her fingers).

Holding out his arms after stripping off his skivvy shirt, he displayed her art work for me. "She done all this. She was somethin' else. I wouldn't let nobody touch me with the needle but her."

Then, gritting his teeth, he said: "That lousy son-of-a-bitch of a bitch. She was workin' on my back on somethin' really big." Then, "Look!"

He turned his back to me and sure enough, it was entirely covered with an admixture of scabs and an heroic landscape scene.

"I was just healin' up from our third session," he growled. "How the hell does that bitch get off killin' herself when she's only half-done? It was the biggest thing she done yet: *The Rock of Ages.*"

I wasn't allowed to write about these remarkable facets and the story, that only stayed in the paper for two editions, just went three paragraphs.

There was also a two paragraph story I covered that had a unique twist I couldn't mention because it might be considered too inhumane. It was about a young escape artist who was given special leave from San Quentin where he was serving time for second degree murder. Under heavy guard, he was allowed to attend his father's funeral. In order not to risk his escape, guards had him handcuffed to his father's casket.

William Randolph Hearst had a thing about animals. This was reflected by the private zoo he maintained in San Simeon. Also, when the news was slow, we reporters had an abundance of animal stories to cover.

On one such afternoon, some damned "tipster" phoned in about a dead dog in the street with a mutt in nearby vigil. I got the story and left with photog Buck Forbes. On the way, I picked up a piece of raw hamburger to stick under the dead dog's neck to lure the mutt so that it would look like it was grieving for my photographer.

But when I stuffed the hunk of hamburger under the dead dog's neck, the mutt refused to eat it, opting to make love to the corpse. As a result, Forbes and I caused an awful stir with my trying to pull the deviate from the dead bitch's behind . . . with Forbes photographing the whole thing.

"You filthy men!" cried one of those who had by now gathered. "You're *sick*," said a woman. "You oughta be locked up!" cried another at the scene. And when a man threw a stone at us, we got the hell out of there without any pictures we could publish.

Along with collecting gallows humor (last words of the condemned before execution), reporters also took interest in asking where several jailed alcoholic felons used to hide their booze. Pretending that newspapers weren't really circumspect, I thought a compilation of these inventive hiding places would one day make a good feature story.

There were the usual places: The inside of vacuum cleaner bags, in the toilet water chamber and in freezer ice trays. But it took a good creative criminal to come up with the unique places, where no one would ever think to look.

I interviewed a wealthy valley man who got hauled in by police for wife-beating while under the influence. Being his first offense—and having a lot of money for an effective attorney— the judge let him off with a stiff fine. He was allowed probation with the proviso that he would not drink or have alcoholic beverages on his property for an entire year.

But before she would let him back into the house, his healing wife threw out all the corked and uncorked hooch from the premises.

However a month later, figuring he wasn't an alcoholic after all, our affluent rancher started erratically driving his tractor when he emerged from his orange groves.

The wife and concerned neighbors—who hated the man anyway—were unable to locate where he was hiding his vodka.

After a time, the anger ebbed to disinterest because our boy was toeing the line in the area of violence. But while entering the grove unannounced one day, his wife caught him standing next to one of his orange trees and sucking hard from a long green tube. It seemed our foxy rancher had been drinking from these tubes which led up to a half-dozen strategically placed green douche bags he'd cleverly camouflaged behind the leaves of his fruit trees.

When the automobile spray windshield cleaner was first introduced, a shrewd Grand Theft Auto felon devised a way to bore a hole through the fire wall of one of his stolen vehicles. Then he rerouted the water supply tube that sprayed the windshield when the wipers were operating. He had also filled the tube's reservoir with gin, and any time he wished to have a drink, he would merely turn on the windshield wiper.

Something else never referred to in print was when reporters arrived on the scene of a liquor store blaze. Firemen would get very irate when we kicked their high hip boots, listening for the clink of bottles they might be sneaking out of the place.

There was a nurse I once interviewed after she was cleared of a murder charge. She had lost her license after passing out while attending a patient under intensive care. Shortly afterwards, there was an explosion in her small apartment that killed her husband. Arson investigators said the explosion hadn't been caused by a leaky gas valve. Therefore, our heavy-drinking Florence Nightingale was being held under suspicion. She finally broke down under questioning, saying: "I thought I'd hidden my bottle of rum very well from my husband. He was trying to get me to stop drinking so I hid my rum in the refrigerator where I thought he'd never find it. It was inside a big hollowed-out meatloaf, and any time I wanted a drink, I'd just open the front end of the meatloaf and take a swig. My husband must have found the meatloaf, and wanting to surprise me, he put it in the oven to cook."

This sounded reasonable to detectives and arson investigators returned to the exploded and burned out apartment. There, they found enough pieces of the 151 proof rum label to clear the nurse.

The original story had been good enough to carry a picture, but the reason for the explosion was never published in a follow up story.

When I interviewed a man for drunk driving during an overnight watch, he gave me a convoluted story which I ached to get into the paper, but the news editor killed it because the O. Henry ending was too vulgar to print. And without it, there was no story.

Late getting home, our D.W.I. said he'd drunk half of a pint bottle of vodka when a physical emergency came up. He had to take a leak in the worst way.

"I was late and didn't want to take the time to stop," he said. "And I couldn't pee all over the family car, no matter how hard I had to go. The smell alone would have been terrible ... but the drive home was long."

He had one alternative: He was too frugal to empty the half-filled vodka bottle, but there was no other place to go, so he went in it.

"But arresting officers said they found an empty bottle in the car," I said.. "There was no vodka."

"I know," said the remorseful fellow. "I could hardly drink it."

When Al Stump was writing a classic sports piece about the first player to be voted into Baseball's Hall of Fame—Ty Cobb— this fierce competitor lay dying of cancer in a northern California hospital. The feature Stump was writing had to do with the stubborn process Cobb went through before giving up to death.[26] But it was edited out of Stump's piece how Cobb successfully fooled his doctors about where he had his vodka in his hospital room. His nurses were also keeping a twenty-four hour watch over the fallen gladiator, also trying to discover the mystery of the hiding place.

Cobb finally surrendered his life and the nurse of duty, following the routine, removed his dentures from the water glass next to his bed and replaced them in the dead ballplayer's mouth. She suspiciously sniffed the air. "This water glass doesn't have water in it," she said ... "This water glass had vodka in it."

Who was the one who had been getting the hard stuff to Cobb? It was Al Stump, naturally. At night, Al would noose a bottle to the cord dangling outside Cobb's first story window. And when his nurse took a short break, the dying man gathered enough energy to haul it in.

"One night when I found the full bottle still dangling from the end of the cord," said Stump, "I knew Ty was dead."

There were occasions, however, when a crafty rewrite made it in print with his otherwise unpublishable story. This was achieved by misdirection or double entendre. Jack Smith was a master with this ploy.

On a particular occasion, there was a woman found nude and dead. Before the autopsy report came in, Jack's story was sparse with detail. But along with the mystery of it all, and in the description of the body, he reported something that went through all

---

[26]Hearst executive feature writer Bob Considine said Stump's 1961 *True Magazine* piece on Ty Cobb, "Fight To Live," was "... the best sports piece I have ever read."

editions of the day. He wrote: "The body had been tattooed. On one, it said, '*Sweet,*' and on the other, '*Sour.*'"

At a later time, Jack wrote about a priest who had died in bed of a heart attack while a client at a whore's residence on Lysol Hill (better known as Bunker Hill). Smith did the piece, but, naturally, didn't write that the dead man was a Catholic clergyman. But not to make his story vague to the attentive reader, he mentioned the following at the end of his piece:

> Draped over a chair next to the double bed was a black coat and matching black trousers. The detachable collar was starched and white. There was no necktie.

HARRY WATSON & FRIEND—When posing with boxers, normal people do it face-to-face. Not photographer Harry Watson (left) sneaking a rabbit punch on heavyweight champion Muhammud Ali. Harry's never posed for a normal picture in his life.

AUTHOR GENE FOWLER'S final inteview with *Times Syndicate* columnist Jack Smith.

XVI

"Quick, Watson, the Camera . . ."

A few years before he made his solo flight over the Atlantic Ocean to Paris in 1927, Charles A. Lindbergh was a barnstormer. He was hired to fly to a mid-west city where there had been a flood disaster. He was to deliver negative film to two different newsreel agencies in New York. One photographer calamitously trusted his competition cameraman to deliver his undeveloped film to Lindbergh. But when the Lone Eagle picked up the film, the foxy newsman who had been trusted by the other photog, handed the aviator his own precious record of the flood . . . along with a roll of blank film that would be delivered to his competition's office. When the film was found out to be blank, Lindbergh was the first at hand to unjustly receive the betrayed news agency executive's broadside. From then on, Lucky Lindy never liked news photographers, or their affiliates, or their constituents.

Fortunately, my suspicious nature would never have allowed me to be that gullible and trusting.

The opposition, I always fought with like hell. But working with one's own photographer was an antithesis.

After being in the field for a time, certain photogs and reporters gravitated toward one-another. Whether by compatible nature or being able to nearly guess what the other's next move was going to be.

A reporter often came up with different picture angles for his cameraman, just as his photog would help with story ideas and quotes.

This became especially important for photogs guiding a cub through his early stories. George O'Day and Buck Forbes were veterans when I came along. They helped me with questions I should ask while covering a police story. They also saw me through cordoned lines with the sight of their 4x5 Speed Graphics held in one hand and a photo plate box slung from an opposite shoulder. To the public, this seemed to have a talisman effect.

When *Times* Pulitzer Prize reporter Gene Sherman was very young and covering a murder with his grizzly photog J.H. McCrory, the veteran suggested on the way back to the office that maybe a good angle not to overlook was that the police had found a Chinese fortune cookie in the dead man's hand. "Just happen to have it with me," said McCrory. It read: "You will live a long, happy life."

I've also seen my own photogs dare things only an imbalanced or very brave man would chance in order to get a picture that often times never made the paper.

Photogs were also great catalysts to break the ice with difficult subjects. They somehow had a gift in identifying themselves with a person in the news and place the interview on a casual plain. This was usually enhanced in that news photographers rarely had been too shackled by inhibitions.

I've also seen my partners climb old wooden oil towers to shoot a close-up of a woman about to leap to her death, then talk her out of it. They also sneaked their cameras into closed meetings where opposing factions were volatile. I'd watched them nearly drown in a flooding river before I helped get them out. Sometimes they'd dash into an incinerating building with rafters collapsing about them . . . just to get the picture.

It was the photographer who was present when there was a raging strike battle being accented with clubs, steel helmets and fists with tear gas exploding all around. The reporter could fill in the blanks later, but it was the photog who was there the moment a mother kissed her dead child farewell after his body was dragged from a lake . . . And God help anyone who get in his way when he was taking a picture.

Among the five newsmen I knew as Pulitzer Prize winners, three of them were still photographers: Frank Filan, Joe Rosenthal and John L. Gaunt, Jr.

Frank Filan won the Prize in 1944 while attached to the Coast Guard when the United States Marines recaptured Tarawa. In their 168 years of existence, this was the Leathernecks' most coveted victory, taking that South Pacific island back from the Japanese. Of the 3,000 American assault troops, only 200 survived. Filan's photo showed a haggard soldier passing several bodies of his comrades with bowed palm trees in the background. Frank captioned his picture: *The Willingness to Die*.

Joe Rosenthal's was the most celebrated photograph to come out of World War II, if not the most dramatic picture ever shot with a still camera. It showed the planting of the American flag at Iwo Jima in 1943.

So vivid was Joe's picture of six Marines in the act of planting the flag at Mount Suribachi's peak that it became the model for our National Monument depicting WW II.

The third Pulitzer winner was John L. Gaunt, Jr., of the *Times*. And during the month after he received this high honor, he was tempted to return the award because of the grief it caused him and his wife.

It was in 1955 when a concerned neighbor ran into Gaunt's patio at Hermosa Beach where Johnny was sunning himself prior to reporting for work on the swing shift. There was a disturbance at the beach. It was believed that a child had drowned.

John ran to his car and headed to the scene where he saw a fire truck arriving. He pulled his camera from the trunk, hurried down the boardwalk, shooting as he ran toward two figures alone at the waterfront. This all happened within only a few minutes.

When he was about 100 yards away, Gaunt made that nth-of-a-second exposure which captured the images of a distraught man being restrained by his wife, holding him from rushing into the threatening waves that had just swallowed up his 19-month-old son.

When the Pulitzer came, so did the letters. The first was from William M. Gallagher of the *Flint* (Mich.) *Journal*, who won the

Pulitzer two year earlier. Because Gaunt's photo dealt with the death of a child, Gallagher warned him to prepare for brutal response from thoughtless people.

When she had learned of John's winning, the *Times* published a feature describing Mrs. Gaunt as "squealing with delight."

Among the hundreds of letters—mostly hate ones—a woman wrote: "I think your wife would have squealed louder if the picture had been taken of *you* instead of *by* you. Why didn't you burn the damned thing?"

A hypocritical attorney from Fulton, Mo., wrote: "How tragic the uncooperative baby did not—at the moment the picture was taken—show himself in the agony of death, poised on the crest of a wave!" The short-sighted attorney didn't realize Gaunt's picture was a warning to parents who didn't prudently watch after their children at the beach.

Until he received a letter from John McDonald of Hermosa Beach, the Gaunts were ready to chuck the medal and award money. But Mr. McDonald had congratulated Gaunt. Mr. McDonald was also *in* the picture. He was the father of the dead child.

A few of these men with the magic boxes I'd worked with were, in fact, walking history pages. Including the young and the old, their professional photographic careers had spanned a century.

George Hailey, who J.B.T. Campbell had on salary, shot the foremost picture of the 1906 San Francisco earthquake and fire disaster for Hearst's *Examiner*.

While drinking on the Barbary Coast the night before the quake hit, Hailey ended up sleeping in a whore's hotel room. When he awakened, Hailey wasn't certain how long he had been asleep because when he peered out the sixth story window, he knew something of great dimension had occurred. The entire city of San Francisco had been leveled and was smoldering. Hailey thought he'd better make a record of whatever happened from his high vantage point. He took his old Graflex camera (which resembled a laundry chute) and snapped his picture, the result of the earthquake he had slept through.

In his blurred mind, one fact stuck with George when he returned to bed with his whore: He knew he would be fired for being missing from the paper so long.

But when the remorseful Hailey turned in his Graflex, a lab man had the presence to develop his glass plates. Among them was this grand panoramic shot of a large section of San Francisco in smoking rubble. It was the photo we grew up with and are accustomed to seeing when we seek "Earthquake" and "San Francisco" in any encyclopedia.

Mr. Hearst was so pleased with George's picture, he was driven to say: "I always want a spot available for Mr. Hailey on a Hearst newspaper for the rest of his life."

When a photographer found himself late to cover a big story, only to discover he'd been scooped, it took imagination to muck his way out of the frightful situation.

One of the few female reporters of the time, Pony Garner of the *Daily News*, was caught in this situation. A nationally prominent politician suffering from severe depression was a patient at Good Samaritan. During an unguarded moment when his nurse had left his side, the politician had decided to end it all and leaped from his hospital room to his death.

By the time Pony arrived with her photog, the body, along with opposition paper reporters, had come and gone.

The enterprising Garner got hold of an attendant who had been on duty when the politician leaped. The attendant filled her in on the story and showed Pony the exact position of the body before it was carted off the the hospital's morgue. "Naturally," he said, "the photographers only took pictures of the blanket covering the body ... Otherwise, it would have been too gory."

Grateful it had been "too gory," Pony located a blanket and waited for hospital personnel to vacate the area. Then Garner lay down on the cement driveway leading to the emergency entrance and covered herself with the prop blanket, unscooping herself with the picture.

Some time later at a city room party, Pony came clean to art department head, Bob Moore. "Bob," said Pony, "that wasn't the real body under the blanket. It was me."

"I know," Mooore said matter-of-factly. "I had to air brush out your high heels."

I have always had a strong inclination to champion the newspaperwoman. Perhaps it was because there were so few of them. Also, the public was inept at fathoming how to treat them . . . or how they expected to be treated when being photographed or interviewed.

Kendis Rochlen of the *Mirror* appreciated my standing up for the newspaperwoman in times of pique. And when it was an unpopular attitude to share with male reporters.

I guess I turned hard-nosed about the way newspaperwomen were being mistreated while covering the vicious motion picture studio strike of 1946.

There were bad feelings between Warner Bros. Studio management and Herb Sorrell's striking painter's union. The nastiness evolved into fighting, a studio guard was shot. And tear gas began exploding along the picket line of union sympathizers.

When management and labor bargaining came to an impasse, editors were requested by Warner Bros. to have news representatives available to attend an informal management question and answer conference.

But for one combination photographer-reporter, we were all men. This woman journalist represented *The Daily Worker*, a newspaper accepted to be affiliated with the Communist Party. Therefore, on this ground, she was denied admittance to the conference.

It was unclear to me at the time if I was being emotionally moved to defend this woman's rights as a woman, or if I was championing her because she carried a legitimate newspaper police card entitling her to all legal privileges granted reporters— man or woman. In the final analysis, I was defending both aspects of the dilemma.

In any event, I refused to cover the conference unless this woman was passed into the studio along with the rest of us.

I pleaded her case on the spot, reasoning that if she wasn't allowed to shoot her pictures and participate in the Q. and A. session, The *Daily Worker* would probably publish stories more damning and distorted. Considering this theory, management allowed her to attend the meeting.

A female photographer—the only one I knew—worked for a metro. She was Helen Marie Brush. And as deceivingly feminine as she seemed, Helen needed no physical assistance from anyone when pursuing a picture.

Helen, a tall, handsome blonde, had been an instructress at a Hollywood rollerdome when she met Gib Brush who was there to do a photo layout of the place.

Gib proposed four times before Helen yielded. After their marriage, Gib took Helen off her skates and put her in a darkroom. She became proficient with the Speed Graphic, and when Gib went off to war, Helen stepped into his spot at the *Daily News*.

When Gib returned, the two became a husband-and-wife team.

When Helen gave birth to her child, she became the first and only woman—in my memory—to photographically record her own baby debuting into the world.

During my final year with the *Her-Ex*, Dave Gershon, who was still covering the harbor beat with Bill Chernus, fell into a situation which would become his final frustration in life.

I had vaguely heard of the story, but newsman Frank Petty further filled me in with the tale of *Sammy, the Skewered Sea Gull*.

It began when Gershon rolled out of bed one morning following a bar-crawling session with Chernus that had started at the Chateau Gardens, went through The Silver Dollar and Fern hotels and ended up at Shanghai Red's.

Dave walked the length of a San Pedro pier just after dawn, breathing deeply of the air, trying to detoxify before going on to look for his daily story. This had become slim-pickings now that national figures were choosing the airliners to-and-from Hawaii and the orient, passing up the leisure life aboard a luxurious liner. The harbor beat was slowly and miserably dying, a victim of progress.

While inhaling deeply of the fresh air, Dave spied what he though was an apparition. It looked like a sea gull with a long arrow thrust right through his body. The old gull was real and it was quietly perched atop a mooring. And that damned wooden missile with arrowhead sticking out one end and feathers out the other rhythmically waiving to-and-fro like a conductor's baton while the aloof bird preened.

Dave cursed himself because he'd broken the photographer's prime commandment: *Thou shalt take thy camera with thee whither thou goest.*

Gershon reasoned no one else in the world had ever taken a picture of a live sea gull with an arrow stuck right through it's belly. But there he was: Sammy, the skewered sea gull.

Dave foggily remembered that such a bird existed. But the one who told him about it was an old salt who mumbled over a mug of rum.

"Dave thought it was a spurious story," said Frank Petty. "But now, on this fateful morning, Sammy was posing as if he was begging Dave to take his picture."

So overwhelmed was Gershon at seeing this picture-of-pictures possibility, he rushed home for his camera. But when he returned, Sammy had flown off.

From that day on, no matter what story he was covering in order to justify his remaining on the harbor beat before that whole God-damned city of San Pedro disappeared, Dave would take French Leave if word came that his hide-and-seek Sammy was in the vicinity.

It finally came to Dave that he must become canny. He began hiding out on the beach for days at a time—sometimes nights. He scanned the sky—through a peephole he had bored in the hull of an overturned beached dinghy.

One afternoon a waterfront informer tapped on the dinghy. Dave crawled from hiding, brushing sand from his face and ears. He was told the elusive Sammy was hanging out at Pier Point Landing.

Petty said it was a rugged 15 miles "as the Gershon flies," and Dave puffed up the pier only to be told by one of the many aware of his hang-up, that Sammy had winged back to his home port; back nearby the dinghy. It was apparent that while Dave had been birdwatching, Sammy had been Gershon-watching.

Then Petty went into a description as though he was reporting on The Mad Hatter of *Alice in Wonderland*:

"The ungullible gull, probably realizing he'd run Dave aground for good, decided on a master stroke to end the game and put him out of his misery.

"Sammy floated around Terminal Island until he spotted a *Life* photographer strolling near the Naval Barracks. Sammy whistled for his attention and landed in front of him. He waited while the man got out his portrait lens and focused in the ground glass, then patiently posed for a series of shots."

When *Life* hit the stands with Skewered Sammy as the full page "Picture of the Week," it was only a matter of minutes before Jim Richardson got hold of Gershon, wanting to know why he hadn't taken this picture that had been living beside him for many a moon. On the phone, Richardson sounded louder than an Italian tenor:

"What the hell does that God-damned initial 'L' in your God-damned name stand for? *Lousy*? or *Lunkhead*?"

No one seems to know what finally became of Sammy, the Skewered. But before he died, the locals used to see Dave Gershon down along the beach at dusk—a shabby, shadowy figure at water's edge, listening to the waves with eyes glazed over, unless—as it sometimes happened—a sea gull settled down on the sand nearby.

Then Dave's red-rimmed eyes would take on a fitful look. He would cackle like a madman and run after the gull and savagely kick at it . . . but always too late.

There were these six brothers, see? Their names were all Watson. And they had an uncle named George Watson who sold his first photograph in 1899 and was awarded a credit line and a bag of jelly beans. Uncle George's picture was of the Colorado State Capitol, and an enterprising Denver general store owner put it in his window. And below the by line, he printed: "If a nine-year-old boy can take a photograph this good, think what YOU can do with our new Brownie No. 1!"

George's father, a Salvation Army Colonel, moved his family to Los Angeles, and during President William McKinley's visit, Uncle George took his picture on the steps of the old city hall on Second and Broadway. McKinley was the first of an unbroken line of ten presidents Uncle George would photograph.

The six Watson brothers in order of the calendar were named Coy, Harry, Delmar, Garry, Billy and Bobs. They all have been newspaper photographers.

I met Harry after World War II and although on opposition papers, we enjoyed each other's company while covering stories. We have remained friends throughout the years, principally because we share similar outlooks regarding the flotsam of interesting characters we have met, mostly of whom never made any front page.

Before becoming a news photographer, Harry Watson strung out his youth as a child actor, appearing in principal roles in the 1930s with Jimmy Stewart, Shirley Temple, Harold Lloyd, Wallace Beery, Fred Astaire, Jimmy Durante and Ronald Colman.

I chronicled Harry in *The Second Handshake* (Lyle Stuart: 1980) about when he appeared with W.C. Fields in Mack Sennett's 1933 short subject, *The Barber Shop*. The redoubtable comedian personally cast his child actors because he was always on the lookout for a boy to shuttle his drinks with dispatch between set and dressing room. Harry was the most adroit in this function and he won the part.

In 1941, Harry enlisted in the Coast Guard, and as a combat photographer, made four South Pacific assault landings in 1944. He was wounded in the first Leyte landing he made with Frank Filan. Harry was subsequently awarded the Purple Heart, and in later years when someone would say, "Oh, you were in the Coast Guard during the war. Then you didn't have to go overseas, did you?"

"Obviously you didn't go overseas to find out," Harry would say.

Watson's combat photographic experiences in World War II made him appear more rugged and husky in appearance than he was when he left for overseas. But he still retained the "you don't have to give me the crap" smile when a reporter was embellishing a story he'd just covered. Nor did his high-pitched voice change.

Each time Harry went on his first assignment, he'd say to himself: "This is going to be the best story of the day."

Beyond his picture taking, it is Harry's wit and puckish sense of humor that survives. He also was always a very quotable guy.

When Harry is cited in the company of one from the present generation, the young person tends to say, "Oh, that's old."

"Certainly it's old," says the old-timer. "Maybe 30, 40 years old. But that was how long ago Watson said it."

Watsonisms would surface. Things such as when someone remarked: "Didn't you notice? I lost 20 pounds." To wit, Harry said, "Turn around. I think I found it." Or when Harry was watching a group of lecherous photographers studying a large-bosomed lady. Harry shrugged: "If you've seen one, you've seen 'em both."

The Watson story with the greatest mileage came when Harry had been refused entrance to a cemetery where 21 gun military rites were being held for four World War II soldiers killed in action and just returned home. Presence of their Gold Star mothers promised to make a strong photographic statement.

But Harry wasn't allowed entrance to the walled cemetery to take his pictures. With retribution in mind, he visited a local poultry store where he purchased an unplucked dead duck hanging outside the vendor's display window. Then he enlisted a Mexican boy to his confidence. He handed him the dead duck, then after reviewing specific instructions for the boy to wait outside the cemetery wall until he heard a loud signal, they returned to the cemetery.

Harry finally gained entrance, promising to stand inconspicuously in the rear and not disturb the military ceremony by using a flash bulb.

The Mexican boy patiently stood outside the wall with his dead duck, waiting for "the signal."

The only thing windy on this sultry day was the minister's sermon. It drew the Gold Star mothers further into remorse.

The chrome-helmeted, white-gloved, cravated honor guard and their sergeant quietly endured, sweating in their heavy woolen uniforms.

The moment for the 21-gun salute eventually arrived, and with orderly precision, the spit-and-polish sergeant clicked his soldiers carrying chrome rifles into position with several grunting "hutt-hutt" commands:

"Ha-*ready!*"

The seven cocked their pieces.

"Ha-*haim!*"

The seven pointed their rifles skyward in preparation for the first of three volleys.

"Ha-*fire!*"

This was undoubtedly the signal for the Mexican boy. And with accurate trajectory, he heaved the dead duck's carcass over the wall.

The bird's body landed a few feet from where the honor guard stood, and nearly a minute passed before the guard regained enough order to get off the next two volleys.

But during this pause, the Four Star mothers broke out into uncontrolled laughter.

There comes a time when one has to take special notice when progress gallops past him, especially if he has settled too comfortable into the easy, pragmatic pursuits of his profession.

This was a painful process for Harry Watson to go through after he began watching television cameramen covering fast-breaking stories on a regular basis.

TV news no longer had to cope with overweight cameras too cumbersome to move about on tripods. Now, the seven local and network stations had installed the latest photographic equipment to completely process 16-millimeter motion picture film for airing uncut in twenty minutes.

This alone had dramatically overtaken the newspapers from coverage time to one-the-street sales by a good three hours. This was a blow, and it made the *extra* obsolete. Now, TV news had the authority to interrupt scheduled programs and air bulletins as they came in.

The Watson brothers were all over town and it was rare when you didn't run into one covering a story. Harry was on the Daily News, and when it folded to merge with the *Mirror* (to become the *Mirror-News*), he decided he would hit the newspapers for an honest try. If this didn't work, he decided to make the break and go over to television.

Jim Richardson, who prided himself as being the firingest city editor in the west, had Watson come in for an interview. When Harry showed, Richardson asked: "Are you one of George Watson's sons?"

"George Watson is my uncle," said Harry.

"Good," said Richardson. "You're hired. Come in on Monday morning."

Watson said, "Okay," and turned to leave.

"Now," said Richardson, "you're fired." He smiled and said to his staff: "I always wanted to fire a Watson."

This broke Dick O'Connor's record for short-time employment. Dick worked an entire morning before getting into an argument with Richardson and being fired. Watson had lasted less than a minute.

This did it. Too many newspapers were going under all over the country. Harry figured he had good time on the 35-mm Imo in combat. Switching over to the 16-mm Filmo camera was no big deal. He went over to KTTV and was hired on the spot.

Harry joined Wayne Clegg at KTTV, and the first piece of scuttlebutt he heard was that Klaus Landsberg was at it again at KTLA. He was working on an innovation to refine a remote TV camera sending unit, trying to trim it down to a weight of 650 pounds by the use of transistors. Landsberg figured he could fit the unit in a helicopter. In this manner, KTLA would be able to get to the scene of a news story long before news teams on the ground arrived. In addition, the helicopter would be capable of covering expanded action in a dramatic panoramic view, which had never been done before. It could *hover*.

As time passed, KTLA crews were kidded by other cameramen with remarks such as, "Does Landsberg still have his remote unit on a diet?" and "When're ya gonna come *swooping* down from the sky on us, fellahs?"

Harry would never forget the day this became a shocking reality. I took place at an expanded site bulldozed flat at the border of East Los Angeles called Chavez Ravine. It was about a week before Walter O'Malley would break ground for his new Los Angeles Dodgers baseball stadium in 1959.

A court order of eviction was about to be served on the last holdout in this vast area of mechanically flattened land. The diehard was a Mexican-American whose family had been living on that spot for four generation. But right now, this land that was registered before automobiles had been invented, was needed to help enlarge O'Malley's parking lot. But with his family, this daring man decided to fight against inevitable defeat.

Excitement ran high when the court order was refused. The sheriffs clicked off the safety on their tear gas guns. It was a matter of minutes now when all hell would break loose.

Then . . . at first, faintly . . . there came a "thrump, thrump, thrump."

The sound grew louder now: *"Thrump, thrump, thrump."*

Officers were about to discharge their gas bombs when everything came to a halt. In confusion, the group looked skyward as the thrump, thrump, thrump swooped from behind a bluff. It was a helicopter ... KTLA's innovation. Instant remote news coverage from the air!

At that moment, something extremely personal was going on between Harry and whoever it was operating that remote camera. He now realized he was glaring up at another mortal enemy. This alien at this very second was vacuuming the story and relaying it in live moving panorama to television receivers throughout the entire country. And it would be another hour before Harry could get his undeveloped film back to KTTV, have processed and put it on the air.

Here Harry was. He had come to television from the newspapers along with progress. And again, he was being scooped.

"How, oh, how, can I do something to blackout this son-of-a-bitch?" Harry mumbled to himself.

With a thought in mind, and refusing out-and-out defeat, Watson defiantly cried out to everyone on the ground:

"Quick, everybody! Lie down and spell out 'FUCK YOU!!'"

It was the best thing Harry could think of just before all hell broke loose.

"MY SECOND FATHER"—In 1974, newspaperman, author, humorist H. Allen Smith visits Fowler upon completion of 40th book, *The Life and Legend of Gene Fowler* ... During 20 years of correspondence, Fowler and the man he referred to as his second father exchanged more than 500 letters. If you can't decipher inscription, it reads: "Dear Will - Guess who's stoned. Allen."

LOVE TRIANGLE—With attorney Grant Cooper, on-and-off-screen temptress Joan Bennett discusses divorce from jealous husband Walter Wanger 24 hours after the motion picture producer shot her lover Jennings Lang across the street from the Beverly Hills Police Department.

XVII

Hookers and the
Snake That Was There

Nineteen-fifty-one was a fascinating news year, especially through the first four months leading up to a two-week suspension J.B.T. imposed upon me beginning April 23.

Starting the new year, the Tournament of Roses Parade and Rose Bowl football game had become a gala news presentation enjoyed on black-and-white television throughout Los Angeles County.

There was an estimated million spectators present at the parade site, and the new breed of TV sportscasters with their play-by-play and commentary mesmerized viewers as Michigan beat California by the score of 14-6.

In the beginning, the Pasadena Rose Parade was incidental to the foot races and tug-of-war contests. They tried football in 1902, but Michigan trounced Stanford's Indians so badly (49-0) that the game was replaced with polo, and in succeeding years, with chariot races. It wasn't until 1916 when football returned on a permanent basis. And it wouldn't be until 1962 when the game was telecast from coast-to-coast beaming Minnesota beating UCLA by 21-to-3.

We reporters showed up at the *Her-Ex* city room at two A.M. where Aggie Underwood gave our four teams instruction. Being an afternoon paper, we focused on hitting the street with the all-important judge's parade float award photos. Commercialism was beginning to be more visible with their entries, therefore it was profitable for parade sponsors to be generous with the blue ribbons to big business. And after color television coverage was introduced, the parade and game became a huge profit-making institution.

Each of our crews was escorted by a privately-paid uniformed LAPD motorcycle officer who would also run negatives back to the paper.

In addition to our overtime, we were given four choice sideline game tickets and a fifth of booze, the last of which we were honor-bound not to drink until we had finished our assignments.

Through the early dark hours, unexpected gale winds proved a hazard for firemen containing bonfires along the parade route. Two store-front glass windows blew out and four floats were involved in accidents while lining up. Home-owners were threatening drivers parking cars on their front lawns, and four beauty queens on the Long Beach float lost their sheer gowns to the violent winds. But at nine A.M. when the parade got under way up Orange Grove Avenue, copies of the *Herald-Express* special edition with picture pages and stories about the winning floats were being sold along the parade route.

This was the year when Maurey Godchaux was assigned to write *Times* sidebars of notables attending the parade. However, the list of prominents was lean, so Godchaux created *Victor M. Frisbie*, an Australian brigadier, whom he quoted as describing the parade as "quite a ruddy good show." But before next New Year's parade, Godchaux was tragically killed.

As a memoriam to Maurie, his staff began perpetuating Frisbie. On ensuing New Year's Days, Frisbie appeared as a prominent alumnus of the visiting football team, a minor official of the Tournament of Roses Association, one of the overnight arrivals to the parade. The staff once even slipped Frisbie's name into the drunk roundup of New Year's Eve. One reporter went so far as to have Frisbie take on the guise of a Marine who had just returned from the Korean War who'd been picked up for drunk by the sheriff's department. But because (as the story was printed), Sgt. Frisbie explained to his jailor that he had never seen a Rose Bowl game, they took pity and let him watch it on their own TV set.

This last piece was so over-documented that a sharp-eyed editor caught onto the bogus story and killed it. This so incensed one *Times* rewrite man that he managed to sneak Frisbie's obituary in the paper's death notice columns.

In later years, it was proven that Frisbies, like old soldiers, never die . . . the ink just fades away. But not for long, because his name began showing up again. If anything, Frisbie had developed new friends and his name began appearing in newspapers other than the *Times*, and he was reported to have been seen in Pasadena on New Year's Day at many different locations at one time.

Now, so many New Year's Days later, there seems to crop up a notation on some city editor's schedule somewhere which reads:

"Sidelights: Victor M. Frisbie."

The international scene that year saw Korean War allied troops abandoning Seoul to the Communists in January and regaining that real estate in mid-March.

In the first month, novelist Sinclair Lewis died in Rome, President Truman turned in a *two year budget* of $140 billion and General Douglas MacArthur celebrated his 71st birthday by reviewing his troops in Tokyo.

Considered to be an international happening, Greta Garbo became a United States citizen on February 9 and Julius and Ethel Rosenberg were sentenced to die in the electric chair for giving Russia atomic bomb secrets. Iran's Premier Ali Pazmara and Jordan's King Abdullah were both assassinated. George Marshall resigned as Secretary of State and Winston Churchill returned to prime ministership. Also, Publisher William Randolph Hearst died of natural causes at the age of 88.

Of principal national interest, there was a price rollback and a freeze on wages, and it was announced that the 1951 draft would snare 641,000 to keep our 3 1/2 million military forces up to full strength. Mary Martin began an extended vacation after washing her hair each night on stage for nearly two years in Rodgers & Hammerstein's *South Pacific*, and to the consternation of news photographers, Miss America Youlande Belbeze of Mobile, Alabama, refused to parade in a bathing suit.

Among the 21 actor-actress divorces I covered locally, were those of Rita Hayworth and Ali Kahn, Barbara Stanwyck and Robert Taylor and Judy Garland and film director Vincent Minnelli. I still vividly recall the splitting up of Linda Darnell and cinematographer Peverell Marley, a man several years her senior. When I interviewed Linda in the Superior Court pressroom, we both were friendly but uncomfortable because we used to date in 1940 and '41 when I was an office boy at Fox Studios.

This was before Linda would star in authoress Kathleen Windsor's torrid best-selling novel, *Forever Amber.*

Linda had a full schedule when we were dating. Movies were made quicker then and during these busy 18 months, she starred in *Brigham Young, The Mark of Zorro, Chad Hanna,* and with Tyrone Power in *Blood and Sand.*

Linda lived with her earthy family in a suburban home where domestic animals wandered in-and-out of the front room. Her mother had a thing about snakes. She loved them and kept quite a few on the grounds. She also used to like to surprise me by poking a vampire in my face.

Eventually, the studio put an end to our dating because I was only an office boy, and this didn't fit into their class distinction observances.

There were five stories on the local level I covered in 1951 that were unique enough to be carried by the wire services. These led up to the fateful day in April when I was to be suspended. The first had to do with a six-year-old boy who died in a Glendale hospital suffering from injuries after leaping from a 20-foot cliff near his home.

It was a quiet Saturday and Art McCarroll was on the desk. He had me go out to Richard Bonham's house to pick up a photo of the dead child for a one-column cut. But when I read the circumstances of the story, I argued with McCarroll that it was worth better art to go with the story. Something better than just a head-and-shoulders picture.

At that time, kids were decorating the landscapes, romping about with beach towels pinned to their shoulders in imitation of "Superman," a role played by George Reeves in a popular TV series. And with the faith only children seem to possess— that everything is possible—Richard ran to the edge of a cliff to soar into the sky. Instead, he plummeted to the ground below, his body shattered. McCarroll demurred and I went out alone to get the picture.

As I drove through the hills nestled by low morning fog, I thought it *was* a good place for a kid to fly. Then, through a window, I saw Richard's parents staring into cold cups of coffee. His father answered my second knock. I told him I was a reporter, had three kids of my own and that I wouldn't blame him if he closed the door on me. He let me in.

When I returned to the paper, I wrote the story in first person, as I had covered it, interviewing the grief-stricken parents, right down to Richard's words in the hospital just before he died: "I really *did* fly, didn't I, Mom?"

Some months later, returning early from vacation because I'd run out of money, I recall coasting down stretches of highway with my clutch disengaged so I wouldn't run out of fuel. My gas tank was as empty as my pocket.

Arriving home, the mail box was filled with bills and advertisements with bills in them. There was a *Readers Digest* envelope. I opened it with he rest of the mail, and I nearly threw away a check for $1,500. It was in payment for the "Little Boy Who Flew" piece I'd sent in and forgotten about. At the time, I was making $125 a week. No amount has since seemed larger than that *Readers Digest* check.

With stories about children seeming to remain foremost in my memory, I recall an 11-year-old girl whose father had pawned her for $10 and a tank of gasoline.

At Georgia Street Juvenile Hall, I found a frail, frightened child dressed in a faded blue cotton print dress sitting on the edge of an oak bench. Shirley Ann O'Brien stared up at me and looked like she wanted someone to hug her, so I picked her up.

The lady juvenile officer told me Shirley Ann, along with her parents and three other children, spent the night at a San Fernando Valley service station. "The owner, a Mr. Cecil

Glover, took them in and fed them," she said. "But then the father," she said referring to her notes, "Mr. William O'Brien, offered to ... actually offered to sell Shirley Ann for the $10 tank of gas."

"Generous guy," I said.

"O'Brien is an itinerant farm worker," she said, "and we have an APB out on him." It had the ring of *Grapes of Wrath* to it.

"Was this Glover planning to keep Shirley Ann?"

"Absolutely," she said. "The only way we got her to Juvenile Hall was through informant neighbors."

"Are you going to press charges against Glover?" I asked.

"What can I do?" she asked.

"How about for receiving stolen goods?" I asked.

Raiding Hollywood whore houses in 1951 wasn't as exalted as it had been during the movie industry's golden years of the 1920s and '30s. In the vintage years, token raids—when the establishments were warned in advance to clear the bagnios of celebrity—were carried on in good spirit on both sides. The town's renowned demimonde Lee Francis waited for the *gendarmerie* with chilled bottles of imported French champagne and dishes of Russian caviar. After the legal pretense was concluded without arrests, officers would sit down and enjoy themselves.

Brenda Allen had been the reigning Hollywood madame following the war, but the filmland's glitter days had stepped down in class.

Lee Francis refused successful raids. Brenda Allen's were becoming costly in payoff money, but in 1951, Barrie Benson was plain knocked out of business.

That depressing April morning, vice squad detective Sgt. Merrill Duncan and eight officers representing robbery, burglary, homicide and police intelligence waited for the front porch light to flick twice from an undercover man already inside the bordello posing as a client. Four more were waiting with officials outside

Madame Benson's 13-room Moorish castle that blended in with other resplendent mansions on Schuyler Road just north of the Sunset Strip. They were news people. Three men and one woman. I was there with my photog Art Wardon, and *Daily News* reporter Don Dwiggins had brought Helen Brush with him.

"Good lord," I said to Helen, "you've gotta be making some kind of history. Has there ever been a woman who broke into a whore house?"

Benson's was a favorite hangout for gangland figures, and new Police Chief William H. Parker intended hers to be the first L.A. whore house to go under. The papers were invited to show that Parker was putting other prostitution ringleaders on notice.

Mobster Mickey Cohen's bodyguard, hulky Sam Farkas, had been picked up a few hours earlier and was presently being shuffled from one station to another so he couldn't make bail. Farkas was one of Benson's regular customers.

The porch light flashed twice and Sgt. Duncan and his congregation, including the press, swooped down.

Inside, it was delightful watching a bevy of surprised young females dashing about in the nude, not knowing exactly where they were going. It was like a fox breaking into the rabbit hutch.

The one most mad was 29-year-old Madame Benson emerging from the "Purple Room" pulling up her brassiere straps. She looked at Helen Bursh and growled: "What the hell are *you* doing in here, anyway?"

"What the hell do you think?" said Helen. "I'm shooting pictures."

Dressed in boxer shorts, the undercover officer stepped forward, handed a $20 bill to Sgt. Duncan and said: "Miss Benson accepted this for services this young lady was about to render me." He patted the backside of a cute redhead who was wrapped in a white beach towel.

As other officers dispersed to gather more evidence, Sgt. Duncan began interrogating Benson. "You mean you're going to question me in front of *her*?" Benson asked while pointing at Helen.

"I won't tell anyone what you say," said Helen. "Talk to my reporter here. I just take pictures."

I began talking to the redhead on the side. Her name was Velma. "How much do you make on a regular trick?" I asked.

"In the Red Room, we get $20, like your undercover man told you," she said. "This is for half-and-half and a head job. In the Purple Room, we get $100 for all night, and $150 if a client wants two of us to play with him at one time."

Velma was sounding so academic, I asked: "Does Miss Benson ever participate?"

"Oh, sure," said Velma. "But only with special clients. She charges them $150 a night ... usually more."

"How are dates made?"

"We have a password," she said. "We have a cocker spaniel named 'Coffee,' and when someone calls for a date, Barrie asked, 'Do you know Coffee?' and if they say something like 'Is that the tall dark man?' Barrie hangs up. But if he says, 'Oh, yes, that's your little cocker,' then Barrie books him."

"What about female clients? Do you have any women clients?"

"Hell, yes," said Velma. "Mostly married middle-aged ladies looking for a strange piece 'cause their husbands are burned out from booze or too busy. This way, they don't take chances getting involved or being caught and losing all that easy living."

"What about the male prostitutes," I asked. "What are they like?"

"They're always hung well and get more money than us because they can't perform nearly as often," said Velma. "But they burn out early, too. Most can't get it up anymore by the time they're 35, especially if they drink a lot."

At this juncture, Barrie Benson figured it was time she put in a call to her attorney while Helen and the rest of us toured the place.

We went into the Red Room and the more lush Purple Room with its king-sized bed, rich carpeting and delicate ivory figurines. Displayed on several tables were framed pictures of popular actors with inscribed certifications such as: "You're an artist" and "Never had any better."

Sgt. Duncan phoned his superior Lt. Carl Shy to say the raid was successful. Shy said he would release Farkas, adding that Cohen's 34-year-old bodyguard told him: "It's a bum beef. I'm just bein' hustled by the cops. They're tryin' to louse me up with my wife."

Now Duncan heard a noise coming from the Purple Room. Helen had flushed the last of Benson's naked doves from under the king-sized bed. The irate blonde screamed at Helen: "You ain't gonna take no picture of *me*, you prick!" She began tossing anything that was throwable and injurious. She hit Art Wardon with her first throw and he bled a bit. But when Blondie discovered it was a woman behind her camera, she exploded with: "I don't believe it! She's gotta be a man in *drag*!"

There was the reclusive "Cobra Woman" whose story no one will believe when I tell it to them. She lived in an out-of-the-way northeastern part of the county. She had no friends because she raised cobra snakes that she milked to supply hospitals with antitoxin.

Felix Paegle and I drove out past Temple City to do a feature on the Cobra Woman during a slow news day. Ever since Linda Darnell's mother shoved snakes in my face, I've always been on guard to put many yards between reptiles and myself. So when the Cobra Woman removed a six-footer from its cage, I immediately checked for the nearest window I could jump through if the damned thing got loose.

And, by God, while she was handling it with a forked hook, the damned cobra bit her on the back of the wrist.

After she returned the snake to its cage, Felix and I started taking her to the car and make a dash for the nearest hospital.

"It's too late," she said with a calm that surprised us. "Nothing can be done now. I forgot to restock my venom antidote."

As she slowly sat down on the living room sofa, I phoned for an ambulance. Helpless to do anything but wait, Paegel picked up his camera and began shooting a series of pictures as she began to die.

With it uppermost in my mind that snakes should never be trusted, there was another female recluse living in the general area of the Cobra Woman's home. She had a snake story of another dimension. This spinster was in her late 60s.

A nearby housing development had enraged pioneer settlers there because, they said: "Modern society is movin' in on us with their God-damned sewer pipelines. We're happy here with our cesspools. These moderns is comin' in here, assessin' us as t' where we put our asses in the mornin'."

A time after the civic sewer strife abated, this spinster phoned the sheriff's substation to complain that "there's a snake in my toilet. Would you mind coming up here and removing it?"

Two deputies were dispatched to investigate the unusual complaint. And after standing some time peering down into her toilet, one said to the other: "This is gettin' pretty ridiculous, standin' here, starin' at a commode, waitin' fer some kinda snake t' show up."

Apologizing for being unable to assist the old lady, the impatient officers departed and began bandying creative speculative conversation on their way into the station.

But sure as sports writers drop clichés, another call came in shortly thereafter. And following a third and fourth unsuccessful visit where the phantom snake refused to make an appearance for deputy sheriffs, a compassionate officer with more duty hash-marks said: "Maybe she's just lonely; wants some company." But he backed up his empathy with a call to the house. And about five minutes into his potty watch, a live boa constrictor raised its head.

The spinster had been vindicated!

"Then she wasn't lonely after all," the substation captain remarked, adding more words with a Rabelaisian bent.

Then it was no time until the spinster watched an S.P.C.A. team noose the snake and hied its slippery long body off to a nearby animal shelter.

After the picture story hit the paper displaying the pot from whence came the eight-foot boa, hardly any time passed until creative city room reporters began coming up with more descriptive headlines than the original that read: SPINSTER DISCOVERS SNAKE IN COMMODE

Some of the unpublishable heads with news affiliations follow:

FOUND: SNAKE WITH NO SENSE OF SMELL
(*Lost & Found*)

DO IT YOURSELF ROTO-ROOTER FOR SALE
(*Classified Ads*)

NEW PETER PRINCIPAL DISCOVERED
(*Popular Mechanics*)

NOSEY BOA AIN'T NO MOAH (*Pop Sheet Songs*)

D.T.'s PROVE HOAX (*Medical Journal*)

STAND UP SHITTING BECOMES POPULAR
(*Free Press*)

NEW CHINESE TORTURE FOR GOOSEY P.W.s
(*Yank*)

SNAKE HOLDS BREATH FOR NEW WORLD'S RECORD (*Sports*)

SETBACK FOR ALCOHOLICS ANONYMOUSE
(*The Grapevine*)

Years later, a reporter friend confided that this episode had made an everlasting impression on him. "Every time I sit down," he confessed, "I always look first."

On December 29, just as New Year's celebrations began to exhilarate, a forlorn middle-aged unemployed laborer, Gordon C. Van Ess, wrote his Last Will in a lonely, seedy downtown Los Angeles hotel room on skid row before taking a fatal dose of poison. The Testament read:

> A will and testament, my small estate &
> bequeeth to my Mother my body to the nearest
> credited Medical school. my soul and heart to
> all the girls, *and my brain to Harry Truman.*

Oh, yes. I've gotten way ahead of myself and passed April 23, when I was hit with my two-week suspension from the paper. I wouldn't for a moment think of further delay, so let's get on with the mean old John B.T. Campbell and what he did to me.

MOVIE STAR'S RECONSTRUCTED FACE—Fowler (center) interviews star Franchot Tone (right) outside courthouse during divorce trial with Barbara Payton. Tone had his face reconstructed after actor Tom Neal maimed him. *Daily News* reporter is at left.

XVIII

Me and
General MacArthur

T he day fast approached when I was to become an unintentional newspaper legend. I would supply the material for future reporters to talk about.

It began taking form on April 11 when the news flashed over wires around the globe that President Harry Truman had relieved General Douglas MacArthur from all four of his commands, including the post of Supreme United Nations Command and Chief of the allied Occupation of Japan where he was treated as an emperor in force.

This was the stunning climax to Truman's and MacArthur's policy standoff over the conduct of the Korean War.

MacArthur first heard of his unconditional release over Armed Forces Radio. It was twenty minutes later that the 50 year veteran of three wars received notification in the form of an envelope marked *Flash*. In the message, Truman stated that "with deep regret," he had concluded that MacArthur was unable to give his "wholehearted support to the policies of the United States Government and the United Nations in matters pertaining to his [MacArthur's] official duties."

The rift between the two was kindled when Truman had flown to the South Pacific and confronted MacArthur about his releasing sensitive statements to the press before clearing them with the White House. In effect, Truman had made the trek to tell the 71-year-old hero of Bataan, the Philippines and the Pacific War to keep his mouth shut.

To compound this irritation, when Truman landed on a God-forsaken Pacific island, MacArthur—who had grown accustomed

to Emperor Hirohito doffing his divinity to go see him—played
a personality game of chess and refused for nearly a half-hour
to make the first move and report to the President's plane.
Through his liaison, the President reminded MacArthur that he
(Truman) was the Commander-in-Chief. "Tell that son-of-a-bitch
to get his ass on over here," he told his aide.

The April 11 firing was the beginning of a story that would
eclipse all other national and international bulletins and not yield
the front pages for a solid month.

The following day's reaction on Capitol Hill was more spectacular than the press had anticipated. Republican legislative
leaders termed the MacArthur removal as "a tragic error" and
a victory of Secretary of State Dean Acheson, which they added
was a preliminary step to a "Far East Munich." Flabbergasted
Democratic leaders were afraid to make any mis-statements and
fall into disfavor with their electorates, so they refrained from
comment.

Senator Richard Nixon entered a resolution of his own asking
the Senate to go on record that President Truman "has not acted
in the best interests of the American people," which really didn't
mean much, but it was an opportunity to keep his name in the
newspapers.

But it was Indiana's Senator Jenner in general session debate
who cried out to demand President Truman's impeachment. To
the Democratic constituency, it was a nightmare when Jenner's
motion was followed by great applause.

The Hearst organization, which long before had planned to back
MacArthur for the Republican candidacy, didn't miss a quote
favorable to the General. An INS correspondent in Korea wrote:
"The G.I.s had come to love Gen. MacArthur for his frequent
visits to the front lines under gun fire."

I was out on the street gathering statements from the angered
Los Angeles citizenry. Dick O'Connor and Jack Smith were putting sidebars together for the front page. These reflected the
feelings of most American voices when one of their heroes got
kicked in the groin.

Her-Ex phone lines jammed. Most communications Mr. Campbell chose to publish had a common theme: "Impeach Truman and reverse his removal of MacArthur." A L.A. Western Union superintendent said the telegraphic "deluge" had begun a few minutes after the announcement was made in Washington City and "had steadily risen into a flood of outrage."

Many tearful complaints came from mothers of sons fighting in Korea. One mother called to say, "I always felt better because my son was fighting under General MacArthur. His whole concern in this mess was to see to it that we weren't fighting in vain . . ."

The country immediately began making preparations to take the General into its arms and create the biggest reception ever to welcome home its fallen hero.

And, indeed, it was a grand hurrah. Following a tumultuous reception in Honolulu, MacArthur's private plane landed in San Francisco on April 18. And following a parade where nearly a million cheered, our champion addressed the throngs at City Hall. With an eloquence he said he learned at his mother's knee, the good General said: "My emotions defy description as I find myself once more among my own people, once more under the spell of the American home which breeds such magnificent men as I left fighting on the battlefields of Korea."

MacArthur emphatically denied he would be a candidate for public office. In political translation, this meant he was hot and ready to be drafted by any emotional constituency.

On this day of celebration, a Mississippi flood raged and took human lives. The *Herald-Express* gave it three paragraphs on page three. A single paragraph reported that 75 were feared dead aboard a sunken submarine. An otherwise headline story about a drastic need for U.A. atom bomb defense received only four paragraphs, and a Korean Communists peace bid was lost among MacArthur picture art on page five. For a straight month, the news would all be MacArthur as—much to the annoyance of Truman—he majestically toured the country from coast-to-coast.

There was a bit of drinking in the *Her-Ex* city room as we pasted up San Francisco wire stories and John B.T. Campbell begrudgingly wrote his headline of the day:

800,000 IN S.F. JOIN
MACARTHUR TRIBUTE

Our managing editor was distressed that his paladin-turned-martyr had chosen to first set foot on San Francisco soil instead of in Los Angeles.

Probably trying to dismiss the thought of personally assassinating Truman for his dastardly directive, Campbell let everyone in earshot know that he had been born the very same year, month, day and hour as was his military hero.

"If he would have only come to Los Angeles instead of that vulgar little city up north," he moaned, "we would have given him tribute never seen before."

The orangeade dispenser had been removed as a result of Perry Fowler's didoes with the gallon of vodka, so a bar was set up back in the photo department.

The latest edition dedicated to MacArthur coverage was passed around the city room and Campbell started all over about how he was exasperated that MacArthur hadn't come to L.A.

This got me to wondering at our four-and-a-half cent mileage allowance how much it would cost to theoretically drive up to San Francisco, kidnap the General and return him to Los Angeles.

The round trip miles, I calculated, would come to $85.68. Then I began thinking about filling out a bogus expense account just for laughs and hand it in to Aggie. The subject matter was a riot.

I also recalled other odd vouchers handed in over the years. Ones that gave pleasure to all but the comptrollers.

There was *Life* magazines's great writer, the late Loudon Wainwright, who covered the second World War from a Navy aircraft carrier. At the end of each expense account he sent in from the South Pacific, Loudon would add sundry amounts to cover "taxi fare." Considering he was putting his life on the line each day, the front office never questioned Wainwright's money chits. But a newly-hired accountant did. Along with a following payment, the bookkeeper enclosed a note:

Please discontinue payment requests
for "taxi fare," as I note you are
stationed aboard a ship.

Paperclipped to his following voucher was Wainwright's note explaining his taxi fare expenses. Two words:

Big ship.

Our veteran Jack Stevens was not to be forgotten. Annually covering the *Youth For Christ* promotion, Jack's bonus was to enter the price of a new Stetson hat on his expense voucher. But this privilege was rescinded during a corporate economy drive.

This didn't stop the persistent Stevens. For two years, he listed his Stetson, but Richardson scratched it out.

On the final occasion, Richardson looked over at Stevens with his wandering eye to say: "I see you didn't put your Stetson down."

"Oh, I did," said Stevens, "but you won't be able to find it."

Gathering more courage to write my Gen. MacArthur expense account, I recalled the foremost swindle sheet turned into the Hearst corporation. It came from my father, whose simple theory was: "Never return with money."

In 1921, a report emanated from the northernmost regions of Ontario that three U.S. Navy aeronauts had been found alive after an unexpected wind had blown them off coarse a month earlier and carried their balloon into the bleak Canadian wilderness near a town named Moose Factory.

Pop was assigned to cover the story and confer with the fortunate explorers who had escaped freezing in sub-zero weather. They were expected to be available to the press a week hence.

My father registered at the King Edward Hotel in Toronto then went on a shopping tour to stock a private railroad car he was about to lease. There was an abundance of fancy food and vintage wine available so his trek into the northern wilds with opposition reporters might be reasonably comfortable.

A week passed and the balloonists arrived in Moose Factory. Their stories were gripping enough to keep them on the front page for a few days.

But during his waiting time, my father had been a constant loser in high-stake poker games. And when he arrived back at the American, he faced the problem of filling out—in detail— how he had spent $1,500 in expense monies during the Canadian caper.

Beyond legitimate expenditures, such as leasing the private car, it was necessary for my father to cover up his poker losses. Therefore, he created a mythical fully-equipped dog team and sled. And in an effort to satisfy a sharp-eyed comptroller, he fantasized, relating the illness of his lead dog requiring medical care following a fierce battle with a malamute. Then he wrote down that the lead dog's mate had pups that had to be paid for. And when the father unexpectedly died, it was necessary to give this brave lead dog a fine funeral.

Within a short time, the voucher was bounced back along with a note from the auditor. It read:

Mr. Fowler:
You have yet to account for $60.

Without thinking much about it, Pop scribbled on the bottom of the accountant's note:

Flowers for bereaved bitch, $60.

I had thought enough on my plan and filled out the mileage voucher for $85.68. At the bottom where it was printed, Explanation, I wrote:

MacArthur pickup—San Francisco.

Then I sat back in the bull pen and waited for a big guffaw from the city desk. It didn't come, so I dismissed the gag like a punctured Moose Factory balloon and went on to other useless pursuits.

The MacArthur San Francisco reception occurred on a Wednesday. On Friday, as the General was delivering his stirring "Old soldiers never die" speech to a joint meeting of Congress in Washington, our pay checks were being distributed. I gave mine a second look because, somehow, my phony voucher had gone through. An additional $85.68 had been added to my regular weekly salary.

Now I found myself in an uncomfortable circumstance. I was fearful about turning it in, so pretending everything would pass, I cashed the check and shared my profits with the gang at Moran's bar. The only thing I could think of was to write a personal check to the auditing department the next day so the news of my backfired joke wouldn't get up to Mr. Campbell. Unfortunately, I'd shared my joke, too.

When I got to the bookkeepers the following afternoon, I was told I was too late; that an interoffice memo had been sent up.

It was late in the afternoon and J.B.T. had left for the day.

The following morning, Aggie was summoned to Campbell's office. She remained there for about five minutes during which time, I watched the two shouting at one another. Odd for Aggie who called Campbell "Mister."

In another half-hour, Campbell's leggy secretary, Mickey, swayed past the bull pen and tacked the managing editor's notice on the bulletin board. It read:

> Mr. Will Fowler, reporter, is suspended without pay for two weeks for a gross exaggeration on his expense account for week ending April 21, which had no basis whatever on monies he had spent. This expense account included $85.68 on "MacArthur pick up—San Francisco." The voucher slipped [by] in routine.
>
> Mr. Fowler is suspended from the *Herald-Express* payroll without pay for a period of two weeks beginnings May 14, 1951, and any further employment entirely depends upon his satisfactory explanation of the affair.
>
> Yours very truly,
John B.T. Campbell
Managing Editor
>
> P.S.: Furthermore, he will return $85.68 to the *Herald-Express* before any further employment will be considered.

I will never understand why letters equivalent to death warrants are most always signed: *Yours very truly*.

During the two short weeks I was off, dozens of half-informed movie actors began admitting to the Kefauver Committee that they were Communists; bandleader Xavier Cugat and glamorous Abbe Lane made ink with their marital problems; World War II's most decorated soldier, Audie Murphey, married an airline stewardess; Violet Berling, a Long Beach music teacher, was found guilty of murdering her 11-year-old girl pupil with an accordion strap; three actresses vaguely attempted suicide; Red Skelton signed a $10 million contract with Proctor & Gamble to appear on television for seven years, and newspapers throughout the country had begun republishing old MacArthur photos because they had run out of new ones.

The first afternoon following my return from exile, Aggie and I ordered a drink at Moran's. I asked her exactly what she and Campbell had discussed about my phony expense account.

Mr. Campbell asked me: 'Shall I fire Fowler?' And I said: 'Hell no. I okayed the voucher and put it through. Fire me.' ''

Noblesse oblige.

XIX

Triangles

When I traveled with my family to the Southland, I was 13 and the kids I went to school with in New York referred to any place in Southern California as "Hollywood."

When we settled in Beverly Hills for the school semester, my parents chose an English Tudor house owned by Marion Davies. When Marion learned Gene Fowler was her leasee, she wanted to give it to him as a present in gesture for the loyal years Pop had spent as a reporter and editor for Hearst. He declined her offer.

It was 1935, only ten years after Beverly Hills was first subdivided. The Beverly Hills Hotel had been constructed at the northern point on Sunset Boulevard where Rodeo, Canon, Beverly and Crescent drives converged. There were wide, box hedge-lined bridal paths running the lengths of Rodeo Drive and Sunset Boulevard. A Southern Pacific train, later leased by Pacific Electric Railways for trolley passenger service, transversed the quiet town twice a day and there were many vacant lots available at reasonable prices.

During these years I became closely acquainted with John Barrymore, Thomas Mitchell, Richard Dix, Lew Cody and W.C. Fields. This is when I used to drive my father to meet with these wassailing raconteurs. Spoiled by their company, I lost interest in most friends my own age. For a half-year after I graduated from high school, I lived with Barrymore and his male nurse Karl Stuevers at Jack's mansion on Tower Road where his last "bus accident," Dolores Costello, had denuded all but three of its 55-rooms.

It wasn't until I became a newspaper reporter in 1944 when I discovered there was a warehouse full of unopened closets and more love triangles than one could shake a geometric figure at.

When I worked on the *Herald-Express*, newspapers, periodicals, radio, television and motion pictures were still considered "pure." The metropolitan papers rarely overstepped moral boundries. The word *damn* wasn't even printed in the papers.

Television had frightened the motion picture industry, though. And as its box office receipts declined at an alarming rate, it was trying to find ways to entice its lost audience away from TV sets and back to the theaters.

Motion picture producers fought back with three dimensional (3D) movies viewed through polarized glasses, showing lions and other threatening things leaping out from the screen. The fad didn't last, so the wide-screen anamorphic lens was introduced—which remains today, but in modified form. Still, these were not innovations to successfully lure TV enthusiasts from their living rooms where they were enjoying free entertainment ... as tedious and unsophisticated as the medium was.

The solution was not in introducing gimmicks. Rather, it was necessary for industry executives to *change the process* of how they were being governed and restricted.

Eric Johnston had taken over the Hays Office, but it wasn't until Jack Valenti was appointed president of the newly inscribed Alliance of Motion Picture and Television Producers that eventually allowed permissiveness to reach the silver screen. So swiftly did this evolve that it was necessary to introduce the GP, R and X rating system, hinting to theater-goers how maturely a picture's subject would be treated.

The industry began thriving again. Inflation soared and producers took more vast amounts from the top of production cost. Nouveau-riche stars went unbridled with their lack of esthetic taste, building tawdry-looking houses in Beverly Hills, purchasing expensive cars and gaudy wardrobes to show off in public.

To the aggravation of other entertainment mediums, television began overpowering them. It was refining and diversifying its services to the public. It was giving what the newspapers and radio were unable to offer: It embraced and extended the senses of vision and hearing beyond their natural limits. The movies stood shoulder-to-shoulder in this respect, but one didn't have to drive to another location and pay money to have the experience. Moreover, the weekly newsreel had disappeared because TV offered up news by the hour.

In its refinements, it had advanced to the point where all TV stations offered filmed news coverage to a multitude of new fans preferring to watch and listen to the day's events rather than read about them. It beat picking up a soaking wet paper on the doorstep when the weather was inclement.

Television was no longer a novelty. It was something to be respected and in some cases, feared. It had grown to be so powerful so early on that—like eating, sleeping and sex—it had become a *way of life*.

Whether it was looked upon as a boon or a cancer, this new medium was responsible for the majority of the nation's newspaper to go bankrupt. Furling their sails, the metropolitans frantically embarked on emergency economics when it was already too late. The next step was to merge with another big paper, hang on and hope to survive.

In the west, however, it was the *Los Angeles Times* that broke the shackles of pragmatism and forged ahead. It worked harder with its creativity and daring regarding its editorial concepts. This was strongly aided by the installation and intensive use of the computer which recently came into the favor of big business.

The paper began serving suburban towns which had lost their prized newspapers. It created "sections" devoted to specialized circulation in these areas. And presuming its readers had already been filled in with the basic hard news by TV, the *Times* concentrated on giving its readers an in-depth view of the subject matter.

During this period in the early '50s, I was reporting for the *Her-Ex* when television's production companies began moving from New York to Los Angeles. And although movie production was picking up in the west again, there was still ample room and major studios welcomed renting set space and hiring out its talent to the new settlers. The final step came when the three networks moved their executive offices to the coast.

With all this entertainment world activity churning, the barometric pressure of Hollywood's movie stars remained in its usual state of flux and continued to supply good copy for our afternoon paper which was still thriving.

This was the period when burly actor Tom Neal nearly killed Franchot Tone—a delicately framed leading man with patrician features—in the early hours of September 14, 1951, on the front lawn of bosomy actress Barbara Payton's house.

It was a love triangle created when this sloe-eyed blonde was unable to decide with whom she preferred to sleep.

Franchot Tone had graduated *magna cum laude* from Cornell and after some little theater experience in the town of his birth, Niagara Falls, New York, he migrated to Hollywood, making his 1932 motion picture debut opposite Joan Crawford in *Today We Live*. During these early years, it was tantamount that Tone be a superior lover because Crawford disallowed mediocrity near her bedchambers. The two were married and a tempestuous life followed. Divorce came a short time later.

Tom Neal was a stocky leading man in quicky "B" movies. He'd built up his body and claimed to have been a professional fighter. But his constant picking on weak, non-athletice men was something a boxer didn't do.

Barbara Payton, an eye-stopper in the form of a tall version of Al Capp's Daisy Mae, was born among the piney woods of Minnesota and made her way into the acting business, relinquishing her lucrative trade as a high-paid prostitute. During one of my later interviews with her, Barbara told me that sex had never gratified her. She could take it or leave it.

There seemed to be a waning in Tone's sexual talents due to excessive drinking. Following the divorce from his second wife, and equally beautiful woman, Jean Wallace, Tone took up with Barbara.

Shortly after the Tone-Neal fracas, *Her-Ex* movie columnist Harrison Carroll was first to break the story. This was made possible by his legman—Army Archerd, dean of trade columnists on *Variety*. Archerd came up with the first Neal quotes:

"First Barbara was going to marry Tone, then she was going to marry me. We had already taken our blood tests and were going to have the wedding ceremony in San Francisco tomorrow afternoon ... First thing I knew of any change in plans was when Barbara went out yesterday with Tone."

Meeting Neal at Barbara's place, Tone ordered him out of the house, and on the lawn, Neal mashed his face in with his fists.

Archerd said that at this point, Barbara came screaming at Neal and he hit her in the eye. But when the two looked at Tone's face that resembled ground meat, Barbara called for an ambulance and Neal fled.

After Bevo Means flashed the report from the sheriff's beat and I was assigned the story, Bevo told me Tone and Barbara had been taking in statuesque stripper Lili St. Cyr's bathtub performance at Ciro's the night before. They had wanted to catch it before the sheriff closed it down following a lady tourist's complaint that it was "lewd."

I told Bevo to check if Neal had a record as a professional boxer. "If he was and Tone lives," I said, "Neal can still be hauled in on a felony warrant for using his fists as lethal weapons."

Before going out to Barbara's house, I checked with Hollywood homicide detective Sgt. A.W. Hubka who said, "You never know about brain concussion injuries, and if Tone dies, we have enough on Neal already to drag him in on a murder charge."

I went out to the Payton place and knocked on the door. I heard movement inside but nobody answered. Next, I visited Barbara's neighbor, Judson O'Connell. He said he was awakened by a woman's scream and "the mechanical pounding" administered to Tone by Neal.

Later, I checked in at California Hospital where Tone was reported in critical condition following emergency surgery. Therefore, we reporters were officially on a death watch. Tone's physician Lee E. Siegel confirmed that in addition to a crushed nose, the actor's jaw had been shattered and his cheek bone was caved in. It was necessary for his face to be reconstructed, he said. But the worry now was that a blood clot caused by the concussion might become lodged in Tone's brain and cause instant death or, at the least, a stroke.

Tone's first demand after being removed from the critical list was that Neal be charged with felonious assault with intent to commit murder. Next, he asked that Barbara be allowed to visit him.

Emerging from Tone's room following a three-hour visit and wearing dark glasses, Barbara made an interesting understatement to the press. She said she'd been on "an emotional teeter-totter for a month" after first announcing her marriage to Tone, then to Neal, then again to Tone.

"Did Tom Neal hit you in the face?" I asked. "It's obvious you have a black right eye." This put her off balance. "If you don't tell us," I said, "District Attorney Roll will."

She broke down and admitted Neal had "walloped me so hard he knocked me out." She said Tone never tried to hit Neal and that when she came to, she found herself draped over Tone's body.

Bevo Means got back to me and said Neal had never had a professional or amateur boxing record. This overruled the felony possibility. But despite Tone's earlier threats, he'd not yet gotten around to signing a complaint.[27]

But the Tone-Payton-Neal love consortium wasn't over yet.

A few weeks after Neal put Tone in the hospital, Hollywood was betting two-to-one that Tone and Barbara would never get married.

But they did.

---

[27]Long after this, Barbara phoned me for dinner to help her with a personal personal problem. At that time, she said she'd talked Tone out of pressing charges because she thought she was still in love with Neal.

Following a hiatus from the front pages, the healing Tone traveled to Cloquet, Minnesota, where, on September 29, the two were wed on the lawn of Barbara's aunt Muriel Redfield's small white house. Hundreds of townspeople gathered to give the couple a noisy impromptu reception. It was so clamorous with teenagers banging on pails and ringing fireballs that relatives requested a few minutes of quiet so the ceremony could continue.

County Judge Ed Johnson had waived the state's mandatory five-day waiting period and performed the ceremony.

After the wedding, Mr. and Mrs. Tone and 16 of her relatives and friends left for dinner at a Duluth nightclub, leaving Judge Johnson alone who remarked: "I have married 400 couples in the past 13 years, but I never saw such a shivaree like this before!"

After only 53 days of marriage, the triangle plot thickened.

Hurrying to beat Barbara filing divorce papers in West Hollywood, Tone won the race with his attorney Henry Herzbrun. The complaint was that Barbara had "contemplated starring in a movie" with Tone's arch rival, Tom Neal! The producer was to be William Cagney, actor Jimmy's brother.

After Barbara said, "I don't want any alimony, I just want Mr. Tone to pay for my furniture," the divorce became final. Immediately after this latest stormy phase of the confused *affaire de coeur*, Cagney cancelled Barbara's contract and she never did make the picture with Neal.

While attempting a comeback in 1962, Barbara, whose leading men included Jimmy Cagney and Gregory Peck, was married to an antique dealer named Jess Rawley. But producers shunned her after several had seen Barbara starring in recent stag films shot in Mexico.

After she and Rawley were divorced, Barbara began to disappear into the fabric of humanity. Some who had known her well were distraught that she had settled in the border town of Tijuana where she worked a crib in a large, multiracial whore house where exotic venereal diseases spread like an epidemic.

I hadn't changed my home number for years, and in 1967, Barbara phoned me in the middle of the night to say she thought she was dying. I was working at Fox at the time, and on the first weekend, my friend Ralph Trejo and I drove to Tiajuana

I hardly recognized Barbara because her body had become swollen. Ralph and I carried her bodily from the crib and delivered her to her parents' home in San Diego. There, on May 8, Barbara, the once voluptuous blonde who had made men whistle, died of cirrhosis of the liver. The reason she had phoned me was that she greatly feared dying and having her body thrown in an unmarked grave.

Because he had lived at such a furious pace for most of his life, Tone grew old quickly. In 1956, at the age of 51, he secretly married a young—and predictably—buxom "budding actress" named Dolores Dora.

In 1968, he played his final role portraying the President of the United States in *The High Commissioner*. The same year, at the age of 63, having outlived Barbara, the *Phi Beta Kappa, cum laude* Cornell graduate, ardent lover of Joan Crawford, and the "perfect matinee idol" of his time, died on September 18, of lung cancer.

Tom Neal was despondent that he was practically unemployable after nearly killing Franchot Tone in 1951. And on April Fool's Day of 1965, the tough guy actor who was prone to land sucker punches on drunks, got into an argument with his third wife, 29-year-old Gail, and shot her to death. He claimed they were fighting over possession of a pistol.

Pleading guilty to a manslaughter charge, Neal was sent to the California Department of Correction and served seven of his one-to-15 year sentence. Upon release, he became a gardener in Palm Springs, a forgotten man. Even failing at this, he moved to a small apartment in North Hollywood and died of a heart attack on August 6, 1972 . . . the tenth anniversary of Marilyn Monroe's death.*

Author's note:

***An obscure Hollywood character named
Robert F. Slatzer approached me in the early**

1970s with a short, unfinished piece he'd hastily put together regarding Marilyn Monroe's death. He asked if I could expand it into a book for him. This would be for the usual speculative fifty-fifty split of all profits and equal author credits.

I said to Slatzer: "Too bad you weren't married to Monroe. That would *really* make a good book."

After I had gotten into the first draft, Slatzer mentioned he *had* been married to Marilyn, but "only for a weekend."

Because of questionable material he was feeding me, I became suspicious. I began investigating some of these "facts" after finishing my second draft whose title, *The Life and Curious Death of Marilyn Monroe* (Pinnacle Books, 1974), was given me by writer Al Stump.

Then when I discovered a personal Walter Winchell letter missing from one of my press books, and after an old boxer Noble "Kid" Chissell told me he was "just tryin' t' help out a friend" when he signed a paper attesting that Slatzer was married to Monroe, I made a decision: As a responsible reporter and biographer, I decided not to share coauthorship

After the book was published, I found it to be filled with fantasies. It has turned into a type of unliterary work that gives Hollywood history a hernia.

Since, Slatzer had made a career of being a pretender, selling gullible TV talk show producers who don't do their research very well, with the deception that he was married to Marilyn.

Until recently I considered Slatzer to be a harmless faker—that is, when he lately deceived an entire network with a made-for-TV movie with a title something like, "Marilyn and Me."

This latest dream was to sell his story to ABC in which he not only weds Monroe, but claims to have had a close relationship with Walter Winchell and a run in with baseball legend Joe DiMaggio.

Take this from the one who removed his name from the book:

Robert Slatzer was never married to Marilyn Monroe. He met the star only once. That was in Niagara Falls, New York, where he had his only pictures taken with her while she was making the movie, *Niagara*, with Joseph Cotten in 1951-52. Slatzer never met Marilyn before or since that time.

Also, Slatzer never even met Walter Winchell or Joe DiMaggio in his life.

Before Walter Wanger shot MCA movie agent Jennings Lang below the organ of increase because he suspected him of sharing sexual kinetics with his wife, actress Joan Bennett, I covered another Hollywood story which fit into these frantic times when television and the newspapers were battling.

As a reminder how well actress Zsa Zsa Gabor has preserved herself over these many years, the 1952 sex symbol star Corrine Calvet phoned Aggie Underwood to say she wanted to challenge Zsa Zsa to a bust-measuring contest. Aggie sent me to interview Corrine to ask how she planned to put on this contest.

When Corrine answered the door, she was wearing nothing more than her charming French accent.

Crossing her bare stemmed legs, Corrine said, "Zsa Zsa said once that I had no breasts at all, and I'm suing her for $1 million for that." She said: "Any time that Hungarian actress wants to make a contest with me, I'll strip like I am now and prove that my bosom is much bigger—without artificial respiration—than Zsa Zsa's." She added: "I know she can't compete with me. I would be far out in front of her."

"I get your point," I said.

Calvet did file the suit, but Gabor wasn't available for comment. Nothing came of it, but Corrine did get herself a lot of publicity which led to new picture contracts.

My story lead went:

"Corrine busted out with a new charge against Zsa Zsa Gabor today."

I suppose the only climax to the following Joan Bennett-Walter Wanger-Jennings Lang love triangle story was in itself the anticlimactic demonstration of how the aloof motion picture industry sheds itself of excess former greatness and fame.

Raven-haired Joan Bennett was known at the pinnacle of her success as a princess in one of the theater's royal families. She was one of three daughters of the late matinee idol Richard Bennett and Adrienne Morrison, who was also a Broadway star.

Joan made her stage debut at age 15, and together with her sisters Barbara and Constance, took the motion picture world by storm.

Joan had started out her career as a blonde, but after their marriage in 1940—and at the suggestion of director Tay Garnett—her husband, producer Walter Wanger, had her dye her hair black. This culminated in giving Bennett a new and more glamorous dimension.

Fifty-seven-year-old Walter Wanger was a towering figure in the film industry. He enjoyed a long series of movie triumphs. Many of the industry's hits bore his name as producer. Among them: *Private Worlds, Algiers* and *Stage Coach*. His most recent effort was *Joan of Arc*, starring Ingrid Bergman.

Wanger had everything going for him, except one: What husband ever had "everything going for him" when he was being cuckolded by a man 16 years his junior?

Fearful he was losing his 39-year-old wife, Wanger had her and her personal agent, Jennings Lang, followed by private investigators in Los Angeles and New York.

Wanger's investigators informed him that his suspicions of Miss Bennett's unfaithfulness were valid. This betrayal burned into the fibers of Wanger's body. He was a Jew and nurtured inbred customs of the time-honored Semitic tribes from which he came. Jennings Lang was also Jewish and acquainted with these religious traditions related to the ancient "unwritten law" in regard to infidelity. The tribal practice for thousands of years was for the cuckolded husband to seek out his transgressor, cut off his testicles and stuff them into the offender' mouth.

Now, on a warm late afternoon of December 13, 1951, once quiet-mannered Wanger decided it was time to take this unresolved situation from the hands of his private detectives.

The diminutive gray-haired man also began loading the .38 caliber revolver he'd bought some years earlier when Sheriff Biscailuz made him an honorary deputy sheriff. This legally allowed Wanger to carry a concealed weapon.

Wanger had also recently purchased a razor-sharp four-inch blade hunting knife which he hid inside his coat pocket—and he fully intended to use it.

Armed with two weapons, Wanger drove to the Music Corporation of America's agency parking lot in Beverly Hills where top talent executive Lang had his offices.

The producer waited for an hour-and-a-half in the lot situated directly across the street from the Beverly Hills City Hall which included Chief Clinton H. Anderson's police department and jail.

As the sun began to set, a blue Cadillac convertible drove into the asphalt parking lot. Joan Bennett was driving. Her passenger was Jennings Lang.

The two sat and talked as Wanger stalked toward them, gripping the .38 pistol.

The two sat and talked as Wanger stalked toward them, gripping the .38 pistol.

Parking lot attendant Samuel Scott was standing 75 feet from the car when Wanger confronted the two. He said: "I was attracted by their loud voices ... Then I heard Miss Bennett scream: 'Don't! Don't!' Then I ran over to the car where I found Mr. Lang slumped over the seat. Miss Bennett was running around the car to his side."

It was then that parking lot owner Sidney Holtzman arrived. He said he watched Lang sink down, "moaning and groaning and holding his crotch with both hands." Holtzman said he thought for certain Lang "had his balls shot clean off."

Despite its close proximity to the parking lot, gunshot reports hadn't been heard at the police department. But at that time, Holtzman helped Joan lift the injured Lang into her Cadillac. Lang moaned: "Get me to my doctor's office on Wilshire Boulevard."

Before the convertible roared off, Wanger dropped his pistol in the front seat. And as they drove to the doctor's office with the heavily bleeding Lang, Holtzman later told Chief Anderson that Joan asked him: "How are we going to avoid the publicity?" Then, "I want you to have this car cleaned thoroughly after you drop us off at Dr. Riemer's place."

Two uniformed police officers arrived at the parking lot and apprehended Wanger who gave no resistance. They escorted him to the station where it was not necessary at the time for him to be booked, fingerprinted or photographed. Instead, he was directly escorted into Anderson's office where the Chief questioned Wanger in a friendly manner in the presence of a recording court stenographer.

At the time, police had no clue as to where Lang and Joan Bennett had disappeared to. They were aware he'd been shot, so an all points bulletin was issued for police to be on the lookout for a man who might be bleeding to death.

Within minutes after arriving at Dr. Riemer's office, the physician had Lang—with Joan by his side—moved to surgery at nearby Midway Hospital. There, Joseph Pollock, M.D., performed a 90-minute procedure described as "delicate surgery" in the area of the talent agent's scrotum. He later said it was miraculous Lang hadn't lost his testicles, much less, his life.

This was a different story to cover for the reason that so many things were simultaneously going on in several different places. Had this story broken a few months later, TV news would have been covering with its new Filmo cameras. Therefore, we newspaper reporters enjoyed these final days when we were still covering exclusively.

Sending me out to the Beverly Hills police station, Aggie said: "I have a hunch Bennett might be showing up, even though she's pissed off at her husband."

Aggie then assigned Dick O'Connor to do the roundup, with Jack Smith handling sidebars coming in from various locations in the field.

While I covered the Beverly Hills police station, other crews were heading toward the $150,000 Wanger mansion in Holmby Hills, the district attorney's office, the hospital where Bevo learned Lang was languishing following the mandatory gunshot wound report. A beat crew also hung out at the Superior Court clerk's office where a writ of habeas corpus was expected to be filed by whichever attorney would be representing Wanger.

Then there were family members and friends to be interviewed before the law and attorneys arrived to silence them: Were Walter and Joan getting along well of late? Had they been fighting? Did anyone have a hint of some clandestine place where the asserted lovers might have been holding clandestine meetings?

Also, in the city room, picture editor Eddie Krauch was shuffling through dozens of Bennett glamor photos.

Smith's first sidebar would get the head:

Parallel In Love Shooting

It would be compared to the 1938 love triangle shooting of singing star Ruth Etting's young playmate, pianist Merl Alderson, by Ruth's older divorced husband, Martin "Moe the Gimp" Snyder.

Photographers filled the police station anteroom and hallways now, waiting for Chief Anderson to finish questioning Wanger before sending him upstairs to the jail where no prisoners happened to be locked up at the time.

As we waited, the proprietor of Beverly Hills' most exclusive restaurant, Mike Romanoff, appeared. The moustached pretender to Russian Tsar Nicholas II's family had shown up with his head waiter and a selection of delicacies protected under sterling silver warmer domes. He planned to personally supervise the serving of Mr. Wanger's dinner in his cell.

My photographer Ed Phillips posed pictures of Romanoff and his *matre d'* with towel draped over one arm, examining the meal.

Actor George Murphy arrived to visit the producer just as a uniformed officer led Wanger—tactfully unmanacled—from Anderson's office.

A heavy set man, Chief Anderson moved slowly and smiled a lot. He liked cigars, but never smoked them outside his office. But he always had a good Havana in his desk drawer for visiting reporters. He scorned looking like the stereotype cop, probably because he'd headed up the Beverly Hills police department since the city was founded in 1925.

Anderson said Wanger made his first phone call to his attorney, Mandel Silberberg. Wanger had said: "Mandel, I'm in the office of Chief Clinton Anderson at the Beverly Hills Police Department. They're holding me for shooting Jennings Lang. I want you to come down here." Then as an afterthought: "But finish your dinner first."

We soon learned that Silberberg phoned Jerry Giesler, who, coincidentally, had also handled the Ruth Etting shooting case. Silberberg officially turned Wanger over to Giesler as a client. Criminal law was out of the contract attorney's realm of practice.

Then Anderson said he'd booked Wanger "with intent to commit murder," and humorously added: "... and we'll also book him on assault with a deadly weapon ... as soon as we find the damned gun."

The the Chief quoted Wanger's time-tattered explanation for his act—a line of dialogue he would probably have disdained to use in one of his prize-winning films. ''Mr. Wanger said, 'I shot Mr. Lang because he broke up my home.' Then he said, 'Please call my home and ask the servants to turn the radios off so the children won't hear the news that way.' '' These were his daughters Stephanie, 8, and Shelly, 3.

Her-Ex reporter Judd Smith was at Midway Hospital when Deputy District Attorney Adolph Alexander arrived to take Lang's statement. But doctors refused him entrance to Lang's room, saying he was too sedated at the time and was being administered a transfusion to offset shock and loss of blood. And when District Attorney Ernie Roll heard Anderson had taken a lengthy statement, he was driven—Code Three—to the Beverly Hills police station.

By this time, Jack Smith had gotten Miss Bennett's daughter Melinda on the phone in New York. The 17-year-old girl was born during Joan's second marriage to playwright Gene Markey. Melinda had phoned her mother when she heard about the shooting and asked if it was all right if she made her TV debut that night on CBS network's ''Star Playhouse.'' Joan wished her luck and said not to worry.

Ernie Roll and Jerry Giesler simultaneously arrived in Beverly Hills. Roll headed for Anderson's office and Giesler for the officer of the day, waving a writ signed by Superior Court Judge Thomas J. Morrison. It would free his client on $5,000 bail. After that, Giesler went upstairs to talk with his new client.

In Anderson's office, Roll learned from deputy Alexander that Lang had gotten word out (secretly through Joan Bennett) that he didn't intend to press charges against Wanger. And when Roll faced us in the anteroom, he said he was hot over Lang not cooperating with Alexander. He said: ''I have a good witness in the shooting, whose name I can't reveal at this time [Scott]. And in spite of Mr. Lang's attitude, I promise you Mr. Wanger will be prosecuted.'' He added that he wouldn't oppose the writ since he'd been assured Lang would recover. After talking with Anderson, Roll disclosed that Wanger had warned Lang a year earlier in New York to stay away from his wife. Wanger had said: "If anybody breaks up my home, I'll shoot him." Roll said both Wanger and Lang had later relayed this conversation to Joan.

Judd Smith called in from the hospital to report that Lang's wife, Pam, had shown up dressed in black and wearing dark glasses. She told Judd she didn't believe her husband and Miss Bennett had engaged in an illicit love affair. "My only concern now is for my family and my husband's physical condition. We have two children and there are no complications in our lives."

When police located the revolver and Holtzman, the parking lot owner was held for five hours as an "uncooperative material witness."

Things started dragging until Joan Bennett made her entrance at the police station. She was wearing a dark dress with page boy collar and cuffs. She was followed in by her publicist Margaret Ettinger and two of her own aides.

Miss Bennett graciously removed her dark glasses for photographers. She appeared to be somewhat shaken but had received good advice to cooperate with the press.

"He must have gone berserk," she told reporters. "He never behaved like this before." When questioned, she denied a triangle involving her with Lang. And to attorney Silberberg, who had also accompanied her (probably to pick up an easy fee), Joan said: "Mr. Wanger's jealousy was purely in his imagination ... My husband was close to a nervous breakdown already because of worry over bankruptcy proceedings against him ... All this stemmed from his financing *Joan of Arc.*" (Although critically acclaimed, the Ingrid Bergman starrer was a disaster at the box office.)

Then Miss Bennett repeated to us what she had told Chief Anderson earlier. She said: "I had an appointment yesterday afternoon with Mr. Lang, and after our office meeting, we drove around Beverly Hills and Hollywood in Mr. Lang's car. Then he brought me back to the MCA parking lot and took me over to my own car when Mr. Wanger[28] joined us."

---

[28]When caught dead to rights, the famous always revert to the third person when referring to their lovers and others.

After Joan departed with her entourage, Wanger was accompanied through the anteroom with Giesler holding on to his arm. "Ducking photographers," Giesler told Wanger earlier, "makes you look guilty as hell."

When I asked Giesler if he planned to evoke the "unwritten law" in this case, he smiled and said: "Could be, Will. Could be."

Directly, Wanger went undercover from the press at the home of an undisclosed friend.

The news-gathering and writing the lead story, along with four sidebars, was coming to an end. It had only been 18 hours since Bevo Means called in the first flash until the *Her-Ex* was put to bed with Campbell's lengthy headline blazed across the front page:

FILM PRODUCER WANGER SHOOTS ESCORT OF WIFE, JOAN BENNETT

Below were three photos. Across the first four columns was a five-inch glamour shot of Bennett reclining on an elbow, sensuously staring into the camera. She was wearing a long draped negligee as black as her hair. It was captioned:

Joan Bennett As Top
Hollywood Glamor Girl

Besides the Ruth Etting triangle story and the piece about Joan's daughter debuting on television, Jack Smith also wrote two more sidebars.

In all, the published *extra* contained nearly 5,000 words covering every story angle we could come up with.

Over the weekend, San Francisco's top criminal lawyer Jake Ehrlich phoned Aggie at her home to say he had been retained by Lang and was on his way by plane to Los Angeles. "Telling me ahead of time was for a past favor," Aggie told me, "so keep it our secret." It was Saturday, an overtime day, and she sent Judd Smith and Ben White back to Midway Hospital where Ernie Roll was scheduled to arrive at 8:30. Perry Fowler and I went out to the Wanger estate in Holmby Hills.

On the dot, Ernie Roll, already in a bad mood because his weekend had been disrupted, arrived at Midway with deputy

Alexander and two stenotypists. A D.A.'s personal involvement in big cases such as this one was imperative when he had the chance to get his name and picture on the front page, so it was expected he'd be ready with a lot of quotes and dramatic disclosures. Roll's intention was to take Lang's statement regarding his involvement in the biggest Hollywood love shooting triangle in years. Ben White shot the D.A. heading past the front desk toward Lang's private room. Again, a nurse barred the entourage, and Lang's on the scene lawyer, Oliver Schwab, disallowed Roll talking to Lang.

Words got hot and Roll shook his finger at Schwab: "In that case, Mr. Lang's refusal to cooperate in the inquiry will be a matter for the grand jury to investigate on the grounds of obstruction of justice."

Deputy Alexander added: "There's also a place called General Hospital prison ward where we can have access to him."

It wasn't until tempers cooled that Roll let photographers shoot pictures of Wanger's hunting knife he just happened to have on him. It had been found in Wanger's coat pocket after he was apprehended.

Another confusing development was the revelation that two reports of private detectives who shadowed Bennett and Lang had been found in a suitcase in Wanger's car following the arrest.

It was believed that some of the papers were in Chief Anderson's possession. Reportedly, Giesler was planning to demand they be returned to his client as possibly supplying motivation for the shooting.

Meanwhile, Perry and I were staked out at the rambling Wanger hilltop home. It was turning into a slow news day until Bennett's attorney Grant Cooper showed up. He was one of the number of big-wheel lawyers who always surfaced defending or representing someone noted in the public's eye. I asked Cooper if there was a divorce in the offing. He said: "I have not discussed this aspect with Miss Bennett, but I don't believe anything along that line is contemplated." To a reporter, this was the same as his saying: "Who the hell knows?"

As Cooper rang the front doorbell, I said: "Then would you pass along to Miss Bennett that 24 hours ago Mr. Wanger told Chief Anderson that the day before the shooting, Wanger and Miss Bennett were, indeed, discussing divorce?" (Ehrlich had given Aggie this information.)

A maid answered, but Cooper, trying to be fair without going against his client's wishes, said: "I'll give you this: Yesterday after Mr. Wanger was released from jail, I made Miss Bennett conveniently absent from the house when Mr. Wanger came up to remove five suitcases filled with clothing. I hear he's rented an apartment in Beverly Hills. Where, I don't know."

Sunday was a quiet day. Friends came to my house for a barbecue and I enjoyed telling them various aspects about the case that hadn't been in the paper. After all, being a newspaper reporter had its moments of importance and interest to his friends. It was amusing living in a neighborhood filled with curious people.

We started all over again in the city room on Monday morning. Among other stories, O'Connor was doing a weekend wrap up on the case, mainly recapping what had happened on Saturday. The *Her-Ex* didn't put out a Sunday paper, so what we did on Monday wasn't too important other than to keep it's readers up on the latest happenings.

Aggie gave me Chief Anderson's home number from her private phone book, and I waited until 7:30 before calling so he'd have time to waken.

The Chief and I played cat-and-mouse. I said: "I just heard you have both Wanger's private eyes' notebooks."

"This early in the morning?" the Chief asked. "Someone told you that this early? Who told you that?"

I could have heard it from Giesler, Cooper, Schwab, Jake Ehrlich, or the D.A.'s office. I made a guess: "Ernie Roll."

"Ernie told you that himself?"

"Someone in the D.A.'s office."

"Who in the D.A.'s office?"

"Jesus, Chief, you expect me to tell you *who*? I have my own sources, too. You expect me to tell you where I got the information?''

"I can't do that," he said, "but I'll tell you this—and it's off the record: I'm keeping the notes to see if we can find any justification for Wanger's suspicions, to see if there's a clue pointing to premeditation."

"Can I use that as a quote?"

"You come up with someone's name in the D.A.'s office and hang it on him."

"I can do that," I said. "Now, how about some addresses? I want some place to start with, where Joan and Lang were sleeping around . . . I figure it's got to be some place handy for a quick matinee . . . You know these Hollywood agents hand out their keys to preferred clients."

"I tell you what," said Anderson, "I'll give you this much: It's a pain in the ass when you reporters start grazing in my pastures at one time . . . So try asking around the Beverly Hills apartment district."

"Jesus, Chief, all the apartments are below Wilshire Boulevard . . . and that's 75 percent of the population. How about narrowing it down?"

"Try above Olympic and between Spalding and Beverly Drive."

"That's no help," I said.

Pay Foley, the dapper beatman who wore a stiff collar and morning coat with a fresh carnation in his buttonhole, was covering the County Grand Jury hearing. It convened Tuesday to consider indictments charging Wanger with assault with intent to commit murder and/or assault with a deadly weapon. But before the jury's convention, it was agreed by the district attorney that it would not be necessary at that time to set an arraignment date.

Witnesses Holtzman and Scott reported what they'd seen at the parking lot, and my friend police chemist Ray Pinker said the gunshot sound wouldn't carry far if Wanger pressed the pistol close to Lang's body. Dr. Riemer testified to the extent of Lang's wound, and Beverly Hills Lt. A.J. Gebhardt told of removing a "long-bladed knife" from Wanger's coat shortly after the producer's arrest.

The indictment charged that Wanger "did willfully and with malice aforethought commit an assault with the intent to kill and murder Jennings Lang."

But before the jury handed down its decision Giesler insisted the return of private investigative reports covering surveillance of Bennett and Lang in Los Angeles and New York, saying: "They [the reports] show much more than just that Miss Bennett and Mr. Lang were meeting at the parking lot where the shooting occurred . . . I have a client to defend and if it is necessary to use the reports in his [Wanger's] defense, I certainly won't hesitate to use them."

The Grand Jury chose the more serious of the two alternative charges presented. The "assault with intent to commit murder" charge carried a sentence of five-to-14 years in prison on conviction.

The gun, knife and Lang's bullet-ridden pants, were presented to the jury as evidence.

Wanger and Giesler waited in a nearby bail bondsman's office when the indictment was handed down by Superior Judge Thomas J. Cunningham. Wanger then surrendered himself for arraignment and posting of a new bond.

Now that Wanger was being held, I started working on locating the apartment where Joan and Lang had been meeting for their trysts.

A veteran reporter never tries the time-consuming door-to-door search in cases such as this one. This is what I did:

Nearby the Beverly Hills City Hall, I waited for the lunch break when I intended to question a relief receptionist at the impressive, formal white colonnaded, red-bricked antebellum MCA building. Relief receptionists were the best to approach because they were rarely clued in on the company's procedures. Therefore, instead of their coming up with something like, "You'll have to come back later,'' they would usually work hard to accommodate someone. They wished to appear efficient.

I went in at 12:30, about when the deal-makers were well into their usual two-hour, three-martini lunches. I approached a chubby receptionist reading a paperback book on the sly. I opened my coat, making certain she got a good look at my .38 calibre revolver. The young lady quickly shoved her book into a drawer. With police and county investigations having been in abundance these past few days, she obviously figured what I might be there for and seemed happy to help me in any way possible.

"I'm investigating the Jennings Lang case," I said.

"What may I do for you, sir?" she said, trying to smile.

"I'm checking on a few of Mr. Lang's business acquaintances," I said. "Could you help me with some of their names?"

"I don't know . . . any of . . . Mr. Lang's friends," she said while opening a lower desk drawer.

I mumbled something like, "I understand" as she laid a typed double-spaced list down on the desk.

(Reporters were adept at reading upside down and backwards. We learned this through years of cadging information from police blotters, motel and hotel registers and deciphering hot picas locked in blocks in newspaper composing rooms.)

While Miss Obese was fingering down the list, I searched for addresses in the area Chief Anderson gave me. There were five employee addresses in the area between Spalding and Beverly. Three started with "Mr." I put the addresses to memory, then said: "Well, don't mind, Miss. I'll come back later when someone more familiar with the situation returns."

I worried I hadn't armed myself with enough information by the time I got to the third residence. It was an expensive-looking duplex at 141 South Bedford Drive and belonged to a Jav Kanter. No one was in, so I started looking for neighbors to talk to— always women in those days.

I located one. She was the landlady next door at 143½. Her name was Mrs. Rowena Nate. Not only was Rowena cooperative, but she filled me in with famous past history tenants who spent some time at Kanter's duplex. Among them, she said, "was Marlon Brando while he was recuperating from a leg wound."

Rowena was a cute middle-ager who also wanted to impress me that she'd been around a few boudoirs in her time. She primped and said: "Oh, yes. For more than six months Joan Bennett and Mr. Lang . . . played house in the afternoons." She smiled and tittered.

This was the first legitimate quote anyone, anywhere had offered in their own name as being witness to the Bennett-Lang trysts.

"Their constant meetings were the talk of the neighborhood. Miss Bennett often stopped to pat children's heads as she arrived and went."

Another neighbor lady, who wouldn't identify herself, noted that "the two lovers often appeared with small packages." She even offered that she had investigated Kanter's garbage and said: "Sometimes they had small picnics for themselves."

Landlady Rowena said Joan and Lang "stayed for three and four hours at Mr. Kanter's duplex, but Miss Bennett always left shortly before dark . . . Miss Bennett in her blue Cadillac and Mr. Lang in his green Cadillac."

The more inquisitive anonymous lady unashamedly told me she watched through her window at the pair moving from room to room, including their lying in bed together, "but I never saw what they eventually did because she always got up and closed the blinds." I could read the disappointment in her face.

In support of all this, however, I wasn't able to locate a neighbor who could recall whether Joan and Lang met at the Kanter place the afternoon of the shooting. This was when Bennett told police she was "driving around Beverly Hills and Hollywood" with her agent of nine years.

When I recapped the day's story angles to Cappy Marek, Taxi Bill and Blind Virginia at Moran's, I was still waiting for the initial blush of traffic to subside before heading home. I slept fitfully, dwelling on interviewing Lang at his house the next day, now that he'd slipped out of Midway Hospital.

When I arrived at Lang's two-story Spanish hacienda the next day, Mrs. Lang escorted us to the tiled stairway with decorative iron railing. She was quiet and looked down at the floor. We reporters didn't know it at the time, but Mrs. Lang was a very sick woman.

Upstairs in the large master bedroom lay the star of the day. Lang was propped up with pillows at his back and a few below his knees. There were about eight of us reporters, and appearing as inconspicuous as possible in a corner sat Jake Ehrlich, a thin, sharp-featured man with flashy eyes. His legs remained crossed throughout the twenty minutes we were there. And he never spoke a word.

Lang's answers to our questions were at best ... terrible. He was filled with mundane Hollywood cliché metaphor. And as it usually happens in a group of interviewing reporters, one eventually ends up doing most of the questioning. In this case, it happened to be me.

"Mr. Lang," I asked. "Exactly what went through your mind when you saw Mr. Wanger coming toward you brandishing a revolver?"

Lang dramatically drew in a breath for effect, then tried to put us down with his motion picture jargon. He said: "Well, gentlemen ... you know what a *montage* is, don't you?"

I was pissed because he'd ignored Aline Mosby's presence. "You mean to say: 'Do Miss Mosby and we gentlemen understand what a *montage* is.' " I was one up on him.

"Ah, yes. Forgive me Miss Mosby," he moaned. "With apologies, I mean: *Do* you know what a *montage* is?"

We chuckled at his attempt to debase and I said: "Yes, Mr. Lang. A *montage* is a film editing function; a series of quick shots ... to bolster a weak story."

The next day, Matt Weinstock's *Daily News* column dwelled more upon what I had said about a *montage* than he did about Jennings Lang's pompous statements.

With the advent of April, both Bennett and Wanger had been wrung dry with press exposure. But as a result of the notoriety, no immediate movie contracts were forthcoming for Joan. Even a national company had had second thoughts and cancelled an ambitious magazine soap commercial campaign.

Wanger appeared pessimistic, expecting the worst regarding a possible one-to-15 year prison sentence hanging over him. He was an apprehensive Damocles at best.

But this was what it was all about when one hired Jerry Giesler to get in the ring with a judge or jury and exercise his jurisprudent infighting.

Giesler had convinced Wanger it would be better to avoid an open trial, permitting the producer's fate to be decided by the testimony already given to the grand jury.

On the morning of the 14th, with his client by his side, Giesler appeared before Justice Harry J. Borde in Santa Monica Superior Court and presented him the grand jury transcripts along with letters from producers Darryl F. Zanuck, Hal B. Wallis and Walt Disney. Also author Fulton Oursler and a U.S. Senator, all begging for clemency.

Waiving a jury trial, Giesler impressed Judge Borde that it would be less publicly taxing for the family children if he would come to a decision regarding the depth of Wanger's guilt away from the press.

This was agreed upon by the court, but when Giesler tried to push harder, Judge Borde refused the criminal lawyer's plea to reduce the grand jury indictment of assault to commit murder to simple assault.

After digesting the grand jury transcripts containing testimonies of the seven witnesses, Judge Borde said to Wanger: "I am reducing your grave indictment because the evidence I have studied has fallen far short of proving that this offense was committed with your intent of murdering Jennings Lang. Therefore, I hereby sentence you to four months in the Los Angeles County Jail."

Judge Borde also allowed Wanger three weeks to get his affairs in order before beginning his term. During this period, unusual and surprising things began happening. Wanger started visiting the Holmby Hills house to have breakfast with the family, and the separated husband and wife were seen in public on occasion to be affectionate toward one another.

On Tuesday, June 3, I asked Sheriff Biscailuz and Chief Jailer Al W. Willey if Wanger would receive any special treatment—as most wealthy and prominent people do—when he surrendered himself the following day. They said "no;" that Wanger's duties as a prisoner would be decided after he took a shower, changed into blue denims and was given a physical examination after he arrived at the Wayside Honor Farm in Castaic.

Friday morning, Wanger boarded a county bus containing security wire windows. One of the two prisoners he was shackled to began ducking photographers, but the other laughed: "You don't have to cover up, man. We've got a celebrity between us. Nobody'll notice you an' me."

The press caravaned the bus from the Hall of Justice to the desert town where the honor farm was located. There, the manacled Wanger requested his picture not be taken while passing through the front gate. I left it to another reporter to say: "What the hell. It's only a gate."

Before retiring in an upper berth, Wanger was asked who should he have notified in case of death, and he said: "My wife, Joan."

He was reported to have slept like a baby. He didn't know the man in the berth below was Evan Charles Thomas, the notorious "Phantom Sniper," infamous for a series of rifle attacks on women.

During his stay at the farm—which was tantamount to a camping vacation—Wanger was given several jobs, any one of which a hardened inmate would have killed for. He arranged athletic contests and religious services, was appointed librarian to succeed an inmate about to graduate, and ran the projection machine on nights movies were screened. He was spared from heavy duty farm labor because he was found to have "flat feet."

During his stay, Joan opened in the play *Bell, Book and Candle* in Chicago.

After serving 102 days, Wanger emerged tan and healthy, wearing a neat gray suit and brown shoes. Hiding no longer from cameras, the producer now insisted on leaving jail "side-by-side" with another freed prisoner, Ralph Hile, an Army top sergeant who had done 100 days for drunkenness and cashing bad checks.

Wanger was also bubbling with ideas for the reform of the state's penal institutions and told reporters he hoped to get to work immediately on a scenario based on his experiences at the honor farm. He spoke highly of his treatment by jailers and deputies, but condemned the California penal institutions as "America's Number One Scandal." Through time though, his enthusiasm flagged and he never did get around to doing all this. The closest he came much later was to produce a picture based on the life of Barbara Graham titled *I Want to Live*, which was a denunciation of capital punishment.

Perhaps the eventual financial failure Wanger suffered in producing *Joan of Arc* sparked this unfortunate affair between his wife and Jennings Lang. He seemed unable to sustain a rational manner while facing bankruptcy. And this obviously spilled over to disrupt a harmonious family life.

But I believe the reason *Joan of Arc* was checkmated at the boxoffice was because the theatre-going public has always been hypocritical and unforgiving of others who got caught doing bad things they, themselves, were lucky enough to get away with.

At the time of the movie's release and through its run, Wanger's star—a married Ingrid Bergman—was also romantically linked with Roberto Rosselini, and eventually bore her Italian producer-director a child out of wedlock.

Following a touted successful reconciliation and second honeymoon, Joan's and Wanger's marriage ultimately failed.

Wanger's ultimate financial fiasco came when he produced the screen epic *Cleopatra* at 20th Century-Fox. It was started in the late 1950s and finally released in 1963. The film was plagued with unrecoupable expenses when overseas production shut down as a result of leading lady Elizabeth Taylor's illnesses. This was compounded by her romantic flare ups with her leading man, Richard Burton. This spelled the end to Wanger's motion picture

career and he departed Fox in acrimony. This and the love
triangle, however, didn't seem to have tolled heavily on him even
though he disappeared from the public's eye. In 1968, at the
age of 72, Wanger died in his New York apartment, and the media
made little of his passing.

In the case of the triangle, who was the one most erupted by
this fling of the glands? Joan Bennett came to star in a successful TV series and was featured in many more pictures. Jennings
Lang went on to become a successful producer. But the one
person who was only fleetingly mentioned in the torrid front page
affair, the one who publicly stated that she refused to believe
her husband had been unfaithful, Mrs. Pam Lang, was driven
into deep depression and a few months after the story quieted
down, she died of a heart attack.

In the entertainment industry, love triangles participated in
by high profile people never work out. Those I've observed and
reported on have ended in total failure. I have also spoken with
a few of the intimates after the fact. The men agreed they should
have kept their flies zipped, and the women wished they had
kept their legs crossed.

ISOSCELES OF A LOVE TRIANGLE—Actress Barbara Payton at peak of her beauty while simultaneously sharing her love with movie star husband Franchot Tone and actor Tom Neal in 1951. The Hollywood split infinitive nearly caused the *Mutiny on the Bounty* star his life at the hands of Neal when they fought over Barbara's affections.

XX

Exit Laughing

When Christmas, New Years or any other legal holiday fell on a Saturday or Sunday, that day was absorbed into the normal weekend. There was no referendum wherein an establishment would reimburse an employee or give him an extra day off That's the way it was back in those days before Alaska and Hawaii had been admitted to statehood. So when the Fourth of July fell on a Friday in 1952, it was like being handed a mini-holiday.

It was only six weeks prior to the Fourth when both Jack Smith and I would be starting on new jobs independent of the newspaper business. What had attracted us most was that these positions would be paying us three times more than the salaries we were receiving on the *Her-Ex*. But for some reason we couldn't explain to ourselves at the time, neither of us cared to let Mr. Campbell find out about our financial windfalls until the eleventh hour.

Jack was striking out to become a special representative for top Hollywood publicity agent Carl Bior and I'd been signed to join John Fenton Murray and Ben Freeman as one of Red Skelton's writers for the comedian's television comedy show, which, according to the national popularity polls was Number One.

Also, during celebration of this patriotic holiday, a 32-year-old woman from San Diego named Florence Chadwick planned to assault the standing 25-year Catalina Channel swim record of 15 hours and ten minutes.

After informing Aggie of our luck in promoting a yacht that weekend, she let Smith, Dick O'Connor and myself off early on Thursday afternoon in order to get an early start on our self-destruction. The yacht belonged to Skelton's business manager Bo Roos. And just in case she wanted to get in touch with us, I gave Aggie the boat's private radio band call letters.

We traveled south on the Pacific Coast Highway and made it to the summer resort town of Newport Beach in my 1949 Ford station wagon along about sunset.

Not only had Roos offered us his yacht, but we were also availed of his apartment at pierside, plus a "Captain" to navigate us to-and-from Catalina Island.

After settling in at the digs, we decided to check out a nearby carnival before shoving off. There, I won a doll for ringing a gong atop a 20-foot-high rail three times. But after we were threatened to be cited for drinking openly from a bottle, we departed after I gave my doll to a little girl.

Itching to join a regatta haphazardly heading toward Catalina, our gray-haired skipper—whom Smith dubbed "Ahab"—cast off and headed out to sea.

The rangy Civil War chronicler O'Connor had never seen a flying fish before, and in his enthusiasm to trap one in flight with a free hand, fell overboard into the channel waters.

Captain Ahab, with intimate knowledge of the erratic currents, put about and in no time, O'Connor was saved along with a fifth of Gilbey's Gin that he steadfastly clinched in his red paw.

Smith calculated that since prehistoric days, Catalina Island had been visited by 67 million people—give or take a press agent more or less—and so it was with a feeling of discovery that we raised our heavy eyebrows and allowed our vision to embrace that spectacular landfall, rising out of the tossing sea as it did with a hearty welcome for the wayfarer.

We finally anchored offshore and a water taxi delivered us to Avalon's pier. Here, ignoring the craft's unsteady mooring, O'Connor leaped from the prow through the keen Pacific air momentarily looking like a figurehead. Smith recalled that O'Connor groped for the bleached and weathered wood of Avalon with his right foot shod in canvas. There was a moment of silence, broken only by the sound of bait being slipped on hooks, and for one dread second, fishing stopped entirely as O'Connor let anger sweep over his pink, peaceful face to shout a fearful refrain:

"Good gravy, gentlemen! Surely there's a liquor store about!"

With a new cache of refreshments—this time champagne—our yacht headed toward the isthmus where we could cheer on Miss Chadwick before her midnight start.

There, we approached an elegant bar where *Her-Ex* columnist Bill Kennedy was enjoying a Tom Collins and the company of Del Mar Beach Club boss Roger Cunningham. Kennedy was expounding that newspapermen no longer were unwashed, uneducated, unwanted and underpaid.

It was just then that O'Connor, wearing his worn skipper's hat, and Smith in dirtied white turtle-neck sweater, and I sporting a frazzled straw headpiece I'd picked up in Tahiti years earlier, appeared.

After searching the heavens for an answer to our shabby condition, Kennedy immediately reversed his pontification, saying to Cunningham:

"What I was telling you about newspapermen was not exactly true." He sucked on his cigarette and staring out over the bay (He couldn't look at someone while telling a lie), continued:

"Newspapermen are *all* unwashed, uneducated, unwanted, underpaid and unpredictable."

Somewhere along the line we ate food as ballast for our stomachs. Then I wandered off seeking Florence Chadwick for an interview. Even though I wasn't working, it seemed the natural thing to do.

I located her while making my way up to the end of the isthmus pier where the press and a thousand spectators were bunched together awaiting the swimmer to show up.

Standing on the beach beneath the pier, I saw Florence in her white rubber cap and six pounds of black grease plastered all over her bathing suit and body.

"My trainer's out there at the end of the pier in our skiff," she pointed. Then, "Well, I guess I'd better get going."

I waded along with her until the water got up the my chin, then said, "So long."

I then wandered back to gather up Smith and O'Connor at the bar where I'd left them. They were talking with Tarzan of the movies Johnny Weismuller. I invited him to accompany us to the mainland aboard Roos's yacht and watch Miss Chadwick do her thing.

After Captain Ahab jockeyed our craft into the reestablished regatta, I noticed the *Thunderbird's* presence. This 75-foot craft was not only loaded to the gunwales, it was bursting with an overflow of landlubber reporters.

I could have pointed out at least a half-dozen maritime violations over-and-above the insufficient number of available like jackets it carried aboard. Also to be taken into consideration was the possibility of an outbreak of *mal de mer* with the majority of news people throwing up over one-another.

The chock-a-block craft was incapable of traveling more than a few knots an hour, about the speed Chadwick was swimming. And if the channel waters grew nasty, there could be a sea disaster that would take precedence over the swim. With this in mind, I checked out Bo Roos's shortwave sending set to find it in working order.

Evident and a sore to our eyes, the new news medium was with us. And for the first time in history, television was covering a live channel swim. As we watched, Smith and I also realized the damned thing was beating the newspapers in the image of network station KNBH.

During the night, Florence paused in her steady 32-stroke pace to swallow broth, sugar and vitamin pills. And a mid-morning, prospects began to change for the worse. A fog had drifted in only to lift later and leave the area overcast and cold. The the treacherous Japanese Current came into the picture, beginning to alter Chadwick's 21-mile course. The ocean swelled and several reporters predictably became sick and hung over the *Thunderbird's* railings.

Florence began complaining about being cold; that her hands, arms and shoulders were growing numb. She had drastically slowed down her pace.

It was then when Johnny Weismuller dived from our boat to offer encouragement to the swimmer. Stroking alongside the English Channel champion, our country's premiere aquatic hero gave one of the most disgraceful demonstrations of the American Crawl I'd ever witnessed.

It wasn't until we hauled Johnny back aboard that the Olympic champion told us he'd suffered severe leg cramps when diving into the chilly waters.

It was about noontime when Florence gave up to the strong sea swells. She pulled alongside her skiff and her trainer called out:

"Is there a doctor around?!"

Smith, O'Connor, Weismuller and I exchanged quick glances, then I shouted back:

"We have a doctor aboard over here!"

I think I was driven to the preposterous lie because television was stealing the show and it would be my last chance to scoop the bastards. And on my day off, to boot.

Quickly, we hauled Chadwick aboard and took her below and out of sight of the TV camera aboard the *Thunderbird*. Then Captain Ahab wrapped her in blankets. She was shivering and had blue skin where the grease had washed away.

We had actually shanghaied Chadwick, and in order to take full advantage of our position, I suggested that Captain Ahab change his coarse and leisurely cruise up-and-down the inlet for a couple of hours while KNBH tried to figure out how to fill in its dead time on the air.

Realizing the swim was over, the other boats began heading for the breakwater while on topside, Smith said: "I wonder what you get these days for kidnapping."

I was interviewing Chadwick below as a *Her-Ex* rewrite man took notes on the other end of Bo Roos's shortwave radio. "The idea was to have the tide with me at the end of the swim,'' she said.

Before I got off the radio, I told Aggie we would continue cruising until she had a circulation truck down at Huntington Beach giving away papers with our exclusive story.

Aggie said: ''Right now, KNBH is running old films of Chadwick's English Channel swim.''

When we hit the dock much later, the opposition was ready to kill us, KNBH had already departed and our circulation truck pulled up with stacks of papers telling about the swim on the front page.

''I'll make it next time,'' was the final quotable quote Chadwick gave the press.

And she surely did. When all things were good and right with nature and the Japanese Current, Florence did it in record time ... both ways ... without stopping.

It was Jack Smith's and my final day at the *Her-Ex* when my father and mother drove down to the paper with Red Skelton and his wife, Georgia, in celebration.

Campbell had to have a few good traits because he'd had the conviction to hire Aggie Underwood as his city editor. Then he had other ways such as the attitude he was displaying this day. He absolutely could not comprehend why anyone had the right to quit him. But in spite of this viewpoint, he was completely affable with Red Skelton and my father. Jack and I, however, were not graced in this manner. Actually, when we approached, he wouldn't even acknowledge our presence.

Later on, before Aggie headed for home, a group of us went down for a final drink at Moran's. The regulars were staring up at Curly's newest appropriation, a television set that Taxi Bill had stolen for him.

It would be the last time I would talk with Cappy Marek. He was as old then as I am now.

And I wouldn't be seeing Blind Virginia still listening for the footsteps of the man who had blinded her so many years ago.

Nor would I be talking again with Cocky Lou, Any Time Annie or Dirty Marie, who still didn't believe that Red Skelton who was with us ... was *really* Red Skelton.

The following working day, Monday, July 21, at 4:53 A.M., a treacherous earthquake struck so hard it rocked the California coast from San Diego to San Francisco. Its epicenter was not located beneath the *Herald-Express* building, but it did practically level the town of Tehachapi.

Maybe the paper's quirky managing editor thought Jack Smith and I were strangely behind the earth-shaking. Who can tell? Nobody ever knew what was going on in Campbell's mind. However, at the end of the day, he had the following note posted on the city room bulletin board:

> *Jack Smith and Will Fowler are hereby banned*
> *from the city room of the Los Angeles Herald-*
> *Express for just and good reason.*
>
> *John B.T. Campbell*

Add End

On Wednesday morning, November 1, 1989, Hearst Corporation executive Robert Danzig was surrounded by more than 100 editorial city room reporters and editors. He stood atop a bullpen desk and began to speak: "It is with great regret ..."

With those and the rest of what he had to relate, the historically fiery *Los Angeles Herald & Examiner*—following 75 years of bias, but never dull journalistic coverage of the news in its time—was executed on the spot.

Women cried and a few male employees glared at Danzig with open hostility.

After the executive concluded his speech, those not active in putting out the farewell edition began packing personal belongings in scavenged cardboard boxes and began filtering from the building, heading for their parked cars and the uncertainty of an immediate future.

The *Her-Ex* had been up for sale for a year. The price was $100 million, but entrepreneurs were not flocking to purchase the battle-scarred sheet from which corporation executives had too often gone to the well and drawn liquid assets to reinvest in other Hearst holdings.

The now creaky money-maker of yesterday had outgrown its "bottom line" usefulness.

Columnists began composing their several departmental obituaries. The headline on the sports section read: *We're Outta Here*. Below the style department's head, *Going In Style*, there were no less than 14 by line pieces. The outsized front page headline mixed sentiment with a touch of hurt. It read: *So Long, L.A.!*

When I issued forth as a naive cub reporter nearly a half-century ago, I stared up in awe at the imposing old Examiner building whose blue and yellow tiled domes sparkled like semiprecious stones in the morning sunlight. As though I had tripped into King

Solomon's mines, it beckoned; dared me to enter its dark caverns to learn of the mysteries of the Fourth Estate.

The years in between have not been kind to the aged establishment that has long ago lost the sheen in its orphanage from uptown architectural progress. The Red Car trolley clangings can only be heard in the minds of old men. The Carillo Hotel across the street has turned into a squalid job corps residence where dope is openly sold at the corners, and dirty shops conduct marginal businesses behind darkly painted-up windows. I can no longer remember which one it was where Jim Murray and I picked out the engagement ring for Miss Gerry Brown. It's as though a collective area has become one in an old body, wandering like a leper; searching for a soul so it might pass over into the next world with a modicum of dignity. As the once grand newspaper edifice waits for the inevitable wrecker's ball, one realizes it's too late for a return performance.

An author never finishes writing his book. Along the way, he must eventually abandon it. And as doing so I lift my invisible glass in a toast to the hard-drinking, hard-working, wisecracking merry marauding newspaper reporters who covered and cranked out stories of lurid murders and scandalous tales as we fiercely competed with one another throughout the mid-twentieth century's last gasp of hell-raising years.

Acknowledgments

For three-quarters-of-a-century, since legendary newspaper publisher William Randolph Hearst hired my father in 1918, there has remained a mutual respect and friendship among our families. And during the writing of *Reporters*, Randolph A. Hearst allowed me full access to his newspaper archives. Without his generous help, this book would have been far more difficult to write and less interesting.

I especially thank my close friends Jim Murray, Jack Smith and Harry Watson for their help. The same goes for my late friends Gus Newman, Richard O'Connor, H. Allen Smith and Agness Underwood, whose memories often crawl into my mind like a warm bowl of milk.

To the others listed below who assisted me, I thank them for helping fill this old reporter's life with excitement:

Army Archerd, John Babcock, Blair Ball, Agnes Bane, Leo Batt, Marian Benson, Bob Bowen, Frank Q. Brown, Stan Chambers, Charles Champlin, Forrest Concannon, Frank Cotten, Jimmy D'Arrgo, Virginia Depew, William Donati, Scott Eyman, Jet Fore, J. William Fowler, Stan Gordon, Maury Green, Charles Hillinger, Jack Hirshberg, Anna Hull, Jerry Hulse, Marjorie Hurd, Roger Hurlburt, Art Jackson, Norman Jacoby, Hal Jacques, Jim Johnston, Hal Kanter, Pat Kindermeyer, Barbara Dempsey Leonard, Paul and Liz Leiss, Lou Mack, Robert Marshall, Bob Martin, Jimmy MacLarnin, Conrad Mercurio, Kendis Rochlin Moss, John Fenton Murray, Nancy Newman, Cathy Newmeyer, Chuck Panama, Robert Pflug, Arthur Pine, George Putnam, Phil Rhodes, Joe Rosenthal, Craig St. Claire, Margaret Scott, Vernon Scott, Leonard Shannon, Burt Sims, Sharry Steichen, Lyle Stuart, Al Stump, Bob Thomas, Tom Thompson, Joe Trocino, George Underwood, Count Billy Varga, Turnley Walker, Art Warden, Richard Webb, Gene Webster, Mary Evelyn Underwood Weed, Bob Yeager, James L. Young and Robert Young, Jr.

Index